FRONTIERS OF
PSYCHEDELIC
CONSCIOUSNESS

"David Jay Brown's *Frontiers of Psychedelic Consciousness* is a quintessential explorer's journal: a trip report on David's own odyssey to track down the pioneering minds of the entheogenic space. New ways of thinking about self and world abound! The new space seems to be *inner space*, and this book is a first-rate psychedelic excursion into this rich new land."

JASON SILVA, EMMY NOMINATED HOST OF
NATIONAL GEOGRAPHIC CHANNEL'S *BRAIN GAMES*

"As the psychedelic renaissance gathers momentum, it seems very timely to revisit the writings of some of the pioneers in the movement who have shed light on the fascinating aspects of consciousness brought about by these substances. David Jay Brown has curated an insightful selection of interviews with some of these movers, whose experiences and understanding continue to pave the way for the reintegration of psychedelics into Western society. A most useful volume."

AMANDA FIELDING, DIRECTOR OF THE BECKLEY FOUNDATION
FOR CONSCIOUSNESS AND DRUG POLICY RESEARCH

"In David's series of interviews, coming as they are from such a diverse range of contributors, a broader, more passionate, and truthful description of humanity's psychedelic trajectory could barely be imagined. Each chapter takes the reader from the precision of hard science and political ethics to the most intensely beautiful personal happenings, in which spirituality and personal growth and development are woven into the interviewee's patchwork quilt of experiences. *Frontiers of Psychedelic Consciousness* works so well because it is not only a gathering of great minds and famous pioneers; it is also a deeply intimate documentation of David talking, in his original, sensitive way, simply with people. It is undoubtedly a powerful educational tool, but above all else it is a testament of great human warmth."

BEN SESSA, M.D., PSYCHIATRIST, PSYCHEDELIC RESEARCHER, AND AUTHOR OF *THE PSYCHEDELIC RENAISSANCE*

"For serious students of psychedelic history this book is a vital and vibrant continuation to his seminal *Mavericks of the Mind*. There is no greater chronicler of psychedelic thinking than David Jay Brown."

BRUCE DAMER, PH.D., AUTHOR OF *AVATARS!: EXPLORING AND BUILDING VIRTUAL WORLDS ON THE INTERNET*

"David Jay Brown is one of the most incisive chroniclers of the second stage of the psychedelic revolution and other alternative movements. His book offers deep dives through the psyche of some of the most intriguing characters of our time."

DANIEL PINCHBECK, AUTHOR OF *BREAKING OPEN THE HEAD* AND *2012: THE RETURN OF QUETZALCOATL*

Acknowledgments

The genesis for this book was sparked while I was working as the guest editor for the Multidisciplinary Association for Psychedelic Studies (MAPS). Founded in 1986, MAPS is a nonprofit research and educational organization that "develops medical, legal, and cultural contexts for people to benefit from the careful uses of psychedelics and marijuana."

I wrote the monthly newsletters for MAPS for a year, and for five years I edited their special theme bulletins on the relationship among psychedelics and technology, ecology, the mind-body connection, death and dying, and popular art.

While I was working on the MAPS bulletins I interviewed numerous psychedelic researchers and took the opportunity to discuss more than was necessary for the bulletin, where only a fraction of the interviews were published. That was because I had in mind this book, which contains all of the interviews in their complete form.

First and foremost I would like to thank everyone at MAPS. It was a real pleasure and honor to work with this cutting-edge organization that is helping to change the world.

I'd also like to extend my deepest gratitude to all of the people who have allowed me to interview them for this collection.

Additionally, I would like to express my sincere appreciation to the following individuals for their generous contributions and valuable support: Carolyn Mary Kleefeld, Maria-Teresa Gutierrez-Macanilla, Hana Fiona Theobald, Jon Graham, Arleen Margulis, Meriana Dinkova, Jacob Andrade, Ania Grycan, Jess Buckner, Danielle Bohmer, Danelle

Benari, Amanda Rose Loveland, Lily Ross, Sara Huntley, Willow Aryn Dellinger, Jessi Daichman, Serena Watman, Buck Noe, Sara Mokhtari-Fox, Selina Reddan, Veronika King, Jesse Ray Houts, Audreanne Rivka Sheehan, Patricia Holt, Linda Parker, Denis Berry, Zach Leary, Maria Grusauskas, Rebecca McClen Novick, Annie Sprinkle, Kelly Hollerbach, Heather Goldstein Greenberg, Brandi Goldstein, Geoffrey and Valerie Goldstein, Louise Reitman, Sammie and Tudie, Rick Doblin, Amy Barnes Excolere, Sherry Hall, Suzie Wouk, Sherri Paris, Robert Forte, Valerie Leveroni Corral, David Wayne Dunn, Robin Rae, Brummbaer, Deed DeBruno, Randy Baker, Steven Ray Brown, B'anna Federico, Anna Damoth, Sandy Oppenheim, Lorey Capelli, Dana Peleg, Mimi Peleg, Bethan Carter, Al Brown, Cheryle and Gene Goldstein, Dina Meyer, Bernadette Wilson, Nick Herbert, Erin Jarvis, Jody Lombardo, Erica Ansberry, Jessica Ansberry-Gagnon, Goo Bear, Maria Ramirez, Rob Bryanton, Linda D'Amato, Nathan West, Paula Rae Mellard, Mike Kawizky, Linda Capetillo-Cunliffe, Boa Cowee, Ivy Summer Abshell, Alan Shoemaker, Massimiliano Geraci, Jeff Rosenbaum, Allisun Shine and Tyler, Mark Van Thillo, Gaie Alling, Liza Gopika Lichtinger, Torrey Peacock, Robert J. Barnhart, Frank Alan Bella, Brittany Nicole, Susanne G. Seller, Teresa King, Ben Osen, Jim Steele, Patrice Villastrigo, Rupert Sheldrake, Tod Barnett, Dragonflower Lyoness, Arlene Istar Lev, Catherine McBride, Rick Strassman, Stanley Krippner, Ralph Metzner, C. Michael Smith, Simon Posford, Jason Silva, Ben Sessa, Bruce Damer, Daniel Pinchbeck, and Dieter Hagenbach.

Special thanks to my worldwide network of Internet friends, who inform me about new scientific developments, support my work, share their creative talents, and challenge my ideas. I am most grateful for everyone's contributions and communications.

Introduction

In my four previous interview books—*Mavericks of the Mind, Voices from the Edge, Conversations on the Edge of Apocalypse,* and *Mavericks of Medicine*—psychedelic drugs and plants played a supporting role. I usually had one or two questions in each interview about how psychedelics had influenced my interviewees' work, and many of the topics that we discussed were inspired by my own psychedelic experiences.

Shamanic journeys with LSD, magic mushrooms, ayahuasca, and cannabis inspired many of the questions I asked, as well as many of my interviewees' responses and the ideas that were discussed. A large percentage of the accomplished scientists, artists, and thinkers whom I've interviewed over the years were inspired by their use of psychedelics, and I felt like it was my sacred duty to record this important historical information for future generations.

In this new collection, psychedelic drugs and plants are the primary focus of the interviews. Psychedelic drugs and plants have played an invaluable role in my own cognitive development. My experiences with LSD and cannabis as a teenager had a profound effect on me. They strongly influenced the direction of my academic studies and, later, the

1

course of my career, as well as my psychological and spiritual perspectives on the nature of reality.

These experiences are documented in my book *The New Science of Psychedelics: At the Nexus of Culture, Consciousness, and Spirituality*, which is available from Inner Traditions. This new collection of interviews serves as a companion volume for that book, exploring some of its ideas in interactive dialogues with experts on how psychedelics affect the mind.

THE PSYCHEDELIC RENAISSANCE

The past eight years have been especially exciting for me. After many dark years of having been zealously repressed, psychedelics are finally coming out of the closet and up from the underground, where they are being healthily integrated into Western society. After almost twenty years without any government-approved clinical studies of psychedelic drugs anywhere on the planet, and a mainstream media that demonized, ridiculed, or ignored them, there are currently more than a dozen clinical studies of psychedelic drugs taking place around the globe, with more on the way—and they're all getting positive media coverage.

Thanks to the Multidisciplinary Association for Psychedelic Studies (MAPS), the Heffter Research Institute, the Beckley Foundation, and the Council on Spiritual Practices, these new medical studies are exploring the wide spectrum of therapeutic applications for LSD, psilocybin, ibogaine, and MDMA.

The renaissance that's presently occurring around the world with psychedelic drug research not only gives me great hope, but it also has allowed me to shift gears with my writing career so that I could write more about the subject that has influenced and interested me the most: psychedelic drugs and plants. I was thrilled to have the opportunity to cover the initial wave of new scientific research on psychedelics for *Scientific American Mind* magazine in 2007 and to be able to edit the special theme bulletins for MAPS about how psychedelics have affected technology, ecology, the mind-body connection, and our view of death and dying.

A summary of all of the clinical psychedelic drug research that has gone on around the world since 1990 can be found in my book *Psychedelic Drug Research: A Comprehensive Review,* which was recently published by Reality Sandwich. In *Frontiers of Psychedelic Consciousness* I interview some of the most influential and interesting people who have explored these powerful, mysterious, and controversial substances; who have helped to change our cultural perspectives about them; and who can offer some valuable insights into their potential.

LOOKING AT THE BIG PICTURE

Our planet's biosphere is currently experiencing a serious crisis. A massive loss of biodiversity, toxic nuclear and petroleum leakage into the oceans, heavy metals spewing into the atmosphere, climate change, and other frightening ecological dangers could easily lead to our own extinction.

Environmental instability and unsustainability exist on many levels, due to our species' lack of foresight and ecological blindness, which places the future of human civilization in great peril. The very perspectives that we need and that we seem to lack as a species—compassion, ecological awareness, empathy, cultural boundary dissolution, creative thought, and spiritual connection—appear to be fostered by the use of psychedelic drugs and plants. Sadly, Western cultures universally prohibit the personal use of these sacred medicines.

However, maybe the situation isn't really as bad as it first appears. I suspect that plant spirits—the wisdom of botanical intelligence— specifically designed psychedelic chemicals in order to activate those parts of the human brain that cause us to question the integrity of our culture, and to place a greater value on genetic or primal intelligence than on cultural beliefs.

Making psychedelic substances culturally forbidden, taboo, and illegal appears to increase their attractiveness to many people, and it spreads the word about their existence, so there may be a secret plan, a divine wink, and a sacred smile behind their draconian prohibition.

Many people think that the widespread use of psychedelic plants and fungi around the world could be the biosphere's decisive response to human patterns of ecological destruction, and that a hidden intelligence in nature may be utilizing psychedelic plants as catalysts to increase our ecological awareness and wake us up—hopefully, before it's too late. To discuss this idea, I interviewed ethnobotanist Dennis McKenna and anthropologist Jeremy Narby.

According to mycologist Paul Stamets, there's actually scientific evidence to support the commonly encountered idea in the psychedelic community that psychedelic plants are here to teach us how to become more ecologically aware.

Psilocybin-containing mushrooms tend to grow in areas that are disturbed by ecological upheavals, such as where roads are freshly cut into forests, where landslides occur, or around the grounds of a new construction site. Magic mushrooms seem to proliferate especially in areas where there has been a lot of disruptive human activity, almost as if they are a response to our use of the planet's resources.

Could it be that psilocybin mushrooms are a response by the biosphere, like a chemical signaling system within the body, to help the wayward human species become more symbiotic with its environment?

Can it really be just a coincidence that a fungus reported to increase ecological awareness specifically proliferates in those very areas that are ecologically damaged? And could it possibly be a seductive plan, designed by botanical intelligence, to hide this visionary fungus and other psychedelics among the party drugs that young, impressionable people take for fun, while the cultural authorities forbid and outlaw their use?

How many people, I wonder, have eaten a handful of magic mushrooms at a party or concert, just for fun, and then unexpectedly wound up having a full-blown mystical experience that totally transformed their lives?

Thanks to human activity, these mind-expanding mushrooms, which were once restricted to very narrow ecosystems, are now flourishing all over the Earth. Magic mushroom and ayahuasca-using cultures, once restricted to a few areas in Central and South America, are also now spreading all over the planet, like a growing mycelium network.

There are currently hundreds of ayahuasca churches that have been established throughout the world, and the U.S. Supreme Court even ruled in favor of allowing one of them to legally operate within U.S. borders. According to anthropologist Luis Eduardo Luna, studies done in Brazil suggest that ayahuasca use tends to make people more sensitive toward ecological issues. Research into the members of ayahuasca churches revealed that many of them decided to change their professions after participating in ayahuasca rituals so that they could work with natural products or on environmental protection issues.

Considering the precariously toxic state of the world at present and what lies at stake, perhaps it might be a good idea to listen to what the people who know the most about these strange substances have to say.

AYAHUASCA, AMAZONIAN SHAMANISM & GENETIC INTELLIGENCE

I suspect that the greatest hope for raising ecological awareness on our wayward planet lies in the power and intelligence of the ancient Amazonian jungle brew known as ayahuasca. This visionary tea, which is composed primarily of two different plants that work together synergistically, is sacred to the indigenous people of the Amazonian rain forest for its healing and spiritual properties.

My personal journeys with ayahuasca in the Peruvian jungle convinced me that an experience with this magical brew is the most valuable of all psychedelic experiences.

In the workshops that I co-teach with psychotherapist Meriana Dinkova about navigating altered states, I always stress that there are three main factors that influence the outcome of a psychedelic experience: set, setting, and dosage.

This is an idea that was developed by the late Harvard psychologist Timothy Leary. A set is one's mental or emotional state, expectations, and intentions, which should be positive, realistic, and clearly envisioned.

The setting is one's immediate environment where the experience occurs, and this space should be as safe, aesthetically pleasing, and secure as possible.

The dosage is simply the amount of the drug or plant that one consumes in relation to one's body weight, and this should be carefully determined by reviewing scientific studies, indigenous use, and anecdotal reports.

However, while undergoing a series of shamanic ayahuasca journeys in the Peruvian Amazon, I realized that there was a fourth factor involved in determining what happens during a psychedelic experience—something I had overlooked before. This is the intelligence and the intention of the plant (or drug) itself, which can serve as a healer or a teacher.

It's easy for the uninitiated to laugh at statements like this, until one encounters the reality of the plant spirit for themselves. This often becomes obvious with a strong dose of ayahuasca, magic mushrooms, iboga, salvia, San Pedro cactus, or peyote, but it can be more subtle on other psychedelic journeys.

However, there's little denial among initiates that the ayahuasca brew, as well as shamanic cacti and fungi, contain a living spirit, an intelligent being, that will communicate with you directly—through vivid imagery, scenes that combine into a kind of meta-language of spoken words and spelled-out words—and that use every sensory channel and symbolic medium possible to make absolutely sure that you get the message.

Virtually everyone who meets this wise and ancient spirit agrees: she clearly knows us better than we know ourselves, and she has much to teach us.

PSYCHEDELICS &
CULTURAL TRANSFORMATION

In this collection we'll not only explore the ancient shamanic secrets of the Amazonian jungle, but we'll also look at the latest medical and scientific research into psychedelic drugs, as well as their effects on modern culture.

I interviewed Johns Hopkins neuroscientist Roland Griffiths about his studies with psilocybin, the psychoactive component of the magic mushroom, which shows that it can produce a mystical experience in some people that is indistinguishable from those reported by mystics throughout history.

I also interviewed psychiatric researcher Rick Strassman about his five-year DMT study at the University of New Mexico, MAPS founder Rick Doblin about the new research with MDMA to help people with post-traumatic stress disorder, and pharmacologist Daniel Siebert about the therapeutic potential of *Salvia divinorum*.

Additionally, I spoke with psychiatrist Stanislav Grof, psychologist Charles Tart, and Roshi Joan Halifax about how psychedelics relate to the near-death experience and psychic phenomena, and how they can be used to help people overcome the anxiety surrounding one's fear of death.

Oh, and what a thrill it was to be able to interview electronica musician Simon Posford (a.k.a., Hallucinogen) of Shpongle—one of my favorite music groups—for this book.

In my interview career I was fortunate enough to be able to speak with two of the most influential psychedelic musicians in history. The interview that I did with Jerry Garcia of the Grateful Dead appears in my book *Voices from the Edge*. In this collection, Posford speaks at length about how his use of LSD and DMT influenced his music.

SAVING THE WORLD

Cultural contributions and medical potentials aside, I think that psychedelic drugs and shamanic plants have the potential to help us survive as a species. I truly believe that psychedelics can help to save the world. I think that they can help to raise ecological awareness, make our sacred interconnection and interdependence on the biosphere obvious, and set many people off on a course of spiritual evolution.

Tripping on psychedelics can also be psychologically risky—no one will argue with that—but, when done correctly, their safety record is hard to beat, and not doing them may be even more dangerous.

I don't think that there's much time left on this planet, as we may be driving ourselves into extinction with runaway pollution and toxic waste. Besides psychedelic drugs and plants, I don't know of anything else that can turn someone around overnight, like Scrooge in *A Christmas Carol,* and make them into a better person.

Psychedelics inspire novel thought, new ideas, and alternative perspectives, and they strengthen problem-solving abilities. They can actually improve creativity and artistic performance. Research by psychologist James Fadiman, psychiatrist Oscar Janiger, and others, has demonstrated that mescaline, LSD, and cannabis can genuinely enhance creativity.

In the pages that follow James Fadiman speaks with me about his research, and we explore the fascinating subject of creativity and psychedelics.

Because creativity lies at the heart of solving every problem that we currently face as a species, this is one of the primary reasons why I believe so strongly in the psychedelic drug research that's going on today and so faithfully support the leading-edge organizations that work to make it happen. I urge you to do the same and to donate to them as generously as you can.

I think that it's an atrocity and an outrage that these sacred medicines are illegal, and I feel that the quickest path toward developing a more conscious and compassionate world is through the intelligent use of psychedelic plants. Currently, the best way to legitimize the use of these important medicines in our society is through the kind of scientific research that MAPS, the Heffter Institute, and their sister organizations are currently doing.

This will eventually allow shamanic sacraments like ayahuasca, cannabis, MDMA, LSD, psilocybin, and DMT to legitimately enter into Western society, first as prescription medicines and then as fully integrated parts of our fast-moving, technophilic culture. Once that happens, the heavens will part, the dark age will end, and the world will never be the same again.

●   ●   ●

Portions of the interviews in this book with Albert Hofmann, Charles Tart, Dennis McKenna, Daniel Seibert, Jeremy Narby, Joan Halifax, Roland Griffiths, Stanislav Grof, and Simon Posford were previously published in *The MAPS Bulletin,* and a portion of my interview with Rick Strassman was previously published in my book *Mavericks of Medicine.*

1
LSD, Science, Consciousness, and Mysticism

*An Interview with **Albert Hofmann***

Albert Hofmann, Ph.D., is the world-renowned Swiss chemist who discovered LSD. The impact that LSD has had on the world is certainly immense, and, although largely incalculable, I think it's fair to say that this superpotent, mind-morphing compound has deeply affected every aspect of human culture, from art to science, politics, medicine, and spirituality.

Hofmann also discovered and first synthesized psilocybin and psilocin, the primary psychoactive components of the "magic" mushroom, as well as the psychoactive lysergic acid alkaloids in morning glory seeds. He also designed the ergot-derived cognitive enhancer Hydergine, which is used as treatment for memory disorders, as a product for Sandoz Pharmaceuticals.

Hofmann was born in Baden, Switzerland, in 1906. He graduated from the University of Zurich in 1929 with a degree in chemistry and then went to work for Sandoz (now Novartis) in Basel. Hofmann's research goal was to work toward the isolation of active principles in known medicinal plants. He worked with the Mediterranean plant squill

Albert Hofmann

for several years before moving on to the study of ergot and ergot alkaloids.

Over the next few years Hofmann worked his way through the lysergic acid derivatives in ergot. In 1938 he synthesized LSD-25 (the twenty-fifth in a series of lysergic acid derivatives) for the first time. However, after minimal testing on laboratory animals with no interesting results, he set the compound aside and continued to work with other derivatives.

Five years later, on April 16, 1943, he resynthesized LSD-25 because he felt that he might have missed something the first time around. This was at the height of World War II, shortly after Enrico Fermi made his discovery that led to the atomic bomb. Hofmann said that he had a "peculiar presentiment" to resynthesize LSD, and that LSD "spoke" to him. Many people have speculated about the possibility of a relationship between the discovery of the psychoactive properties of LSD and the first nuclear explosions, as LSD is thought by many to be something of a spiritual antidote to the aggressive and toxic tendencies of the human species.

After Hofmann resynthesized LSD, he wrote in his laboratory journal these famous words: "Last Friday . . . I was forced to interrupt my work in the laboratory in the middle of the afternoon and proceed home, being affected by a remarkable restlessness, combined with a slight dizziness. At home I lay down and sank into a not unpleasant intoxicated condition, characterized by an extremely stimulated imagination. In a dreamlike state, with eyes closed . . . I perceived an uninterrupted stream of fantastic pictures, extraordinary shapes with intense, kaleidoscopic play of colors. After some two hours this condition faded away."

Apparently Hofmann accidentally ingested a minute amount of the LSD—possibly through his fingertips—and because the drug is active in such small doses (measured in micrograms), Hofmann became the first person in human history to experience the psychedelic effects of LSD. Three days later, on April 19, he decided to verify his results by intentionally ingesting 250 micrograms of LSD. Compared to other known drugs, none of which were known to have effects in such small quantities, this would have appeared to be a very conservative dose.

As it turns out, 250 micrograms is actually quite a hefty dose of LSD, and Hofmann had a powerful and rather frightening experience that forced him to bicycle home from the lab and spend the day in bed, where he fully recovered in a few hours. The anniversary of this day, April 19, has become known to many appreciative people as Bicycle

Albert Hofmann and author David Jay Brown

Day, in honor of Hofmann's famous hallucinogenic journey through the streets of Basel while traveling home.

Hofmann told me that he was "convinced from the very beginning of the fundamental impact" of LSD. Although Hofmann has always seen great spiritual value and creative potential in LSD, he was often dismayed by the way that many young people used it merely to enhance sensory experiences and by the strict prohibitive reactions toward the drug by virtually every government in the world. Because of the enormous controversy that surrounds LSD, Hofmann referred to this mighty mind-morphing molecule as his problem child.

Hofmann continued to work for Sandoz until 1971, when he retired as director of research for the Department of Natural Products. After that time he continued to write and lecture. Hofmann told the story of how he discovered LSD and reflected on the impact it has had in the world in his book *LSD: My Problem Child*. He was also the author of *Insight Outlook* and coauthor of *Plants of the Gods* and *The Road to Eleusis*.

Hofmann was a fellow of the World Academy of Sciences, a member of the International Society of Plant Research, and the American Society of Pharmacognosy. To find out more about his work, visit www .lsd.info.

Hofmann turned a hundred years old on January 11, 2006. He was remarkably healthy and acutely mentally focused when I spent time with him. I attended his centennial birthday celebration and LSD symposium, "LSD—Problem Child and Wonder Drug," in Basel from January 13 to 15, 2006.

Thousands of unusually creative and deeply appreciative people gathered from around the world to honor Hofmann's work with the kind of reverence that is usually reserved for saints and religious sages. It was the largest conference ever held on psychedelics, and some of the most brilliant and accomplished scientists, artists, writers, and musicians on this planet were there to honor Hofmann.

———————————————————— @ ————————————————————

I interviewed Hofmann with the help of my friend Dieter Hagenbach, who organized the event in Basel. Dieter translated my questions and Hofmann's German responses. Although Albert was feeling quite exhausted from the barrage of media attention around his hundredth birthday celebration, he graciously agreed to answer my questions. His answers were generally brief; however, they are, I think, succinctly eloquent and profoundly wise. Albert spoke about how he became interested in chemistry, how psychedelics have affected his view of the world, and what he thought about the future evolution of the human species. Hofmann passed away two years later, on April 29, 2008, at the age of 102.

What originally inspired your interest in chemistry?

ALBERT: My interest in chemistry was inspired by a fundamental philosophical question: Is the material world a manifestation of the spiritual world? I hoped to find deep, sound answers from the solid laws of chemistry to answer this question, and to apply these answers to the external problems and open questions of the spiritual dimensions of life.

When you first discovered LSD did you have an intuitive sense that this drug would have the enormous impact on the world that it has, or were you generally surprised by what followed?

ALBERT: I was convinced from the very beginning of the fundamental impact.

What motivated or inspired you to go back and synthesize LSD a second time in 1943?

ALBERT: I synthesized LSD a second time for a deeper pharmacological investigation.

How has your own use of LSD affected your philosophy of life?

ALBERT: LSD showed me the inseparable interaction between the material and the spiritual world.

What sort of association do you see between LSD and creativity?

ALBERT: Since LSD opens up what Aldous Huxley called the Doors of Perception, it enhances the fields of creative activity.

Do you think that LSD has affected human evolution?

ALBERT: I do not know if it has affected human evolution, but I hope so.

What are your thoughts on why LSD is almost universally prohibited by governments around the world?

ALBERT: LSD belongs to a class of psychoactive substances that provide the user with a new concept of life, and this new way of looking at life is opposite to the officially accepted view.

What role do you see LSD playing in the future?

ALBERT: In the future, I hope that LSD provides to the individual a new worldview which is in harmony with nature and its laws.

What do you think happens to consciousness after death?

ALBERT: I think that each individual's consciousness becomes part of the universal mind.

What is your perspective on the concept of God and spirituality?

ALBERT: God is the name of the universal creative spirit.

What sort of relationship do you see between science and mysticism?

ALBERT: Science is objective knowledge, and mysticism is personal spiritual experience.

What do you attribute your long life to?

ALBERT: I don't know.

Are you hopeful about the future, and how do you envision the future evolution of the human species?

ALBERT: I am hopeful about the future evolution of the human species. I am hopeful because I have the impression that more and more human individuals are becoming conscious and that the creative spirit, which we call God, speaks to us through his creation—through the endlessness of the starry sky, through the beauty and wonder of the living individuals of the plant, the animal, and the human kingdoms.

We human beings are able to understand this message because we possess the divine gift of consciousness. This connects us to the universal mind and gives us divine creativity. Any means that help to expand our individual consciousness—by opening up and sharpening our inner and outer eyes, in order to understand the divine universal message—will help humanity to survive. An understanding of the divine message, in its universal language, would bring an end to the war between the religions of the world.

2

The Nonordinary Mind, Psychedelics, and Psychology

*An Interview with **Stanislav Grof***

Few people on this planet know more about nonordinary states of consciousness than Czech American psychiatric researcher **Stanislav Grof, M.D., Ph.D.** Grof is one of the founders of the field of transpersonal psychology; the codeveloper, with his late wife, Christina Grof, of Holotropic Breathwork therapy; and a pioneering researcher, for more than fifty years, into the use of nonordinary states of consciousness for the purposes of healing, personal growth, and spiritual transformation.

Grof is also one of the world's experts on LSD psychotherapy and has supervised more legal LSD sessions than anyone else on the planet. Grof's near-legendary work at the Spring Grove Hospital Center in Maryland—treating alcoholics and terminally ill cancer patients with LSD—is some of the most important psychedelic drug research of all time.

Although initially interested in filmmaking, Grof received his M.D. from Charles University in Prague in 1956, and he completed his Ph.D. from the Czechoslovak Academy of Sciences in 1965. He also completed a seven-year training as a Freudian psychoanalyst. Grof became the principal investigator of a program that explored the therapeutic and heuristic potential of psychedelic substances at the Psychiatric Research Institute in Prague.

In 1967 he came to the United States as a clinical and research fellow at Johns Hopkins University School of Medicine and at the Maryland Psychiatric Research Center (MPRC). He went on to become assistant professor of psychiatry at Johns Hopkins and chief of psychiatric research at MPRC. During this time, Grof, Walter Pahnke, Sanford Unger, and others ran studies at the Spring Grove Hospital Center treating alcoholics and terminally ill cancer patients with LSD. The results from these studies, which ran from 1967 to 1972, were extremely encouraging.

From 1973 through 1987, Grof was a scholar in residence at the Esalen Institute in Big Sur, California. During this time, he and his wife, Christina, developed Holotropic Breathwork therapy as a non-pharmaceutical means for inducing an LSD-like nonordinary state of consciousness for self-exploration, personal growth, and therapy. They also founded the Spiritual Emergency Network (SEN), an affiliation of psychologists and psychiatrists who offer psychological help to people undergoing a psychospiritual crisis.

In fact, the Grofs coined the term *spiritual emergency* to distinguish certain psychologically transformative episodes from schizophrenia and other forms of psychosis. This concept inspired the creation of a new category, Religious and Spiritual Problems, in the official Diagnostic and Statistical Manual (DSM-IV). In 1987 the Grofs founded Grof Transpersonal Training (GTT), for the training and certification of practitioners in Holotropic Breathwork. Together they presented workshops and lectures throughout the world.

Grof was the founding president of the International Transpersonal Association (ITA), established in 1977, and he is the originator of some very compelling psychological theories. Grof developed a theoretical framework for understanding LSD experiences and spiritually transformative states of consciousness that is based on a memory of one's experience in the womb or a trauma from the birth process. This theory

Photo by Michael Jang

Stanislav Grof

postulates four basic perinatal matrices (BPMs) that correspond to different stages in the birth process.

Grof also described and mapped another new, large domain in the unconscious that he calls the transpersonal. These concepts are discussed at length in a number of Grof's books. Grof is the author or coauthor of more than twenty books, including *Realms of the Human Unconscious*, *LSD Psychotherapy*, *Beyond the Brain*, *The Cosmic Game*, *When the Impossible*

Happens, The Ultimate Journey, The Stormy Search for the Self, and *Spiritual Emergency* (the last two coauthored with Christina Grof).

Grof is currently a distinguished adjunct faculty member at the California Institute of Integral Studies (CIIS) in San Francisco, where he teaches, and he continues to lecture throughout the world. Grof has had more than 140 articles published in different scientific journals, and he served on the editorial boards of the *Journal of Transpersonal Psychology,* the *Journal of Humanistic Psychology, ReVision,* and others. Grof received the prestigious Vision 97 Award, which was granted by the Dagmar and Václav Havel Foundation in Prague on October 5, 2007. For more information about Grof's work see www.holotropic.com and www.stanislavgrof.com.

I interviewed Stan Grof on March 23, 2007. I found him to be unusually elegant with words, and his ideas were simply mesmerizing. We spoke about psychedelics and creativity, the reality of encounters with otherworldly beings, what happens to consciousness after death, and the difference between a spiritual emergency and a psychotic episode.

What originally inspired your interest in psychiatric medicine?

STAN: When I was eighteen years old I was finishing what we call gymnasium in Europe—the equivalent of high school in America. I love to draw and paint, and my original plan was to work in animated movies. I had already had an introductory interview with the brilliant Czech artist and film producer Jirí Trnka, and I was supposed to start working in the Barrandov film studios in Prague. But that situation changed radically when a friend of mine lent me Freud's *Introductory Lectures on Psychoanalysis.* I started reading the book that very evening, and I couldn't put it down. I read through the night and into the next day. Then, within a few days, I decided that I wanted to be a psychoanalyst, and I let the animated movies go. I enrolled in the medical school and got in touch with a small group of people in Prague interested in psychoanalysis; it was led by Dr. Theodor Dosužkov, the only psycho-analyst who had survived the Second World War in Czechoslovakia. Most of the psychoanalysts were Jewish, and those who did not leave ended up in gas chambers.

How did you become interested in psychedelics and nonordinary states of consciousness?

STAN: When I began my career as a psychiatrist I was initially very excited about psychoanalysis. But then when I tried to apply psycho-analysis in my clinical practice I started seeing its great limitations. I was still very excited about the theory of psychoanalysis but was increasingly disappointed with what you can do with it as a clinical tool. I was realizing that there was a very narrow indication range. You had to meet very special criteria to be considered a good candi-date for psychoanalysis, and even if you met those criteria, you had to be prepared not for months, but for years. And I realized that even after years, the results were not exactly breathtaking. I found it very difficult to understand why a system that seemed to explain every-thing would not offer some more effective solutions for emotional and psychosomatic disorders.

In order to become a psychoanalyst one had to first study medicine. In medicine, if you really understand a problem, you are usually able to do something quite effective about it—or if you cannot, then you can at least understand the reasons for your failure. We know exactly what would have to change in relation to cancer or AIDS for us to be able to be more successful in the treatment of these diseases. But in psychoanalysis I was asked to believe that we have full understanding of what's happening in the psyche, and yet we can do so little over such a long period of time. So I found myself in a crisis where I started to regret that I had chosen psychiatry as my profession. I was thinking back nostalgically about the animated movies, wondering if that would have been a better career choice.

At that time, I worked at the psychiatric department of the school of medicine [at Charles University] in Prague and we had just finished a large study of Mellaril, one of the early tranquilizers. This was the beginning of the "golden era of psychopharmacology." The first tranquilizers and antidepressants were being developed, and it was believed that most of the problems in psychiatry would be solved by chemistry. So we conducted a large study with Mellaril, which came from the pharmaceutical company in Switzerland called Sandoz. We had a very good working relationship with Sandoz, which meant the usual fringe benefits that psychiatrists get from pharmaceutical companies: compensation for the trips to conferences where one reports about their preparations, supply of relevant literature, and free samples of various new preparations that they produce.

As part of this exchange, the psychiatric department where I worked received a large box full of ampoules of LSD. It came with a letter which said this was a new investigational substance that had been discovered in the laboratories of Sandoz by Dr. Albert Hofmann, who happened to intoxicate himself accidentally when he was synthesizing it. The letter described how the son of Albert Hofmann's boss, Zurich psychiatrist Werner Stoll, conducted an early pilot study with a group of psychiatric patients and a group of normal volunteers. He came to the conclusion that LSD could have some very interesting uses in psychiatry or psychology. So Sandoz was now sending samples of LSD to different universities, research institutes, and individual therapists, asking for feedback if there was a legitimate use for these substance in these disciplines. In this letter they suggested two possible uses.

One suggestion was that LSD might be used to induce an experimental psychosis. It could be administered to normal volunteers and [used to] conduct all kinds of tests—psychological, biochemical, physiological, electrophysiological—before, during, and after the session. This would provide insight as to what is happening, biologically and biochemically, in the organism at the time when the mental functioning is so profoundly influenced by the substance. This could be a way of discovering what is happening in naturally occurring psychoses. The basic idea behind it was that it is possible that, under certain circumstances, the human body could produce a substance like LSD and that psychoses, particularly schizophrenia, would actually be chemical aberrations, not mental diseases. And if we could identify the chemical culprit, then we could also find another substance which would neutralize it. Such a test-tube solution for schizophrenia would, of course, be the Holy Grail of psychiatry.

So this was very exciting. The Sandoz letter also offered another little tip, which became my destiny. It suggested that this substance might also be used as a very unconventional training or educational tool for psychiatrists, psychologists, nurses, and students of psychology and psychiatry. The idea was that LSD would give these people a chance to spend a few hours in a world that would be very much like the world of their patients. As a result they would be able to understand them better, be able to communicate with them more effectively, and, hopefully, be more successful in treating them. So this was something that I wouldn't have missed for anything in the world. I was in a deep professional crisis, feeling very disappointed with the therapeutic means we had at our disposal at the time. So I became one of the early Czech volunteers and had a profound experience that radically changed my life and sent me professionally and personally to a whole other direction.

How can LSD psychotherapy be helpful in overcoming traumatic life experiences, alcoholism, or a diagnosis of terminal illness?

STAN: We have done studies in all those areas. Psychedelic therapy revealed a wide array of previously unknown therapeutic mechanisms, but the most profound positive changes happened in connection with mystical experiences. We were very impressed with what you could do with very difficult conditions, like chronic alcoholism and narcotic drug abuse. But the most interesting and the most moving study that we did at the Maryland Psychiatric Research Center was the one that involved terminal cancer patients. We found out that if these patients had powerful experiences of psychospiritual death/rebirth and cosmic unity, it profoundly changed their emotional condition and it took away the fear of death. It made it possible for them to spend the rest of their lives living one day at a time. We also found out that in many patients LSD had very profound effect on pain, even pain that didn't respond to narcotics.

Why do you think that holotropic states of consciousness have so much healing potential, and do you think that psychedelics can enhance the placebo effect?

STAN: What do you mean by the placebo effect in connection with psychedelics?

The placebo effect demonstrates the power of the mind over the body. We know that placebos—or biologically inactive substances—can have a measurable healing effect simply because people believe in their power. Do you think that part of the healing potential of psychedelics comes from enhancing what we call the placebo effect in medicine?

STAN: Well, when you call something a placebo, you assume that there is no real biochemical effect.

I don't mean placebos; I mean what's been called the placebo effect, which one can measure. The whole reason that we use placebos in medical studies, when we're testing a new drug, is because of the placebo effect—because our beliefs have the power to influence our well-being in measurable ways. We know that just believing something will have an effect can create a measurable effect, and neuroscientist Candace Pert's research showed that positive emotions can affect the immune system and neuropeptide levels. Do you think that what psychedelics are actually doing, when they assist with healing, is enhancing that power of the mind to affect the body's own natural healing system?

STAN: Well, I never thought about psychedelics as enhancing the placebo effect, because their psychological effects are so obvious and dramatic; one of the major problems we had in psychedelic research was actually to find a believable placebo for them. But I guess if you put it the way that you put it, you could see it as enhancing the placebo effect—because it certainly enhances the power of the mind over the emotional psychosomatic processes.

Can you talk a little about the relationship between certain psychological conflicts and the development of certain cancers, which you witnessed as a result of some psychedelic sessions that you ran?

STAN: We have never really systematically studied this. What I have written in the book *The Ultimate Journey* are mostly anecdotal reports of the insights that came from the patients themselves. For example, sometimes patients had the feeling that their cancer had something to do with their self-destructive tendencies, or that it had something to do with an energetic blockage that occurred in a certain part of their body as a result of traumatic experiences. Sometimes they actually made attempts during their sessions to find psychological ways to heal their cancer, but we never studied this systematically to the point that I could make any definitive statements about it.

Carl Simonton made a large study where he tried to demonstrate participation of emotional factors in the etiology of cancer. One finding was particularly interesting and constant: a pattern of serious loss eighteen months prior to the diagnosis of cancer. But I think that those cases are all really anecdotal, and I don't think anybody has really shown this beyond any reasonable doubt.

One thing that I would like to add is that because of my medical background I used to doubt that cancer could have something to do with emotions. This was at a time when it seemed that the key problem in the genesis of cancer was what transforms a cell into a cancer cell. This changed radically when new research showed that the human body produces cancer cells all the time. So the problem is not what makes a cell a cancer cell, but what causes the immune system to fail destroying them. And it is certainly possible to imagine that psychological factors could cause a breakdown of the immune system, either generally or in certain specific parts of the body.

What kind of an effect do you think that psychedelics have on creativity and problem-solving abilities?

STAN: Oh, a tremendous effect. We have extensive evidence in that regard. In the 1960s James Fadiman, Robert McKim, Willis Harman, Myron Stolaroff, and Robert Mogar conducted a pilot study of the effects of psychedelics on the creative process, using administration of mescaline to enhance inspiration and problem solving in a group of highly talented individuals. In 1993 molecular biologist and DNA chemist Kary Mullis received a Nobel Prize for his development of the polymerase chain reaction (PCR), which allows the amplification of specific DNA sequences; it is a central technique in biochemistry and molecular biology. During a symposium in Basel celebrating Albert Hofmann's hundredth birthday, Albert revealed that he was told by Kary Mullis that LSD had helped him develop the polymerase chain reaction. Francis Crick, the Nobel Prize–winning father of modern genetics, was under the influence of LSD when he discovered the double-helix structure of DNA. He told a fellow scientist that he often used small doses of LSD to boost his power of thought. He said it was LSD that helped him to unravel the structure of DNA, the discovery that won him the Nobel Prize.

In his book *What the Dormouse Said: How the Sixties Counterculture Shaped the Personal Computer Industry,* John Markoff described the history of the personal computer. He showed that there is a direct connection between the psychedelic use in the American counterculture of the 1950s and 1960s and the development of the computer industry. Steve Jobs said taking LSD was among the two or three most important things he had done in his life. He has stated that people around him, who did not share his countercultural roots, could not fully relate to his thinking.

Willis Harman collected in his book *Higher Creativity* many examples of high-level problem solving in nonordinary states of consciousness. I think that studying the effect on creativity is by far the most interesting area where psychedelics could be used. Offer them to people who are experts in certain areas, such as cosmology, quantum-relativistic physics, biology, evolutionary theory, and so on—individuals who hold an enormous amount of information about a particular field and who are aware of the problems which need to be solved. Several of my friends from the Bay Area who are physicists, such as Fred Alan Wolf, Jack Sarfatti, Nick Herbert, and Fritjof Capra, have had some really interesting insights into physics in nonordinary states of consciousness. Some had spontaneous experiences of nonordinary states of consciousness and others psychedelic sessions. For example, Fred Wolf spent some time in South America doing ayahuasca.

Nick Herbert lives nearby and is a good friend. We've actually discussed the following question quite a bit. Many people report unexplained phenomena while under the influence of psychedelics, such as telepathic communication or uncanny synchronicities. What do you make of these types of experiences, which conventional science has great difficulty explaining, and which seem to provide evidence for psychic phenomena?

STAN: The number of these seemingly unexplainable phenomena is growing, and it's occurring in all kinds of disciplines. In astrophysics you have the anthropic principle. In quantum physics you have a vast array of problems that cannot be explained, such as Bell's theorem, which points to nonlocality in the universe. We can add some of the dilemmas that Rupert Sheldrake points out in biology when he talks about the need to think in terms of morphogenetic fields and so on. Ervin Laszlo, in his book *The Connectivity Hypothesis,* actually looked at all these different disciplines and showed all the so-called anomalous phenomena that these current theories cannot explain. He also specifically discusses transpersonal psychology and all the challenging observations that cannot be explained by current theories in psychology or psychiatry. I think Ervin's concept of the psi-, or Akashic, field is the most promising approach to these paradigm-breaking phenomena.

So I think that all this points to the fact that the current monistic/materialistic worldview is seriously defective, and that we need a completely different way of looking at reality. But there is tremendous resistance against the new observations in the academic world, because the revision that is necessary is too radical, something that cannot be handled by a little patchwork, by little ad hoc hypotheses here and there. We would have to admit that the basic philosophy of the Western scientific worldview is seriously wrong and that in many ways shamans from illiterate cultures and ancient cultures have had a more adequate understanding of reality than we do. We have learned a lot about the world of matter, but in terms of basic metaphysical understanding of reality, Western science went astray.

What sort of lessons do you think a conventional Western physician could learn from an indigenous shaman?

STAN: It would be above all the knowledge concerning the healing, transformative, and heuristic potential of nonordinary states of consciousness. This would be especially true for shamans who are using in their practice psychedelic plants. They use these extraordinary tools that provide insights into the psyche and therapeutic possibilities that by far surpass anything available in Western psychiatry and psychotherapy. When I had my first psychedelic sessions and started working with psychedelics, I felt very apologetic toward shamans. The image of shamans that I inherited from my teachers at the university was very conceited and dismissive; it described them as primitives, riddled with superstitions and engaged in magical thinking. Our own rational approaches to the study of the human psyche, such as behaviorism or psychoanalysis, were seen as superior to anything the shamans were doing.

So when I discovered the power of psychedelics, I saw the arrogance of this kind of attitude. The potential of the methods used by modern psychiatry did not even come close to that inherent in psychedelics or in various native technologies of the sacred, which induce nonordinary states by nonpharmacological means. Then I began understanding what had happened historically. Three hundred years ago, the industrial and scientific revolutions brought some important scientific discoveries, which spawned technological inventions that started radically changing our world. This led to glorification of rationality and intoxication with the power of reason. For example, during the French Revolution the Notre Dame Cathedral in Paris was declared the Temple of Reason. In its juvenile hubris, the Cult of Reason rejected without discrimination everything that was not rational as embarrassing leftovers from the infancy of humanity and from the Dark Ages. The overzealous reformers did not realize that not everything that is not rational is irrational; there exist phenomena which are transrational. The mystics are not irrational; they can be perfectly rational in everyday situations, but as a result of their experiences they also transcend the realm of the rational. We are now slowly realizing that in this historical process the baby was thrown out with the bathwater and are learning to make the distinction between the irrational and transrational.

What are your thoughts on the extraterrestrial encounters that many people report on high-dose psychedelics, and do you think that the beings encountered on high-dose psychedelic experiences, such as DMT or ayahuasca, actually have an independent existence?

STAN: I have seen those experiences frequently. We have seen them in psychedelic sessions, in Holotropic Breathwork, and in some spiritual emergencies. I have spent a lot of time with my close friend John Mack, who conducted at Harvard extensive research of the alien abduction phenomena. Did you know John?

I interviewed John for my book Conversations on the Edge of the
Apocalypse.

STAN: Unfortunately he was killed by a drunken driver in London
and is not with us anymore. Like John, I believe that these experiences
belong to the category of anomalous phenomena, paradigm-breaking
observations for which we do not have explanations within the current conceptual frameworks. The kind of explanations that have been
given by traditional researchers just are not satisfactory—that these
phenomena are hallucinations; various meteorological events; new
secret U.S. spacecrafts; balloons; birds; satellites, planets, and stars;
or optical effects such as reflections, mirages, sprites, sun dogs, and
refractions caused by inversion layers in the atmosphere.

I think that these are painfully inadequate, and that there are
significant aspects of the UFO-abduction phenomena or even UFO
sightings that simply cannot be explained within the current scientific worldview. One possible explanation is that the source of these
phenomena is the collective unconscious, as C. G. Jung suggested in
his book *Flying Saucers: A Modern Myth of Things Seen in the Skies.*
As Bud Hopkins and others have shown, people who have the UFO
experiences often report very similar things, often with great detail,
even if these observations occur completely independently and there
is no connection between these people. One of the most astonishing
examples was a sighting in Africa, which involved a group of schoolchildren and a teacher. The interviews with these witnesses were done
by John Mack and resulted in a remarkable video.

In the past similar things were described in the Bible, in the Book
of Ezekiel, and other places. Jung has shown that these sightings have
been described repeatedly in certain periods of human history. The collective unconscious certainly is a reasonable source of these phenomena.
If something comes from the collective unconscious, then individual
people can have intrapsychic access to it, but, at the same time, they
can receive consensual validation from other witnesses, in the same way

in which consensus can be reached on visions of archetypal figures or realms from different mythologies. The distinction between the subjective and objective is transcended. Jungians refer to this realm as imaginal to distinguish it from the imaginary.

When I think about the collective unconscious, I see the parallels with the world that we have created with modern electronics. As we are sitting here right now, we are immersed in an ocean of information. It's coming from the different short-wave radio stations around the world, from the television satellites, from the Internet, the iPhones, and so on. So if we had what it takes to access this information, we could have a vast array of experiences right here, where we are sitting, and it would not be your experiences or my experiences. We would be tapping in to something that is objectively real, although under normal circumstances it is invisible. When different people tune in to these programs, they can reach a consensus that they have experienced the same kind of thing. So from this perspective, the UFOs would be phenomena that are not just intrapsychic or just objective in the usual sense, but would lie in the twilight zone in between the two.

Do you think that the archetypes and information that are stored in the human collective unconscious are of a genetic origin—that is, stored in our DNA—or do you see them as being more like a morphic field that permeates the biosphere and incorporates cultural as well as genetic information?

STAN: I don't think it's in the DNA or in the brain. I don't think it's in anything that we can consider to be material substrate, at least not in the ordinary sense.

So do you see it more like a morphic field?

STAN: Yes. The best model that we currently have is Ervin Laszlo's concept of what he used to call a psi-field; now he calls it the Akashic field. In his last two books, *The Connectivity Hypothesis* and *Science and the Akashic Field,* he describes it as a subquantum field, where everything that has ever happened in the universe remains holograph-ically recorded, so that under certain circumstances we can tune in to it and have the corresponding experiences. For example, in nonordi-nary states of consciousness, we can have experiences of scenes from ancient Egypt or the French Revolution, because there's an objectively existing record of these events in that field, and people who tap that information can reach consensus that they experienced the same kind of things.

How does transpersonal psychology differ from conventional psy-chology, and could you talk a little about your involvement with it?

STAN: I was part of the small group that formulated the basic principles of transpersonal psychology, together with Abe Maslow, Tony Sutich, Jim Fadiman, Miles Vich, and Sonja Margulies. Transpersonal psychol-ogy was a reaction to a number of anomalous phenomena described by mystics of all ages, scholars of the great Eastern religions, anthropolo-gists who had done field research with shamans and native cultures, and psychedelic researchers.

In the first half of the twentieth century, psychology was dominated by two schools of thought: Freudian psychoanalysis and behaviorism. In the 1950s, there was increasing dissatisfaction with the limitations of these two systems, and Abe Maslow became the main spokesman for this increasing dissent. He and Tony Sutich launched humanistic psy-chology, which in a very short time became very popular in professional as well as lay circles. However, within the first ten years of the existence of humanistic psychology, Abe and Tony became dissatisfied with the field they had created, because it did not include important aspects of human nature, particularly the spiritual and mystical dimensions, cre-ativity, meditation states, ecstatic experiences, and so on. When I met them, they were working on yet another new branch of psychology that would incorporate the elements that humanistic psychology was lacking.

They originally wanted to call this new psychology transhumanistic—going beyond humanistic psychology. I brought into this group the data from ten years of my psychedelic research in Prague and a vastly extended cartography of the psyche that had emerged from this work. Part of this cartography was a category of experiences that I called transpersonal, meaning transcending the limits of our personal identity, of the body-ego. Abe and Tony liked this term very much, and they decided to change their original term, *transhumanistic psychology*, to *transpersonal psychology*.

The best way of describing transpersonal psychology would be to say that it studies the entire spectrum of human experience, including what I call holotropic experiences. This includes the experiences of shamans and their clients; of initiates in the rites of passage, in healing ceremonies, and other native rituals; of the initiates in the ancient mysteries of death and rebirth; of the yogis, Buddhists, Taoists, Christian mystics, Kabbalists, and so on. Transpersonal psychology includes all of these experiences.

What's the difference between a spiritual emergency and a psychotic episode?

STAN: After we had had extensive experience working with psychedelic therapy and with the Holotropic Breathwork, it became increasingly difficult to see many of the spontaneously occurring episodes of nonordinary (holotropic) states as being pathological. They included the same elements as the psychedelic sessions and the sessions of Holotropic Breathwork: experiences of psychospiritual death and rebirth, past-life experiences, archetypal experiences, and so on. And if they were properly understood and supported, they were actually healing and often led to a positive personality transformation.

So [the episodes of nonordinary states] became increasingly difficult to see as pathological experiences, which a sample of normal people in our workshops and training would have after forty-five minutes of faster breathing. Moreover, if these experiences could be healing and transformative when they are induced by faster breathing and music, or by minuscule dosages of LSD, why should they be considered pathological when they occur without any known causes? So we coined for these spontaneously occurring episodes the term *spiritual emergencies*. It is actually a play on words, because it shows the potential positive value of these experiences. They certainly are a nuisance in people's lives and can produce a crisis, an emergency, but if correctly understood and properly supported they can also help these individuals to emerge to a whole other level of consciousness and of functioning.

Now, the question that you ask—the question concerning differential diagnosis—is difficult to answer for the following reasons: The concept of differential diagnosis comes from medicine, where it is possible to accurately diagnose diseases on the basis of what you find in the blood, in the urine, in the cerebral spinal fluid, on the X-rays, and so on. You can accurately establish the diagnosis, and if you make a mistake, another doctor can show you that you made a wrong diagnosis and, as a result, prescribed the wrong treatment. In psychiatry, this is possible only for those conditions that have an organic cause. There is a group of psychotic states where this is the case—the so-called organic psychoses. However, there exists a large group of conditions diagnosed as psychoses for which no biological causes have been found. These are called functional or endogenous psychoses.

Anybody familiar with medicine knows that this essentially means admission of ignorance wrapped in a fancy title [*endogenous* means "generated from within"]. This is not a medical diagnosis backed by laboratory data. It is a situation characterized by unusual experiences and behaviors for which the current conceptual framework of psychiatry has no explanation. To make a differential diagnosis, we would first have to have a diagnosis established as rigorously as it is done in somatic medicine. Because that is not the case, we have to use a different approach. We can try to identify the criteria that would make the person experiencing a nonordinary state of consciousness a good candidate for deep inner work. If they meet these criteria, we try to work with them psychologically to help them get through this experience, rather than indiscriminately suppressing their symptoms with psychopharmacological agents.

The first criterion there is the phenomenology of the individual's condition. A positive indication is the presence of elements that we see daily in participants in Holotropic Breathwork sessions or psychedelic sessions: reliving of traumatic memories from infancy or childhood; reliving of biological birth or episodes of prenatal existence; the experience of psychospiritual death and rebirth, past-life experiences, visions of archetypal beings, or visits to archetypal realms. Additional positive indications are experiences of oneness with other people, with nature, with the universe, with God.

The second important criterion is the person's attitude. The individual in spiritual crisis has to have some sense of understanding that this is a process which is happening internally. Very bad candidates for alternative psychological work are people who use a lot of projections, who deny that they have a problem and that they are dealing with an internal process. They are convinced that all their problems are caused by outside forces: it is the neighbor who is poisoning their soup and placing bugging devices in their house, it is the Ku Klux Klan trying to destroy them, it is a mad scientist attacking them by a diabolic machine, or the invading Martians. So there is a tendency to blame that condition on somebody or something outside of them, and being unwilling to accept the possibility that there is something within their own psyche that they can work on. So unless that attitude changes, it is very difficult to do this type of work.

Why do you think that the conditions surrounding one's birth have such a lasting effect on one's outlook toward life?

STAN: Birth is an extremely powerful, elemental event that for many children is a matter of life and death. This is especially true for those who were born severely asphyxiated—dead or half-dead—and had to be resuscitated. In any case, it is a major trauma that has a physical as well as an emotional dimension. The position of current psychiatry and psychology toward birth is unbelievable. Contrary to elementary logic, we see a massive denial of the fact that birth is a major psychotrauma. The usual reason given for the fact that birth is psychologically irrelevant—inadequate myelinization of the newborn's cortex—is hard to take seriously. It is in sharp contrast with data from both postnatal and prenatal life.

There exists general agreement among child psychiatrists that the experience of nursing is of paramount importance for the rest of the individual's emotional life. Obstetricians and pediatricians even talk about the importance of bonding—the exchange of looks between the mother and the child immediately after the child is born—as the foundation of the future mother-child relationship. And extensive prenatal research of people like Alfred Tomatis has shown extreme sensitivity of the fetus already in the prenatal period. How should we reconcile this with the belief that the hours of life-and-death struggle in the birth canal are psychologically irrelevant?

It seems really bizarre that psychiatrists and psychologists believe that there is no consciousness in the child during the passage through the birth canal, but then suddenly appears as soon as the newborn emerges into the world. And the argument about the lack of myelinization of the newborn's cortex violates elementary logic and doesn't make any sense either. We know from biology that memory does not require a cerebral cortex, let alone a myelinized one. There are organisms that don't have any cortex at all and they certainly can form memories. Several years ago, the Nobel Prize was given to Austrian American researcher Eric Kandel for studying memory mechanisms in a sea slug called *Aplysia*. So it's very difficult to imagine how people in the academic circle think, if they can accept that the sea slug can form memories but a newborn child, with an extremely highly developed nervous system and brain, would not be able to create a memory record of the hours spent in the birth canal.

What do you think of applying Konrad Lorenz's notion of bio-logical imprinting, as opposed to conditioning or learning, to the lasting psychological effect that psychedelic experiences often produce?

STAN: The term *imprinting* is most relevant here in relation to the very early situations in an organism's development. As you know, ethologists have shown that the early experiences of life are extremely influential. For example, there is a period of about sixteen hours in the early life of ducklings when whatever moves around becomes for them the mother. So if you walk around in red rubber shoes, they ignore their mother and follow the shoes. Psychedelics can induce deep age regression to the early periods in one's life and offer the opportunity for a corrective psychobiological experience. This new experience then seems to have the same powerful influence on the individual's life as the natural imprinting.

I ultimately don't believe that the memories we experience in psychedelic sessions are stored in the brain—certainly not all of them. I think that many of them obviously don't have any material substrate in the conventional sense—ancestral, collective, phylogenetic, and karmic memories, archetypal matrices, et cetera. Recently, there has been much discussion about memory without a material substrate—for example, Rupert Sheldrake's morphogenetic fields or Ervin Laszlo's Akashic field. So I don't believe that what we experience is stored in the brain. I believe that the brain is mediating consciousness but does not generate it, and that it mediates memories but does not store them.

Why do you think it is that the LSD experiences have such a lasting effect on people?

STAN: Isn't that true about every powerful experience? The more powerful the experience is, the more of an effect it has. It is true even for experiences that we have forgotten, repressed, dissociated from consciousness. Everything that we experience in life is shaping us with a lasting effect. Some of these influences are more subtle and some of them more dramatic, but certainly traumas that people experience in childhood can have tremendous impact. Events in human life can have everlasting impact of people.

What do you personally think happens to consciousness after death?

STAN: I have had experiences in my psychedelic sessions—quite a few of them—when I was sure I was in the same territory that we enter after death. In several of my sessions, I was absolutely certain that it had already happened and I was surprised when I came back, when I ended up in the situation where I took the substance. So the experience of being in a bardo in these experiences is extremely convincing. We now also have many clinical observations suggesting that consciousness can operate independently of the brain, the prime example being out-of-body experiences in near-death situations.

Some out-of-body experiences can happen to people not only when they are in a state of cardiac death, but also when they are brain-dead. Cardiologist Michael Sabom described a patient he called Pam, who had a major aneurysm on the basilar artery and had to undergo a risky operation. In order to operate on her, they had to basically freeze her brain to the point that she stopped producing brain waves. And at the same time she had one of the most powerful out-of-body experiences ever observed, with accurate perception of the environment. Following her operation she was able to give an accurate description of the operation and to draw the instruments they were using.

So what these observations suggest is that consciousness can operate independently of our body when we are alive, which makes it fairly plausible that something like that is possible after our body is dead. So both the experiential evidence from my own sessions and what you find in the thanatological literature certainly suggest that survival of consciousness after death is a very real possibility.

What is your perspective on the concept of God?

STAN: When Jung was over eighty years old he had an interview with a BBC reporter. At one point this BBC reporter asked him, "Dr. Jung, do you believe in God?" A smile appeared on Jung's face and he said, "No, I don't." Any Jungians who are watching this tape cannot believe it. "What? Dr. Jung doesn't believe in God?" Then, after a dramatic pause, Jung says, "I know. I had the experience of being grabbed by something that was by far more powerful than I could even imagine." Like Jung, I had experiences—actually quite a few of them over the years—of what I would refer to as God.

I have experienced in my sessions many gods—archetypal figures of many forms from different cultures of the world. But when I refer to God, I am talking about an experience which is beyond any forms. What I experienced as God is difficult to describe; as you know, the mystics often refer to their experiences as ineffable. It could be best described as an incredibly powerful source of light, with an intensity that I earlier couldn't even have imagined. But it doesn't really do it justice to refer to it as light, because it was much more than that. It seemed to contain all of existence in a completely abstract form, and it transcended all imaginable polarities. There was a sense of infinite boundless creativity. There was a sense of personality and even a sense of humor (of a cosmic variety).

The experience of God seems to be, under certain circumstances, available to all human beings. If you haven't had the experience, then there's no point in talking about it. As long as people have to talk about believing in God or not believing in God or, for that matter, believing in past lives or not believing in past lives, it is irrelevant, because they do not have anything to go by. Their opinion doesn't have any real basis; it reflects the influences of their parents, their preacher, or something they have read. Once you had the experiences, you know that the experiences were real and very convincing.

What types of research and therapies do you foresee for psyche-delics in the future?

STAN: I think that the most interesting area waiting to be explored is to use psychedelics for enhancing creativity, as we talked about earlier. It is something that would facilitate completely new ways of looking at various areas and generate extraordinary new insights into the nature of reality. But I am afraid it will take some time before we see research of this kind. The most difficult challenge has always been to get permission to use psychedelics in populations where there is no serious clinical reason—that is, terminal cancer, chronic alcoholism, et cetera.

What are you currently working on?

STAN: Christina and I are writing a long overdue book on the theory and practice of Holotropic Breathwork.* It will be a very comprehensive book, covering a wide range of topics from the history of the breath-work to the therapeutic use of breathwork sessions and its social impli-cations. It will include the description how to prepare a session and how to run a session, as well as the complementary methods that you can use following the session. It discusses the therapeutic effects, the pos-sibilities of developing a new worldview and new life strategies, as well as the possible importance of working with holotropic states as a means of alleviating the current global crisis.

Is there anything that we didn't speak about that you would like to add?

STAN: One of the areas I am particularly interested in is the revolution-ary development on various scientific disciplines and the emergence of the new paradigm. I firmly believe that we are rapidly moving toward a radically new worldview and that transpersonal psychology and spiri-tuality will be integral parts of it. A worldview that will synthesize

---

*Author's note: This interview was conducted before the death of Christina Grof in 2014.

the best of science and the best of spirituality and would demonstrate that there is really no incompatibility between science and spirituality, if both of them are properly understood. The other area that I am very deeply interested in has to do with the phenomenal digital special effects, which are now available in the movie industry.

Are you still interested in making animated films?

STAN: It is ironical, isn't it? As I look at it, my career has not changed as much as I initially thought when I became interested in psychiatric research. Psychedelic experiences, with their rich imagery, are not that far from animated movies. But I am not interested anymore in making animated movies; what I am interested in is the spiritual potential of these new special effects. I believe that the special effects are so powerful these days that they could not only portray mystical experience, but they could actually induce them in people if they were properly constructed. If we could combine what we know about the inner logic of these experiences with these new special effects, the results could be truly extraordinary. Unfortunately, the new special effects are being used mostly for portraying destructive movies scenes.

Hollywood movies portray with formidable power scenes reflecting what I call BPM III—the violent and sexual imagery associated typically with the final stages of birth. The destructive scenes are so boringly stereotypical that they are almost [interchangeable] from movie to movie. Only the danger takes different forms—alien invaders, natural disasters, dinosaurs or other monsters, demonic beings, and all kinds of dangerous villains threatening to destroy the planet. Most of these movies end up in a situation where the enemy is overcome and people celebrate the victory on a trashed, devastated planet. What is missing is the shift to BPM IV, lifting the experience to the transcendental level, to spiritual death/rebirth experience. I don't know if you know that Christina and I were consultants on the movie called *Brainstorm,* which was an attempt to portray a transcendental experience.

I had read that and found that very interesting, as Brainstorm is one of my favorite films. I thought that there were a lot of fascinating ideas in it.

STAN: That was an effort to bring to the screen the transcendental aspects of the death experience. Unfortunately, the special effects were very compromised, because of the tragic death of Natalie Wood shortly before the movie was finished. MGM didn't want to put any more money into the movie; they believed that it was not viable, because there were three scenes of principal photography with Natalie that were still missing. Doug Trumbull convinced the MGM people that he could finish the movie. He did his best to put it together, but it didn't really come out very well. If you watch the movie, it is not only the lack of the special effects, but there is a kind of a logical gap; you can tell that there is something missing. But I think that the topic of the movie is so interesting that it deserves a remake, as they are remaking all kinds of other movies. I think that this is one that deserves to be remade and done really well.

3
Creativity, Problem Solving, and Psychedelics

An Interview with **James Fadiman**

James Fadiman is one of the few psychologists fortunate enough to have been able to study the effects of psychedelic drugs on creativity, and he is now the world's leading expert on the subject.

In 1966, Fadiman was part of the team that conducted the well-known study in Menlo Park, California, on how psychedelics affect problem-solving abilities. The study provided compelling evidence that mescaline and LSD can enhance creativity and problem-solving abilities among various types of professionals.

Fadiman was introduced to psilocybin by his former professor and friend Ram Dass (Richard Alpert) in 1961, a year after he graduated from Harvard University. He received his Ph.D. in psychology from Stanford University in 1965. In 1974, Fadiman cofounded the Institute of Transpersonal Psychology (now part of Sofia University), where he continues to lecture on psychedelic studies. He was the president of the Association for Transpersonal Psychology from 1972 to 1975 and the director of the Institute of Noetic Sciences from 1975 to 1977. Fadiman worked as a private consultant for major corporations and universities for a number of years. His last business card read: UNUSUAL PROBLEMS. UNIQUE SOLUTIONS.

Fadiman is also the author of several books, both fiction and non-fiction, including *The Psychedelic Explorer's Guide: Safe, Therapeutic, and Sacred Journeys,* which summarizes his groundbreaking research and offers some of the very best guidance that has ever been written for running a therapeutic psychedelic session.

Jim Fadiman currently teaches, lectures, and leads workshops around the world about psychedelics and creativity.

I interviewed Jim on April 4, 2014. He has a warm smile and a golden heart and is one of the kindest people that I've ever had the pleasure of knowing. We spoke about his creativity research, the future of psychology, and where psychedelic drug research may be leading us.

How did you become interested in psychology?

JAMES: By the beginning of my sophomore year in college, I was an unhappy and unsuccessful physics major. I literally read through the entire course catalog for courses that were more interesting (and easier). In one class, a young assistant professor, Richard Alpert, suggested that psychology was not only a good major but would be helpful in whatever else I wanted to do with my life. It was good advice. (Years later, he turned me on to psychedelics.) I was not attracted to psychology as a "science," because coming off physics, it didn't really look like one. The promise of understanding human beings and the possibility of understanding myself won me over.

How have Eastern philosophical systems influenced your perspective on psychology?

JAMES: After my initial exposures to psychedelic experience, I began searching for anything to help me understand my now much wider worldview. Western psychology was then no more than 150 years old, while older systems, especially Buddhism, had been struggling with basic psychological questions for several thousand years. They were obviously far more sophisticated in their understanding of different states of consciousness, as well as having well-developed, complex systems for consciousness exploration. The realization that there were many other systematic attempts to map and amplify awareness led me not to abandon psychology but to actively work to expand it to include what we now call the transpersonal, which extends beyond the limits of individual personality and assumes spiritual experience to be normal.

In addition, I've taught a class for over twenty-five years using Sufi poems and stories as tools for personal awakening. Conventional psychology, still attempting to look as much like a physical science as possible, simply was inadequate for what I was needing to learn. A discipline that hopes to reduce consciousness to brain states, chemical or electrical reactions while denying, except as pathology, even the possibility of higher states of consciousness, spiritual experiences, the paranormal, and intelligence across the spectrum of living beings, can hardly be expected to be useful if one intends serious internal exploration.

What inspired you to cofound the Institute of Transpersonal Psychology?

JAMES: A short answer would have to be incredible lack of knowledge and an invitation to be of real service. Bob Frager and I had become close friends and were working on a different kind of textbook for classes in personality theories. Ours was the first text to include chapters on women—almost all theories seemed to be by and about men—and non-Western psychologies, including Zen Buddhism, yoga, and Sufism. We also had the usual chapters on Freud, Jung, Skinner, et cetera. As the book was about and titled *Personality and Personal Growth,* we thought about how a full education would include emotional, intellectual, physical, and spiritual development. We wrote a very short paper

Photo by Scott Kline

James Fadiman

describing our vision that was published in the transpersonal newsletter with a very small circulation. To our amazement, students from all over the country wrote to us, asking, "Where is the school?" At the same time, Bob was turned down for tenure, even though his classes were extremely popular; he had founded a thriving campus aikido club, had a few publications, plus our textbook.

Although in retrospect it seems foolish, if not downright crazy, at the time it seemed eminently sensible to proclaim that we were establishing a full graduate school of transpersonal psychology and would admit students that fall. We had no money; had never had a business, let alone a school; had no curriculum, no faculty, and no location. Equally amazing was that students applied, sent in their tuition, and eventually arrived.

The on-the-ground reality is that Bob Frager founded and ran the school as well as sat in on all the classes during the first year. I had other work and helped out often, especially as a facilitator, when there were problems. Students would decide what they wanted to learn; we would find a faculty to come in and teach that material. Our original campus was the downstairs of the home in Woodside, California, which included a living room, a kitchen, a bathroom, and an outdoor hot tub. It was clearly an era of experimentation in the Bay Area, as several other alternative graduate schools formed at about the same time. A full answer includes that we founded the school because students risked a lot to get the education we promised, we believed in our model, and Bob needed a job.

How do you envision the future of psychology?

JAMES: If psychology continues on its current reductionist path, it will continue to decline in popularity and value. There is a term in oil-and-gas exploration, *running out of hole,* when you can't attach any more pipes, you have already used up the smallest-diameter pipe available. Psychology's unwillingness to incorporate not only transpersonal psychology, psychedelic experience, parapsychology, and spiritual systems, but also to ignore the massive interest and literature of self-help, suggests that it is diminishing itself on purpose, that it has run out of hole.

Psychology saved itself from becoming irrelevant after World War II, when it pioneered clinical psychology on a massive scale. It recently has become enraptured with neuroscience, incorporating endless discoveries about brain mechanisms, chemistry, and so forth. However, its rejection of vast sweeps of human experience still remains. Albert

Hofmann wrote about the limits of the materialism, but his comments are equally true for psychology. He says it lacks "any physically or chemically inaccessible dimensions of being, to which the essential signs of life belong. Love, joy, beauty, creative spirit, ethics, morality are neither weighable nor measurable, thus they are not present in the materialistic, scientific worldview." Most of academic psychology is not what most people care about.

Fortunately, in the last few decades, there has been an explosion of spiritual texts being translated and new ones being written that grapple with the questions that most people had hoped psychology could answer: *How can I live better? How can I be kinder? How can I treat myself and others with love and compassion?* While I can't point to much in conventional psychology that can help answer these kinds of questions, I can easily direct people to teachers, trainings, writings, and, of course, guided psychedelic journeys that can be enormously helpful.

What kind of relationship do you see between creativity and psychedelics?

JAMES: There are at least six ways to use psychedelics to generate specific kinds of experiences. These include spiritual breakthrough, psychotherapeutic insight, creative problem solving, reuniting with the natural world, recreational use, and microdosing. Creative problem solving is probably the least known but has had the most impact on modern life. In my book I devote almost a quarter of it to lengthy descriptions of how scientists used psychedelics to work on extremely difficult problems in physical science, mathematics, theoretical physics, architecture, et cetera.

The fact that, in almost every case, in a carefully controlled, safe environment, subjects were able to make significant progress and in many cases full solutions was remarkable at the time. No one quite believed that people would focus away from their own personal experience and work entirely on external problems. The relationship now is clear: psychedelics, using a moderate dose, with highly motivated individuals, allows people to utilize their expanded awareness, their enhanced capacity for pattern recognition, visual and metaphoric thinking, plus their increased ideational flexibility for breakthrough solutions.

What would you say were the most important results that you gathered from your study of psychedelics on creative problem solving?

JAMES: Aside from the actual solutions that emerged and later proved to be valued, becoming patents, products, and publications, what was most important is what is called in science proof of concept. For example, does what you are looking for exist?

When we began the research, we were hopeful but not convinced that it would work. After the first group of scientists had worked successfully and gone home, the research team danced around like small children. We were as excited with the success of the method as the scientists were with its results. That the research was prematurely stopped when the government stopped all research with psychedelics has delayed establishment recognition of our findings, but, as predicted, encouraged more underground use. That we demonstrated that it was possible to focus even the intense opening that happens during psychedelic experiences was not lost on the next generation of inventive entrepreneurs.

What kind of new studies would you like to see done with creativity and psychedelics?

JAMES: Fortunately, there are groups of researchers in England and in the U.S. who are about to replicate our original work. Once that happens and is published, then more people will find other ways to work creatively with these substances. And, quite divorced from the slow, steady progress of researchers, there is already one ongoing, massive experiment combining all sorts of psychedelics with all sorts of set and settings and a vast range of problems. I'm talking about Burning Man, a yearly tidal wave of original constructions, ranging from huge temporary buildings to unusual body paint and large rituals, much of it fueled by psychedelically augmented innovations. What the government never understood is that trying to deny people the opportunity to use their minds more fully only creates a self-supporting underground. As [Alexander] Shulgin has said, "The urge to become more aware is always present." People will always use tools that increase awareness, no matter what the legal or religious obstacles may be.

I'd like to see some studies begun in education, using low or microdoses to assist students in becoming more aware of basic patterns in nature, art, and in their own relationships to them. Given that we are still far away from evidence-based regulations of any of these substances, it will be awhile before they become just one more tool available to educators. Imagine, if you will, how much more valuable a field trip for students in botany or ecology or geology would be if even slightly enhanced. And, just like the fifty thousand burners are not waiting for the government to approve the use of psychedelics for creative problem solving, it is hard to imagine that the same students who regularly drop one psychedelic or another at concerts won't be already doing that for field trips.

My problem is, whenever I imagine a future study, I also often find out from my fieldwork that the millions and millions of people who have experimented with psychedelics are way ahead of me.

What are some of the other areas that you would like to see psychedelic drug research look in to and explore more?

JAMES: One of my interests is in how to give people the best possible experience at any dose level. What I have found is that having a skilled guide to assist someone during their journey of discovery allows them to go further and deeper than they would on their own, and certainly deeper than when they are in a group with no one guiding. I would like to see more people trained to be guides. This is being done in some of the new clinical studies as these studies move closer to full medical acceptance. However, right now, about 99 percent of all psychedelic use is outside of any supervision. It seems to me invaluable to ensure those 99 percent of all experiences, as they have the potential to be life changing, to be safe and healthy. There are some underground groups doing excellent training, and there are some manuals available, including my own, but we can do lots better. When LSD was the most widely researched psychiatric drug in the world, before it became illegal, there was a training program in what is now the Czech Republic for health professionals to become psychedelic therapists. In order to be certified, you had to take five individual, supervised sessions and run thirty sessions where you were observed and supervised. That's one area that seems fairly obvious to me.

And here is a study I'd love to see: I know two cases where stuttering was cured during one self-guided mushroom session. It would be easy research to do and well worth doing.

I'm also fascinated by microdosing, taking such a small amount of psychedelic that there are no obvious perceptual changes. As one user describes it, "The rocks don't glitter, even a little." Albert Hofmann considered this low-dose area as a major under-researched area.

I have been collecting individuals' experiences using these very low doses—different substances, different ways of using, and a wide range of results. Microdoses may be an alternative to antidepressants, and a safer alternative to Adderall and the other amphetamine-based, so-called cognitive enhancers. I have one report of a psilocybin-like designer drug that is not only a mood enhancer and a general energizer, but seems to have improved the experimenter's vision. He reports needing his glasses less. Another report is from a Parkinson's patient who microdosed for a month. While it did not appear to make much difference in his physical symptoms, he found himself significantly more outgoing and social. Other people have reported increased productivity, overcoming writer's block, and being more tolerant of other people's failings. Anyone reading this interview who is experimenting with microdoses is very welcome to contact me at fadimanevents@gmail.com. Please don't ask me to send you any illegal drugs, but do let me know how you're using them and the results.

Do you think that the entities that people often report encountering while on DMT or ayahuasca have a genuine independent existence or not?

JAMES: I love this question. Since every culture and every religious system that I know of talks about entities, some who apparently care for and like human beings, and others who don't, I defer to the shamans about their reality. They make use of the specific talents and knowledge of individual entities to heal and help others and to protect themselves and their patients from malevolent forces. As for the world of alternate realities that opens for the few minutes that DMT lasts, they give every appearance of being independent of the person experiencing them, but, then again, so do almost all the entities in dreams, most of which are actually aspects of ourselves. While I have no doubt that there were other levels of reality and other beings, I have not yet found that my belief or lack of belief makes any difference to them, except that if I don't believe in them, it is much harder for them to help me. I've been helped often enough to be grateful for their presence.

As to their form, I recall two incidents. One when Dorothy Maclean, the person who saw the fairies and other beings at Findhorn, was talking with them one day and one said to her, "You know we don't look like this." She asked what did they look like? Their answer was that they were more like energy beings but took the forms that she saw because that made her feel more comfortable.

The second incident is personal. I have worked with a shaman on and off for some years, and she has introduced me to several entities, who, she said, were my helpers. One is a small bear, one a blue deer, and so on. At one point, with guidance, they came to me and said that they are not those animals at all, but as your shaman likes to work with animal-like spirits, that is how she sees us. Therefore, I remain a little skeptical about the actual corporeal reality of beings from DMT-revealed worlds. Most of the beings that appear in ayahuasca sessions are understood by all parties to take various forms. The actual teacher or the spirit of the plant, however, is of a very different order and entirely real.

What do you think happens to consciousness after death?

JAMES: It is a remarkably common experience that those of us who have had a transcendental or entheogenic or classical mystical experience worry far less about death than we did before. What it looks like is that something—call it consciousness—takes on or merges with a physical being near or after birth. That physical being grows, develops, goes through its life cycle, and eventually dies. The consciousness, however, does not appear to die, nor does it appear to have been born. A very different consideration is what happens to my personality at death. It looks like, for most people, the personal identity dissolves back into component parts. However, there are clear cases of consciousness hanging around after death, which we call ghosts or the spirits of the departed. There is well-documented evidence that now and then personality reappears in a new body and remembers its former identity—where it had been born and lived—and can easily identify people it knew in its former life.

My own feeling and personal experience is that I am like a drop of water that has a defined form for a while and eventually returns to the ocean. There it loses its specificity, and parts of it adhere to parts of other former drops so that, perhaps, when once again it evaporates and eventually forms a water droplet, that drop contains portions, call them memories, of the other partial drops that it is made of.

Therefore, the memories I have of past lives, especially those proved to be valid, may be my direct lineage, but also may be the memories of other beings that I have merged with. I certainly would like there to be some kind of reincarnation, since I've been acquiring knowledge for a long time and I hate to think of it just being recycled without being reused. However, there's a great deal to be said for the Jim Fadiman personality to be finished when the Jim Fadiman body dies. When someone says, "I must've known you in another life," it is more often a pickup line than a moment of serious recognition. And, of course, if I'm wrong, it's unlikely that I will remember it in the next life anyway.

What is your perspective on the concept of God?

JAMES: Even before I'd used psychedelics, the notion that God resembled an elderly Jewish man sitting on a throne seemed highly unlikely. I'm always a little sad when I hear an atheist attacking the notion of God but who seems only to know the origin stories of the monotheistic trio of Judaism, Christianity, and Islam. There are more stories available, and many of them closer to my experience. It makes far more sense to me that the universe has some kind of intelligence, and certainly an appreciation of beauty, than to imagine that it is a seven-day wonder or just a bunch of stuff that blew up a long time ago and now clots a bit, and in some of the clots, life forms. It seems self-evident that there is a drive toward increasing complexity and awareness of interrelationships, as well as a drive toward falling apart and reforming over and over. That prayers are answered, that miracles occur, and that deities abound makes life richer and more understandable, whatever we call God. For me to imagine that I could describe the energy that underlies the visible material universe and all living things is above my pay grade.

I recall a time during a journey when I had taken an entheogenic-size dose of LSD and became part of an energy or an entity or a being far vaster than myself. I realized that I knew everything: time, space, human awareness, the creation of galaxies, the interrelationship of all things, et cetera. Then the being made it clear to me that there was no way that Jim Fadiman, with his teeny little brain on a teeny speck of dirt around a small star in one small galaxy, would ever be able to hold that kind of knowledge. The suggestion I was given was to enjoy whatever conception I'd like, knowing that it was as likely for that to be as accurate as if a single parrot fish could comprehend and explain the full complexity of the ecological habitat of its tropical reef. Since then, I worry less about the nature of the universe and more about the world that I actually inhabit. To paraphrase Alan Watts: all existence is a single energy, and that energy is my own being. Or, in terms of your question: everything is part of God—baby clothes, panty hose, anthrax, Hitler's mother, the Alps—everything.

If you could summarize the basic message of your life in a few words or sentences, what would they be?

JAMES: That you learn as much or more from happiness as you can from suffering. That inside of everyone is a divine spark, even though sometimes it is almost impossible to discover it. That the best word to describe the energy that generates and pervades the universe is *loving*. And that eventually you discover that hurting anyone else hurts you as well. I also know that the people who run the world don't seem to share these ideas and that the world would be a far better place if they did.

Is there anything that we haven't spoken about that you would like to add?

JAMES: After some reflection, what came was this: I realize that I am more and more grateful to more and more people and more and more places and things as I get older, and death becomes an eventuality rather than a remote possibility. I have been especially fortunate in how many people I have been able to love, and I'm glad I'm not done yet.

I made a discovery once that I expect everyone else has made as well, but that becomes more important as I've gotten older. I once took my father, who was then eighty-five, to visit his brother, who was ninety-one. At dinner I asked them what were their subjective ages.

After a moment's reflection, my uncle said that he was seven, explaining that had been the age when he was learning the most and had become aware of his own personality. I turned to my father, who said that he was twenty-one, and that it was the age in which he felt most fully alive and open to experience. I'm not sure of my own inner age, but I am delightfully aware that it is not the same age as my body. It is a curious pleasure to notice, and reaffirms my belief that my consciousness and, to some extent, my personality, are independent of this box that carries them around.

4
Exploring Anomalous Experiences

*An Interview with **Stanley Krippner***

Stanley Krippner, Ph.D., is a humanistic psychologist and one of the world's leading experts on altered states of consciousness, dreaming, psychic phenomena, psychedelics, post-traumatic stress disorder, anomalous experiences, indigenous healing, and shamanism.

Krippner was formerly the director of the Kent State University Child Study Center in Ohio and the director of the Maimonides Medical Center Dream Laboratory in Brooklyn. He is currently an executive professor at Saybrook University in San Francisco, where he holds the Alan Watts Chair in Consciousness Studies.

At the Dream Laboratory in Brooklyn, Krippner conducted studies to determine whether people could receive telepathic communications while they were dreaming. The results were quite compelling, and Krippner coauthored a wonderful book on the subject called *Dream Telepathy*. He is the author, editor, coeditor, or coauthor of thirty-seven other books.

Krippner has received many awards for his valuable work, including the Distinguished Lifetime Contributions to Humanistic Psychology

Award in 2013 and the American Psychological Association's Award for Distinguished Contributions to the International Advancement of Psychology in 2000.

————————————————— ☺ —————————————————

I interviewed Stanley on February 17, 2014. We spoke about the future of psychology, psychedelic drug research, dreaming, and whether the entities that people often report encountering while on DMT or ayahuasca have a genuine independent existence or not.

Please tell me a little about how you first became interested in psychology and parapsychology.

STANLEY: I was born in 1932 and grew up on a farm in Wisconsin. In our community I observed a wide range of human behavior—incest, infidelity, child abuse, spouse abuse, bullying, and suicide on the one hand, and generosity, sacrifice, compassion, and integrity on the other hand. I read popular psychology articles about these topics and was fascinated by the information and explanations given.

I was an avid reader, and when I was twelve years of age I asked my parents to buy me a set of encyclopedias. They explained they could not afford the hundred dollars they would cost, and I retired to my bedroom in tears. Then I had an inspiration. I had one rich relative, my uncle Max, and I would ask him to lend me the money. Suddenly I sensed that this would not work out, because my uncle Max was dead. At that moment there was a phone call.

My mother answered the phone and began to scream. Her sister's husband, my uncle Max, had died suddenly of a heart attack. I did not mention this incident for years, but it broadened my reading vista to include premonitions, telepathy, and other parapsychological topics.

How have traditional shamanic systems influenced your perspective on psychology?

Stanley Krippner

STANLEY: I have been interested in Native American culture all of my life. When my father plowed his fields, he often uncovered Indian arrowheads, and my sister and I amassed quite a collection of them. So I started to read about Native Americans, especially the tribes that had lived in our part of Wisconsin. I read about medicine men, medicine women, and shamans, but did not meet one until I began working at Maimonides Medical Center in the 1960s.

I was invited to speak on a panel that included Grandmother Twylah Nitsch, a Seneca Indian shaman. What she, and other medicine people, said about ecology and caring for the Earth resonated with my own worldview. My father was one of the first in the area to practice organic farming, and so I could see the practical applications of becoming a part of nature rather than exploiting nature.

When I met Alan Watts, the philosopher who popularized Eastern thought in the United States, I discovered that this perspective was an important part of his personal philosophy. So I was an ecopsychologist before the word was even coined. Back in 1972, Alan Watts, Rolling Thunder (a renowned medicine man), and I conducted a joint series of seminars at the University of New Mexico in Las Cruces. The students were surprised that we were all delivering similar messages from three different perspectives—psychology, philosophy, and Native American teachings.

How do you envision the future of psychology?

STANLEY: Psychology in the twenty-first century will maintain its focus on such customary topics as personality, motivation, emotions, relationships, learning, sexuality, imagination, memory, and psychotherapy, but will not speak in one voice. Currently the voice getting the most airtime is that of neuropsychology.

Psychology is the scientific study of behavior and experience, both human and nonhuman. Neuropsychology studies behavior and experience through the lens of what we know about the brain and nervous system. I designed three courses at Saybrook University on neuropsychology, so I appreciate the insights that this field has provided, especially in regard to human decision making, mental disorders, sleep and dreams, and many more.

But I also have followed evolutionary psychology with great interest, and this voice is becoming more prominent. Evolutionary psychologists view behavior and experience through the lens of evolution—how traits that were adaptive usually survived, and those that were not adaptive usually disappeared. For example, early shamans treated their patients with plant remedies, rituals, and social support. Many of the plants they utilized had medicinal properties, but many did not. Nonetheless, they worked for a large number of people through what we call the placebo effect.

Individuals who were not suggestible, who did not respond to placebos, and who did not respond to the aid of their community tended not to survive and their genes dropped out of the gene pool. Hence, shamans played a major role in human evolution, and contemporary psychotherapists often use hypnosis, suggestion, expectation, and family and community support to the benefit of their clients. But genetic mutations are not the only way that new traits are introduced into the genetic heritage. There are more maladaptive mutations than adaptive mutations, and so there needs to be other ways that helpful traits can appear.

Tribal healers found ways to activate people's "inner shamans," the self-regulatory capacities of the human psyche. Activities such as meditation, imagery, and multisensory rituals (dancing, drumming, chanting, artistic expression, et cetera) can actually change—for the better—the gene placement on chromosomes. The discipline that studies these phenomena is called epigenetics, and I believe that this field will have a major impact upon psychological theory and practice. We may be observing this today in what is called transgenerational trauma; some studies indicate that survivors of genocide display both positive and negative traits that show up in their children and grandchildren.

Their family environment accounts for much of this, but I do not think it can account for all of it, because some descendants grow up with little knowledge of what went on in the African diaspora, the Nazi Holocaust, the many Indian Trails of Tears, and other episodes of human horror. If Rupert Sheldrake's morphic fields are confirmed by additional research, this would be another input to evolution, both human and nonhuman, as would be the effect of psychoactive plants on the development of early humans' brains.

But the psychology of the future will also identify two other "brains"—the heart and the gut. The field of psychoneuroimmunology has led to a new understanding of the "molecules of emotion" and has discovered that there are as many or more neurotransmitters in the heart and the abdomen as there are in the brain.

Both neuropsychology and evolutionary psychology are important aspects of consciousness—the pattern of thinking, feeling, and perceiving that characterizes an organism at any given point in time—and the study of consciousness will continue to expand in the twenty-first century. Consciousness studies have emerged rapidly since I received my doctorate from Northwestern University in 1961, after a splendid graduate education, but one in which the word *consciousness* was rarely mentioned.

Parapsychology pioneered many of the methods used to study consciousness, although it is rarely given credit. However, parapsychological research is receiving some attention, albeit grudgingly, especially when mainstream psychology is faced with the widespread reports of near-death experiences, out-of-body experiences, past-life experiences, lucid-dream experiences, and other unusual phenomena whose explanations strain the boundaries of conventional psychology.

Psychological models such as those developed by pioneers such as Stanislav Grof don't get much respect by mainstream psychologists, but they do have the advantage of having great explanatory value when it comes to anomalous experiences. Indeed, one of the emerging debates of twentieth-century psychology will be the role of consciousness: Is it an epiphenomenon? Or is it primary, predating the big bang itself? This suggestion sounds outrageous, but some quantum physicists have come close to making this a tenable hypothesis.

What are some of the areas that you would like to see psychedelic drug research look in to and explore more?

STANLEY: Since I had my first psilocybin experience in 1961, I have maintained that psychedelics are uniquely positioned to enhance psychotherapy, to illuminate the study of creativity, and to enhance human problem solving. My dear friend Albert Hofmann made a premature discovery in 1943, and it has taken decades for psychology and other disciplines to begin to realize the potential benefits of LSD and similar substances. And it was Albert Hofmann who echoed Native Americans when he urged people to take walks in the woods, appreciate sunsets, and find other ways of maintaining their connection with the rest of nature.

Strictly speaking, MDMA, or Ecstasy, is not a psychedelic, but it is a potential entheogen—a substance that enables the user to discover his or her inner divinity. MDMA therapy has had long-lasting positive effects on people diagnosed with post-traumatic stress disorder (PTSD), but current governmental regulations limit its use to a few dozen combat veterans. I have published three books on war trauma and know that there is a critical need for cost-effective and time-effective therapies to prevent the broken relationships, the outbreaks of violence, and the suicidal acts that often accompany PTSD.

It takes nothing away from the many existing treatments for PTSD, humanistic-existential and cognitive-behavioral approaches among them, to suggest that MDMA be an overlooked resource. In addition, there are anecdotal reports of therapeutic effects of ayahuasca rituals, and there are published studies demonstrating that ayahuasca evokes no long-term negative effects. In fact, it often produces positive sequelae, such as the cessation of the abuse of alcohol and other drugs. But the use of these plant medicines needs to be linked to the proper set and setting, and not treated casually.

While in Brazil, I once participated in a ritual with a Guarani shaman in which we ingested no fewer than six psychoactive substances—with quite positive outcomes and no deleterious aftereffects. Several decades ago, the anthropologist Michael Winkelman and I participated in a mushroom *velada* [healing vigil] with Maria Sabina, arguably the most important shaman of the twentieth century. Doña Maria claimed that Jesus Christ had come to her in a dream, permitting her to tell the visiting gringos from Boston that when the invading Spaniards banned pagan activities such as mushroom veladas, the Mazatec Indians took them underground.

But the time had come to reveal this secret, in the hopes that the veladas would help to stop human destruction of the natural environment. I had read an account of Maria Sabina's revelation in *LIFE Magazine* back in the 1950s, never realizing that I would meet her one day. Winkelman, of course, went on to write a classic book on shamanism, one in which he refers to psychedelics as psychointegrators that unite the left and right sides of the brain as well as the older and the newer brain structures.

It is this brain plasticity that also responds to spiritual disciplines; meditation, prayer, and contemplation can produce positive structural changes in the brain—and effective psychotherapy can produce similar long-lasting changes.

What do you think dreams really are, and do you think it's possible that the worlds that we visit in our dreams may have a genuine and independent existence outside of our brains?

STANLEY: A dream report is a series of images, recounted in narrative form, that occur during sleep. But a dream report is never the actual dream, and a certain amount of reconstruction probably enters into the recall. As I read the literature, it appears that rapid eye movement [REM] sleep, during which the most vivid dreams occur, served several adaptive purposes in the process of evolution: information storage, rehearsal of future activities, problem solving, downloading of emotions, and completion of incomplete thoughts and feelings.

I have talked with shamans who believe that they can travel to other dimensions of reality during their dreams, and perhaps they can. Psychologists know very little about the imaginal world, that terrain that goes by such names as the collective unconscious and the Akashic field.

Many ordinary people have dreams about future events or about what another person is doing or thinking, but to claim that they enter a parallel universe every night is a notion that lacks empirical evidence. And such a claim diminishes the wonders of the neuropsychology of dreams. From an evolutionary point of view, people who lacked REM sleep did not function very well in society. For example, during REM sleep, one's large muscles are immobilized.

If a member of a tribal society acted out his or her dreams by fighting other people in the tent or the cave, this action could produce injury and disturb the equilibrium and balance of the society. It was not unusual for those people to be exiled—and their genes would not be passed on to future generations.

Also imagine baby monkeys whose mother observed their rapid eye movements. The concerned mother would pay more attention to those babies than to other children who lacked REM activity. The latter would often fall prey to predators; once again, their genes would drop out of the gene pool, while the monkeys with REM would pass on this trait to their own children.

There are many unanswered questions about sleep and dreams, but what we know displays the marvelous way that the sleep-dream cycle became adaptive not only in human evolution but among several other species as well. There is now evidence that the same areas of rats' brains light up during sleep as they did during the day, when the rats were successfully running mazes and finding cheese.

Again, the rats' memories are being stored in a way that will be helpful in the future, giving them more cheese in future maze-running experiments. I disagree with the British biologist Richard Dawkins on many topics, but I agree with him that evolution is the "greatest show on Earth."

Do you think that the entities that people often report encountering while on DMT or ayahuasca have a genuine independent existence or not?

STANLEY: Most of the time, the entities encountered during psyche-delic sessions resemble those described when people wake up from dreams. The psyche has the marvelous capacity to condense experi-ence, and so a stranger in a dream or a DMT session might represent a host of people from waking life who shared a particular trait or role.

However, alterations in consciousness can transport some people into what I referred to earlier as imaginal realms, those aspects of the psyche that contain entities that exist beyond one's imagination, enti-ties that shamans often refer to as spirits, some of whom once lived on Earth and some who have their own abode.

Their reality is taken for granted by shamans such as Twylah Nitsch, Maria Sabina, and Rolling Thunder. But those imbued with Western worldviews ask if they are true. Truth consists of a correspon-dence between one's reported experience and what scientists refer to as facts.

But the philosopher Massimo Pigliucci reminds us that facts come in a variety of flavors—empirical, mathematical, logical, ethical, esthetic, et cetera. This is why I tell my students to refrain from using the word *proved* when referring to psychological experiments. The term *proof* can be applied to abstract logical and mathematical theorems—and to whiskey—but to little else.

What do you think happens to consciousness after death?

STANLEY: One can certainly make a case that some aspect of conscious-ness survives death. Parapsychologists have studied this topic for over a century, and there are hundreds of well-attested instances of survival that can be found in the literature on mediumship, reincarnation, and near-death experiences (NDEs).

For me, the amusing aspects of NDEs is that people who come back from Heaven (or sometimes from Hell) provide reports that are not con-sistent with descriptions given by mainstream Western religions. There are instances in which a departed loved one will appear in a dream, or even in a psychedelic session, giving specific directions on where a lost object can be found, or what decision should be made on a puzzling life issue.

I was lecturing in Mexico when Rolling Thunder's wife, Spotted Fawn, died. That night I dreamed that she came to me to say good-bye, commenting, "You know, I won't be seeing you anymore."

There are numerous examples of what I call visitation dreams, and I doubt that all of them can be written off as coincidence, prevarication, or wish fulfillment. As to what happens to consciousness, I suppose that sooner or later it returns to what is often called the Godhead. But it can take its time, at least according to those who hypothesize that there is a gauntlet of lives that must be passed through first. Western logic maintains that when the body dies, the mind also dies.

But that is taking a limited view of the body. Many Native American traditions speak of the long body, which is embedded in a community and that can extend itself through space and time. This long body can exist after so-called physical death, and can even show up in the future. Rolling Thunder told me that he remembers his past life very well and can recall portions of two previous lives. For Rolling Thunder and other Native American shamans and sages, there was no mind-body problem, the issue that has perplexed Western philosophers for centuries.

What is your perspective on the concept of God?

STANLEY: I have been interested in general systems theory since I met Ludwig von Bertalanffy, the forerunner of evolutionary systems theory, at Northwestern University. Since then I have read books on the topic as well as its offshoots, chaos theory and complexity theory. I have written a few articles about their application to dreams, which seem to organize themselves around a chaotic attractor, a central image that makes emotional linkages to other images in the dreamer's psyche.

I do not conceptualize God as an entity that created the universe from an external vantage point. Rather, there is a self-organizing force that is responsible for the cosmos as we know it. And if people want to call this principle of self-organization God, I would not object.

If you could summarize the basic message of your life in a few words or sentences, what would they be?

STANLEY: When I was a high school student in Fort Atkinson, Wisconsin, Senator Alexander Wiley paid us a visit and gave us some very good advice. He told us to laugh, love, and live, and gave us several examples of all three that had characterized his life and career. Years later, I visited his office in Washington, D.C., and he took me on a ride to the Senate chamber on the famous underground railcar.

He was in good humor all during the short ride, and told a few interesting stories before we disembarked. Since that time, my life has not been easy. I have had my share of failures, hardships, and crises. But I try not to take myself too seriously, to live every day to the fullest, and extend love to my fellow human beings and to the projects I find worthy of my time and effort. And we have talked about many of those projects today.

Is there anything that we haven't spoken about that you would like to add?

STANLEY: You have conducted a very comprehensive interview and there is little that I can add. However, when I was at Northwestern University, I attended a series of three lectures given by Dr. Martin Luther King Jr. I even took him on a tour of the campus, so I had a chance to talk with him privately. My contact with Dr. King turned me into a social activist, and I have done considerable work in developing countries and with indigenous people.

My interest in shamanism provided me with a way to combine activism and scholarship, as did my work with combat veterans with

PTSD, and my several trips to the former U.S.S.R. to interact with Soviet parapsychologists during the height of the Cold War.

I have written papers on marginalized groups such as handicapped children, African Americans who were targets of racism, and transsexuals whose dreams revealed their struggles to establish their identity. I was once introduced as a psychologist who "has his head in the air but his feet on the ground." I considered that to be a splendid compliment.

5
Alchemy, Ecology, and Psychedelics

*An Interview with **Ralph Metzner***

Ralph Metzner is a psychologist, researcher, and one of the world's leading experts in altered states of consciousness. While still a graduate student at Harvard University, Metzner participated in the well-known psilocybin research studies that Timothy Leary and Richard Alpert (a.k.a., Ram Dass) conducted in the early 1960s. After receiving his Ph.D. in clinical psychology in 1962, Metzner continued to explore the potential of psychedelics with Leary and Alpert at the Millbrook Estate in New York, and he became the editor of *The Psychedelic Review*. During the 1970s Metzner spent ten years studying and practicing a meditative system called Angi Yoga. From 1979 to 1988, Metzner was the academic dean of the California Institute of Integral Studies in San Francisco. He is currently professor emeritus there, and he continues to teach courses about the interface between psychology and ecology.

Metzner is cofounder and president of the Green Earth Foundation, an educational organization devoted to the "healing and harmonizing of the relations between humanity and the Earth."

Metzner also maintains a part-time psychotherapy practice, and he regularly conducts workshops around the world on consciousness transformation.

Metzner is the author, coauthor, or editor of more than fifteen books, including *The Psychedelic Experience, The Ecstatic Adventure, Maps of Consciousness, Know Your Type, Opening to Inner Light, The Unfolding Self,* and *Green Psychology.* To find out more about his work, see www .greenearthfound.org.

———————————————— ☺ ————————————————

I spoke with Ralph on November 16, 2013. Ralph has a unique way of blending a scholarly aristocratic presence with his warmly approachable personality. We discussed shamanism, the future of psychology, and the relationship between ecology and psychedelics.

How did you first become interested in psychology, and how did this lead to studying the expansion of consciousness?

RALPH: I think my basic interest in psychology—trying to understand how and why people did the things they did—came from my childhood experience. I was born in Germany in 1936 and lived in Berlin, in a secure, bourgeois existence, with a German father and Scots-English mother, for the first nine years of my life. I remember wondering at the fact that while other schoolchildren and propaganda media would talk glibly about the English as enemies that would be "driven into the sea," my parents and their friends did not talk like that at all. Their primary concerns were the disasters of war and how and when it would end. Later, in my adolescent years, when I attended a boarding school in the north of Scotland, I was exposed to schoolboy taunts about being a "filthy Kraut." Only much later did I come to appreciate these experiences as teaching me early lessons about the subjective relativity of enemies—that enemies are made or designated and don't have any independent reality.

Living in Berlin until 1945, our family experienced bombing raids

Photo by Sophia Marija Metzner

Ralph Metzner

marked by sirens, during which we would all go to the underground shelter. After the sudden end of the war and the collapse of the regime, I became a refugee in an occupied country, experiencing starvation and deprivation and incomprehensibly dangerous situations. My childhood experiences of war and societal collapse undoubtedly contributed to my lifelong, almost obsessive interest in the causes of war and how to end it. In my book *The Roots of War and Domination,* published in 2008 as part of the Ecology of Consciousness series, I discuss a variety of views, traditional and more esoteric, as shown in some of the chapter titles: "Psychological Roots of Violence," "Historical and Prehistorical Roots in Tribal Competition," "Ecological and Evolutionary Aspects of Domination Behavior," and "Mythic Dimensions of Domination and War."

From the perspective reflected in my later writings on the soul's choice of incarnation, I would say now that my conception and birth to a set of parents coming from countries that were about to engage in murderous war with each other reflects a kind of predestination—a soul's choice of parents that is indicative of the soul's mission to work toward the amelioration of international conflict. I've come to think that when a couple from different or warring nations, or religions or cultures, or different economic classes marry and have children, then that choice is itself a kind of pointer toward a commitment to the bridging of those differences. It's the story of *Romeo and Juliet* and countless other stories and films of couples who choose to make love, not war, committing to life and growth, despite the presence of fear, danger, and conflict.

Only recently have I come to a more complete understanding of the psychological effects of my childhood war experiences. I wrote about this in *Worlds Within and Worlds Beyond* (2013): "When I was already in my later years, after five decades of consciousness exploration . . . I came to a rather shocking realization related to my own personal history: I had lived more or less completely identified with a hell realm of withdrawn depression and isolation from the age of nine to the age of twenty-five, that is, throughout my adolescence and early adult years. In 1945, as a young boy in Germany, I was traumatized by the terrifying destruction of war, starvation, separation from my family, and the collapse of ordinary civic life. I withdrew into myself, like a turtle withdrawing into its shell. This depressed withdrawal lasted until 1961, when I first took psilocybin, as a graduate student at Harvard under the auspices of Timothy Leary. At that time, my consciousness expanded to ecstatic, mystical dimensions, transforming forever my worldview and basic orientation" [pp. 49–50].

One of the things that most impressed me when looking back at that turning point of expanding consciousness is that I had absolutely no conception, or even a way of imagining, that such an expansion of awareness was even possible. The worldview that looked painfully, even absurdly, narrow in retrospect was simply what I accepted as reality—the way the world was, period.

As a graduate student at Harvard, 1958 to 1962, I was involved in research based on the currently fashionable behaviorist paradigm, with a smattering of psychoanalytic theorizing. I remember being attracted by the animated voices of my fellow graduate students who were talking about their initial psychedelic experiences, and by the enthusiasm of the charismatic Timothy Leary. And so I volunteered to work on a research project giving psilocybin to incarcerated convicts, for the purposes of bringing about insight and behavior change—knowing that, according to Leary's participatory paradigm, I would also get to experience the substance myself.

I've written about my initial life-changing experience with psilocybin in the autobiographical *Birth of a Psychedelic Culture* [2010; coauthored with Ram Dass and Gary Bravo]: "I understood how my normal perception of the world was constricted and limited by many prohibitions that I had somehow accepted. For example, I went outside (of the house where the session was taking place) and on the porch was a box. I looked inside and saw that it had a garbage can, and automatically turned away. Suddenly I realized I didn't have to turn away, that it was okay to look at it, if I wanted to, that I had a choice and was not bound by a set of preprogrammed rules regarding what could or could not be experienced and perceived. That simple thought was perhaps the most significant revelation of this experience: that I was basically in charge of what I could perceive and think about, that I was not bound by external forces, but rather made choices that determined the extent and quality of my awareness" [p. 19]. Of course, I knew that having the basic insight into the conditioning of our experience was only the first step in what would inevitably be a protracted and yet exciting process of liberating one's consciousness.

In recent years I've come to no longer use the notion of altered states of consciousness, because it suggests that there is a kind of normal, constant state, and *altered* implies an abnormal, even castrated or powerless state. On the contrary, it is clear that profound alterations of one's state of consciousness are, in fact, as common as the cycle of sleeping, dreaming, meditating, and ordinary waking states. In addition, the term *altered*—in the passive grammatical construction—suggests that something was done to you. Whereas the key psychological and ethical issue is having the knowledge and the choice to alter one's own consciousness and not being subjected to manipulation of one's state by any outside agency, without consent. My own linguistic preference now is to talk about expansions, contractions, and alterations of consciousness states—which then leaves the empirical question of how the changes come about open for inquiry.

How have traditional mystic and shamanic systems influenced your perspective on consciousness?

RALPH: After my initial exposure to the consciousness-expanding effects of psilocybin and other psychedelic drugs in the various projects the Leary projects initiated at Harvard, I naturally became interested in the pharmacology and brain science underlying different states. I received a postdoctoral research fellowship at the Harvard Medical School to take the second-year pharmacology course for medical students and write a long review essay on the pharmacology of psychedelic drugs. [This was published in the first issue of *The Psychedelic Review*, a quarterly journal that the Harvard project put out for several years.] I also became interested in the various Eastern and Western spiritual traditions that used plant-based and nondrug methods, such as meditation, to expand and alter consciousness.

In my recent writings I've discussed three major systems of disciplined psychospiritual consciousness development: shamanism, yoga, and alchemy. Each of these work on multiple levels for physical healing, emotional balance, mental understanding, and spiritual connection with divine forces, although they may focus or specialize more in some areas than others. Of these shamanism is definitely the oldest, dating back on all continents to the Paleolithic, whereas yoga and alchemy could be regarded as the Eastern and Western extensions of shamanism, respectively. I've written about these historical roots and precursors of modern disciplines of healing and psychotherapy in my book *Alchemical Divination.*

In my book *The Expansion of Consciousness,* I discuss the traditional mythic alchemical conception of the philosopher's stone, with special reference to the work of two giants, both of them Swiss, who each made profound contributions to the scientific understanding of the links between spirit and matter—C. G. Jung and Albert Hofmann. Jung wrote four volumes of his collected works analyzing the obscure texts of the alchemists, decoding them as written in a secret symbol language of psychospiritual transformation. The alchemists were scientists and also what we would nowadays call spiritual seekers and natural philosophers. Their seemingly obscure texts were written in a symbolic code so that their consciousness-liberating practices could escape the censors and prosecutors of the Inquisition.

I pointed out that Jung, who was not familiar with the consciousness-expanding potential of psychedelic drugs, did not include in his discussions the possibility that there could be physical substances that facilitate or bring about spiritual experiences or visions. On the other hand, Albert Hofmann, being trained as a twentieth-century materialist chemist, though with a deeply spiritual interest, did not have any awareness that the medieval alchemical literature presented an integrated spiritual and material philosophy. He personally thanked me for making him aware of the esoteric European alchemical tradition—a kind of precursor of his life work as the "mystic chemist."

In my book *MindSpace and TimeStream,* I discuss the concept of a state of consciousness as a period of time during which consciousness (thoughts, feelings, perceptions, et cetera, and especially our perception of time and space) function in specific ways, differently in each state. For example, time and space are completely different in the dream state than in the waking state. Psychedelic states are notorious for their varied temporal characteristics—one can experience vast realms of thoughts, images, and perceptions within the space of a few minutes or even seconds of real time. And one may also find themselves in timeless states akin to those recorded by the mystics. So I argue that to make the most effective use of psychedelic states, we must learn to navigate through them according to our intentions, the set, which, in turn, determines the environment and choice of setting.

In fact, the set and setting determinants apply to all our states—both the expansive states that occur in meditation, contemplation, creative arts or invention, and the contractive states of concentration for precision performance, whether mental, artistic or physical, and technical. Intention and practice are always the essential keys: When we fall into expansive states without intention or awareness, we get aimless spaciness, lack of direction, and distraction. When we fall into contracted states without intention or awareness, we are in the realm of addictions and fixations, whether eating or drinking or having sex or watching TV to excess, or doing anything obsessively and compulsively—to the detriment of other natural aspects of our lives, like family, creativity, and livelihood.

During the Harvard project we were deeply influenced by the writings on psychedelic drug states by the religious philosophers Aldous Huxley, Alan Watts, and Huston Smith—all of whom participated in and advised on our project. Following Huxley's suggestion we wrote *The Psychedelic Experience* as a guidebook based on the *Tibetan Book of the Dead,* describing the psychedelic-induced, ego-transcending states by analogy to the after-death states in Buddhist philosophy. Over the years, my coauthors and I have many times heard people tell us how much they appreciated having that conceptual-spiritual framework for their psychedelic explorations—

even if their specific experiences didn't follow the exact sequence of the Buddhist text.

I think the significance of this Tibetan Buddhist paradigm was mainly that it offered a psychospiritual perspective on psychedelic experience, which would have been difficult to integrate with the religious tradition or upbringing of most Westerners. Of course, such a spiritual framework for psychedelic experiences cannot be and should not be imposed on people. But it was helpful to those who wanted something more than the purely psychotherapeutic frames with which psychedelic drugs had been originally associated—and the more recreational, hedonistic use paradigms with which it also became associated later. For myself, I will always be grateful to Huxley and to Leary for having opened my mind to the profound beauty and depth of the Tibetan Buddhist teachings.

In my recently published book, *The Life Cycle of the Human Soul,* I revisit these Buddhist writings and teachings in the light of forty years of subsequent experience, relating them to recent research findings on prenatal and near-death experiences. This has led me to a somewhat different, and, I think, deeper understanding of the bardo teachings on the actual death and afterlife than we had in the 1960s. I now think that the third bardo state, called the bardo of rebirth in *The Tibetan Book of the Dead,* actually and literally refers to the prenatal phase of our lives, from the soul's choosing to incarnate to the conception event, and ending with the actual birth, after which we cycle through the ordinary in-life bardo states of waking, sleeping, and dreaming.

Another breakthrough in my understanding of psychedelic states of consciousness occurred when I came into contact with and started to practice and learn from the shamanic journey methods described by anthropologist Michael Harner. Having studied both the practices involving South American psychoactive plants like yagé and the shamanic journey methods involving rhythmic drumming, more commonly used by shamans in America, and Europe, Harner argued, in contrast to R. G. Wasson and others, that the drumming method was originally more widespread in Europe but was suppressed during the Middle Ages because the sound of the drum attracted the enforcers of the Inquisition. In any case, I took courses and began to practice the shamanic journey method using rhythmic drumming as the technique of entering into an altered state, rather than drugs. Both methods have the same basic three-phase pattern: first, leaving the ordinary world with specific conscious intentions; two, exploring nonordinary reality for healing, insight, and visions; and three, returning to one's home base to apply the lessons learned.

One big advantage of the drumming method over the psycho-active plants or fungi methods, I came to realize, is that drumming journeys (the preferred metaphor for a state of consciousness in which one has the sense of moving while the physical body is lying still) usually last only thirty to forty minutes and don't have the pronounced and potentially distracting physical sensations or side effects of drug-induced trips. One could practice three or four drumming journeys in a day or an afternoon. I used to meet with several friends for the purpose of practicing this, taking turns drumming for one another. When you connect with a given spirit being or vision both on a drug trip and on a drumming journey, or a meditation, this supports the recognition that spirit beings are real, and not just hallucinatory imaginings or drug effects.

Of course, one can also have illusory perceptions in any state of consciousness—waking, dreaming, drug induced, or drum induced. All our visions, insights, and perceptions, in any world and any state of consciousness, are always subject to interpretation as well as verification and testing by the usual methods. A spirit's advice or guidance on healing, for example, is applied in the given problem situation; just like a human doctor's advice would be applied and tested in the real illness or wound. The practitioner, whether with ordinary or nonordinary states and practices, is interested in healing results, and not so much concerned with proving or disproving any theories—

which is the general agenda of the empirical-knowledge sciences.

In comparing shamanic journey methods, whether by plant medicines or drumming, with the meditative methods of expanding consciousness, the key point to remember, as I and many others have recognized, is that meditation does not per se aim at inducing a heightened or expanded state of consciousness. Some of the Japanese Zen texts specifically discourage the meditator from seeking what they think of as illusion visions. In such traditions the goal, if there is a goal, is to bring about a gradual, progressive heightening of our everyday awareness—living and doing everything more mindfully. Or, as the Buddhist meditation teacher Jack Kornfield says, "After the ecstasy, the laundry."

For myself, I prefer and advocate for an integrative approach that practices journey methods of various kinds as well as mindfulness and concentrative meditations, together and separately, as one is guided by one's inner or outer teachers and guides—whether human, divine, angelic, animal, plant, fungal, or extraterrestrial.

How do you envision the future of psychology?

RALPH: Psychology, like all the other social and natural sciences, is the inheritor of the scientific-paradigm revolutions of the sixteenth and seventeenth centuries, in which the founding fathers of modern scientific rationalism—Copernicus, Galileo, Bacon, Newton, Descartes, and others—managed to establish their right to free and independent experimentation from the dogmatic restrictions of the church. In my book *Green Psychology,* I pointed out, as have other scholars, that this freedom to pursue knowledge of the material world was purchased at the expense of denying any reality to the realms of spirit, psyche, or the sacred—a kind of self-imposed and self-accepted limitation that still haunts the modern worldview. I called this the root pathology of Western civilization and traced its origins to even earlier roots in male-god monotheisms and patriarchal social power systems in the ancient world.

This root pathology, which assumes that it is the right and purpose of civilization to control and dominate nature, and, by extension, everything associated with nature—that is, women, children, animals, plants, the Earth itself—is a deeply ingrained attitude that has pervaded intellectual and social paradigms in the West for centuries and is still reflected in the economic and political struggles of our time. I came to recognize, in part through psychedelic experiences, how pervasive this man-over-nature domination pattern is, by contrast to the worldviews of indigenous cultures in which humans are seen as having familial relationships of mutuality and respect with plants, animals, and Mother Earth. I saw too how this recognition of human mutuality with the Earth's so-called environment was another crucial element of the consciousness revolutions of the 1960s, along with women's liberation and the antiwar movement.

The field of psychology, including psychotherapy, which I taught for thirty years at the California Institute of Integral Studies, is still locked within this paradigmatic-behaviorist box. Even though giant strides have been made in linking various mental states to neurophysiological changes in the brain, the study of states of consciousness in their own right is still very much a minor concern in academic psychology training programs.

I also think the lack of recognition of the spiritual dimensions, indeed the spiritual essence of life, is a stumbling block for Western sciences, both the natural and the social. One aspect of that becomes particularly clear in relationship to reincarnation and the afterlife, which is accepted as an obvious fact in virtually all Eastern religions and indigenous traditions. Even although Ian Stevenson published thousands of cases of children remembering verifiable details of their previous lives, the commonly accepted view in sophisticated, Western-educated circles is that we should assume that nothing happens after death. Reincarnation itself is not regarded seriously, much less the possibility that some of our current problems may be caused by past-life karma, and that present actions could have beneficial or harmful karmic consequences in future lives. The Dalai Lama has often talked about how in the Tibetan Buddhist culture the acceptance of karmic consequences in future lives is a major factor in heightening ethical awareness—basically you can't kid yourself that you can get away with things you know you shouldn't be doing.

It's interesting to observe that in many other non-Western countries, there is not nearly the same degree of resistance to the idea of reincarnation, which was extirpated from Christian doctrine at the fifth-century Council of Nicaea. Health educator and nurse Dr. Emma Bragdon, in her book *Spiritism and Mental Health,* has pointed out that in Brazil, where spiritist teachings are widely accepted, there are actually fifty spiritist hospitals, in which past-lives diagnosis and therapy is practiced alongside medical, surgical, psychological, and social-work interventions. I think such centers are harbingers of future, truly integrative health systems, where the physical, psychological, social, and spiritual dimensions of illness and health are equally addressed.

For myself, I have for many years now included past-life regression methods in my psychotherapy practice, if the search for causal factors of present problems in childhood or in prenatal experience, as well as from parental influences, has been unproductive. Past-life regression therapy uses a light hypnotic trance state, in which the practitioner guides the client to ask questions of their inner/higher self—questions about past-life connections to their current-life issues. Such approaches can be very revealing and bring about profoundly healing changes in attitudes. Successful past-life regression therapy does not require commitment to any particular belief system or theory of reincarnation. An openness to the possibility is the only prerequisite and, as in any healing practice, it is the results that count.

Many people, myself included, have reported flashes of insights and seeming memories of other lives during group or shared psychedelic experiences. For past-life therapy, on the other hand, one needs to have the therapist ask and guide the patient/subject to look at specific events in the past life—the childhood, the place and time, the major life issues, and the karmic conditions connected to the present-life issue. This can obviously not be done in a group session, but it could be done in the context of individual psychotherapy. However, I suspect that because the spontaneously emerging visions in a psychedelic session can be extremely powerful and engaging, a specific sequence of questions might be contraindicated. A light hypnotic trance, without amplification, is my preferred method of past-life regression.

What are some of the areas you would like to see psychedelic drug research look at and explore more?

RALPH: I think the various psychedelic research programs currently being pursued are exciting in their potential, and at the same time it is depressing to contemplate how research has been held back for over thirty years for purely political reasons having nothing to do with the demonstrated and potential values of these substances. The political and economic stranglehold that the medical-pharmaceutical-prison-industrial complex exerts on any research not emanating out of pharmaceutical companies, or the university research programs financed by them, has blocked and continues to block the possibilities of realizing the enormous healing potentials of these nonpatentable medicines. It takes heroic efforts of persistence and private fund-raising for any formal research on psychedelic drugs to be first approved and then actually conducted.

The prime areas that are being pursued now and should be expanded dramatically if researchers were really supported in their efforts are:

One, the treatment of the contractions of consciousness involved in alcoholism; drug addictions; obsessions; compulsions; and other fixated, repetitive states with consciousness-expanding states, supported, of course, with psychotherapy.

Two, extreme examples of contracted, fixated states such as PTSD deriving from war or other trauma, in which MDMA-supported therapy is demonstrably the best, relatively short-acting treatment. The special virtue of MDMA, also known as an empathogen or Ecstasy, is that it doesn't produce any perceptual hallucinations or distortions, just a very normal feeling of empathy for self and others, without fear. The traumatized person can calmly review his or her experiences, while the adrenal stress system appears to be in rest mode. Recent research by the German psychiatrist Torsten Passie at the Hannover University has demonstrated that MDMA increases the blood and brain levels of the nursing hormone, prolactin, as well as the "cuddle hormone," oxytocin.

The emotional state of the nursing infant is probably the archetypal paradigm of feeling safe and supported. Used as an adjunct to psychotherapy, the MDMA state allows the client to contemplate the traumatizing event within an aura of safety and well-being. Incidentally, this feeling of nonsexual emotional intimacy has also been observed as being a crucial element of the safety of Ecstasy-fueled rave events, with thousands of dancers who may be hugging and smiling at one another but generally not hitting on others sexually.

Three, to my mind, the most important and far-reaching application potential of psychedelics is in helping people prepare for the ultimate transition of dying. Here the pioneering work of Stanislav Grof and Walter Pahnke in the 1960s, and of Charles Grob currently, has shown the potentials of psychedelics like psilocybin and LSD to help people come to terms with the inevitable ending of life.

In a minor but significant bureaucratic breakthrough, researchers have been given permission, within particular research projects, to give entheogens to patients with terminal illness, not for cure or treatment, but for alleviation of the anxiety around death. And since dying is an inevitable event in everybody's life—one almost universally accompanied by fear and resistance, as well as profound misunderstanding and confusion—the potentials here for social and community benefit are enormous. On my website I've published, with permission, two filmed interviews with terminal patients who were given psilocybin in this project, and they are profoundly moving and beautiful to watch.

There is not space, in the context of this essay, to go into the misplaced political persecution of cannabis growers and producers, as well as the physicians and their patients who are using this ancient medicinal herb with negligible unwanted side-effects and vanishingly low toxicity.

Here too we can see how the enormous potential and individual and social benefits of psychedelic substances are being blocked from realization and application by an inappropriate and distorted system of medical-political control that functions to maximize the profits of the medical-pharmaceutical complex, instead of sponsoring research to benefit suffering individuals and their physicians. Because even when the benefits of these substances have been demonstrated in small double-blind controlled experiments, this does not mean the substance is available to use by those who need it. Results of MDMA therapy with a dozen or so traumatized veterans have been enormously promising. But how much closer are the estimated 350,000 veterans suffering from PTSD to being able to access this medicine through their doctors?

Actually and surprisingly, it turns out they may be closer than one might think. Thanks to the fact of the enormous number of underground Ecstasy users and suppliers, it's probably easier for a veteran to obtain both MDMA and a guiding friend to help him deal with his trauma than it is for a researcher to set up a research project that demonstrates its efficacy. And that can only be considered a blessing.

Do you think the entities that one encounters while on DMT or ayahuasca have a genuine independent existence or not?

RALPH: DMT entities have acquired a semimythical status in the psychedelic underground literature, with questions swirling about their reality. Actually, in the two collections I've edited and published of ayahuasca experiences and of psilocybe mushroom experiences, there are numerous reports of encounters or visions with disembodied *spirits,* which is the traditional terminology. In previous collections which I edited, compiling experiences with MDMA in the 1980s and experiences with LSD in the 1960s, there are also several accounts of visions and conversations with spirits. In the literature of accounts with experiences with the shamanic-drumming journey methods, connections and conversations with spirits seen and heard and conversed with are commonplace. The anthropologist Michael Harner has staked his academic reputation on asserting the reality of spirits.

I think it's somewhat of a red herring to associate entities or spirits with the drug, as if they were a drug effect, when actually the drug only extends perceptual sensitivity so that one can perceive beings and realities that are not visible in the ordinary state of waking consciousness. Such beings may also become visible in dreams, in meditative visions, or in natural settings spontaneously. People may have visions and dreams of the spirits of deceased ancestors, or of their spiritual teachers or gurus, or of saints and deities, or of their spirit animal, both with and without drugs. Some naturally clairvoyant persons can see spirits all the time, but usually it will be in a healing or meditative context. Actually, I think that if you see a vision of a spirit in a drug trip and then also see that same or similar spirit in a nondrug shamanic journey or in a dream, then it enhances the reality status of who or what you saw.

The reality status or independent existence of such spirit beings cannot simply be either accepted or denied. Perceptions in nonordinary states of consciousness can be real or illusory, just like perceptions in the ordinary waking state. They might be perceptions, or they could be fantasies. How do you tell the difference between imagination and reality? Perceptions and visions must be tested and verified. I may, in an ordinary waking state, look out the window and see a man walking down the street, only to realize, as the figure comes closer, that it's actually a woman dressed as a man. We constantly test and verify and repeat our perceptions. One of my teachers, who was a high-level clairvoyant, told me that he always tested and verified his perceptions, sometimes five or six times, if they were especially unusual or unexpected.

The idea that DMT or ayahuasca is somehow the source of these entities comes from a residual attachment to the materialist worldview, according to which only material bodies or objects actually exist. This is an outdated worldview [that] needs to expand to recognize that there are multiple dimensions of reality, and multiple classes of beings in these different dimensions, that all have their own reality status, independent of humans. At the same time, humans, of course, can and do create all kinds of nonmaterial images and fantasy entities, giving them, then, a reality in their own minds that can have significant effects, both healthy and unhealthy, on their lives.

What role do you think psychedelics have had on environmental awareness and ecology?

RALPH: This is an issue in which I have some personal sensitivity. In my book *Green Psychology,* I described how a vastly increased environmental awareness can be one of the consequences of the use of consciousness-expanding substances. I argued, based on my own experience and that of many friends and acquaintances, that environmental activism could arise from psychedelic experiences. When people extended their perceptions to the environment around them with psychedelics, some . . . became aware of the spoiling of the environment and [were] moved to take action to protect and restore it. I pointed out that Rachel Carson's book *Silent Spring,* published in 1962 and widely acknowledged as a major catalyst of the American environmental movement, describes the consciousness-expanding experience, without psychedelics, of asking yourself, "Why are the birds not singing?" Which, then, in turn could lead you to undertake research and remedial action.

Of course, I knew and we all know full well that such action-inspiring experiences in nature can and do occur without plants or drugs. Furthermore, experiences with sacred plants do not necessarily lead to adopting ecological values, for example, in those who take psychedelics mostly for recreational purposes. Some environmental activists took me to task for seemingly encouraging escapist drug experiences when what was needed was energetic action.

In *Green Psychology* there are two chapters that deal with entheo-gens. In chapter five, "The Role of Psychoactive Plant Medicines," I dis-cuss psychedelic plants used as sacrament or recreation; their potential as gnostic catalysts; and their historical role in shamanism, yoga, and alchemy. "I regard shamanic ritual use of such plants, along with herbal medicine and organic farming, as part of a worldwide movement toward a balanced and more conscious relationship with the plant realm." In chapter ten, "Reunification of the Sacred and the Natural," I suggested that "the revival of interest in shamanic practices, including the inten-tional use of entheogenic plant sacraments, is among the most hopeful signs that the split between the sacred and the natural can be healed again."

During the 1980s and 1990s, when I was researching and writing on the topics in *Green Psychology,* I came into contact with and learned from several outstanding teachers and writers, [such as] Theodore Roszak, cultural historian and author of *The Voice of the Earth,* who wrote a foreword to my book, [and] John Seed, Australian rainfor-est activist and coauthor of *Thinking Like a Mountain,* who wrote an epilogue. I had asked visionary eco-philosopher Thomas Berry, whose talks and writings I was deeply influenced by, to write a foreword, as he had read and appreciated some of the essays in the book. He eventually declined, though, asking to be released from his promise, because the two chapters dealing with what he called mind-assisting plants touched on areas he didn't feel qualified to comment on, out of ignorance. I deeply appreciated that he told me that he did not doubt the validity of the insights that can come from the use of these plants. I dedicated the book, then, to four elders who have inspired me in this area: Hildegard von Bingen, the eleventh-century Benedictine nun with her visions of "mystical greenness"; Thomas Berry; Marija Gimbutas, with her groundbreaking archaeological discoveries of the Earth honoring, pre-Indo-European cultures of Old Europe; and Paul Shepard, ecologist and historian, with his insightful analysis of the split between humans and nature.

What do you think happens to consciousness after death?

RALPH: This is and always has been the great mystery: "For in that sleep of death what dreams may come . . ." as Shakespeare's Hamlet muses. The Mystery religions and orphic cults of ancient times created secret and sacred rituals to address our fear of that unknown bourn from which "no traveler returns." When my colleagues and I at Harvard published a guide to psychedelic experiences based on *The Tibetan Book of the Dead,* we treated the Buddhist text as a metaphorical description of consciousness journeys that carried one beyond the so-called death of the ego. In some high-dose psychedelic experiences, a person may encounter the fear of dying and seemingly struggle for dear life. In actual fact, people don't die physically in these drug experiences, except if there are external causes, such as jumping out of a window.

In the past thirty or forty years, though, there has appeared a rather large body of accounts of near-death experiences (NDEs) in which people have actually died, with the heart stopping, whether in accidents or surgery, and then returning to full consciousness. Personal accounts of NDEs continue to appear with some regularity every year, and always seem to land on the bestseller lists for a while, which is a testimony to the enduring fascination for travelers that have returned from that undiscovered country. This literature has been surveyed and analyzed by psychologists such as Raymond Moody and Kenneth Ring, and certain common key features described. I myself have never had an NDE, though I've once or twice, during a near accident, had a taste of that suspended time sense.

In my book *The Life Cycle of the Human Soul,* I describe what we have learned from the NDE research and how that correlates with descriptions of the afterlife from the classic mystical literature of East and West. Common themes of the dying process from such accounts are a sudden sense of discontinuity, a lifting-off into an out-of-body state, and entering into an upward-sloping tunnel of increasing brightness.

This may then be followed by meeting with previously deceased parents or ancestors, accompanied by a sense of welcoming and homecoming, and sometimes a rapid review of scenes, both positive and negative, of their life. Some of the NDE accounts tell of meeting a spirit guide or angelic being and receiving divine wisdom and guidance for their return to physical life.

Of course, we have no way of knowing to what extent these accounts of NDEs describe the typical dying process of those who don't return to life. But we have no reason to assume otherwise. The most striking aspect, to my mind, is the universally positive, even ecstatic and blissful, nature of the afterlife, once the physical release has happened. This is such a contrast from the huge cloud of unknowing anxiety that surrounds the idea and prospect of death. And here is the reason for the tremendous healing benefit that could come for people who are able use psychedelics, and, of course, also meditation, to prepare themselves for a dying that is already in their imminent prognosis.

In my book I relate an experience which was told to me by the person who experienced it, that illustrated the suspension of the time sense that is common to both psychedelic and near-death experiences. During the 1960s a man took a substantial dose of LSD in the company of friends, on a rooftop somewhere in Detroit, at night in the dark. In the midst of the drug-induced high he at one point stepped off the edge of some kind of rooftop box structure only two or three feet high. Since it was both dark and he was high and hallucinating, he thought that he had stepped off the edge of the roof and would now be dying. In the split-second interval of the two-foot drop, he experienced the whole classic life-review scene that reportedly can accompany dying.

What is your perspective on the concept of God?

RALPH: My perspectives on the God concept have changed and evolved in many directions over the fifty years that I have been involved in psychedelic research. In *Green Psychology,* in a chapter on the black goddess, the green god, and the wild human, I described how, prior to the rise of transcendental monotheisms, the religious worldview of the ancient world was polytheistic, pantheistic, animistic, and shamanistic. "Gods and goddesses, the living intelligences of nature, were perceived and worshipped in forest groves and sacred springs, on mountaintops and in great stone circles." I cannot tell to what extent this is true of my fellow human explorers of consciousness, but for myself, the recognition of and connections with deities and divinities inherent and intrinsic with all of nature, both terrestrial and cosmic, has only deepened over the years.

Of course, it is everyone's right, which I totally respect, to focus their religious visioning and prayer on one chosen divinity—*ishta devata,* as it's known in Sanskrit—but we have historically, and even currently, seen far too much bigotry, prejudice, violence, and warfare in the name of the one, true God of this or that group, to make that kind of ideology appealing. And now that science has revealed to us a world of infinite diversity and multiplicity, not only on this Earth planet, but the inconceivable numbers of other planetary worlds and galaxies of star systems, isn't it about time that we expanded our view of the creative forces and creator spirits beyond those of our one little planet?

In the chapter cited above I describe some of the suprahuman deities and divinities associated with different cultures on our planet Earth that I've come to connect with and commune with from time to time, just like I've come to connect and communicate with varieties of different humans on this Earth. I've perceived and learned from, in dreams and visions, the black goddess of the fertile earth in ancient times that became the Black Madonna in the Christian West; the green god or Green Man of plants and trees; the pre-Olympian Dionysus, deity of wine, music, dance, and holy celebration; the Egyptian pair of Isis and Osiris, teachers and guides to growth and healing, [and] the mysteries of death and regeneration; great Pan, the lord of animals; the Indian sacred pair of Shiva, lord of yogis and transcendent consciousness, and his consort, the life-giving and life-taking Shakti; the Norse goddess Freya, who embodies not only the Venusian qualities of love and feminine beauty, but also clairvoyant seership; Hermes, the divine messenger and communicator, who is the teacher-guide of the Hermetic tradition of the secret sciences of consciousness; the Norse-Germanic Odin/Wodan, teacher of shamans who travel to and learn from multiple worlds of consciousness and the multiple classes of beings inhabiting them, of which humans are one, but certainly not the ruling class, as they arrogantly assume.

At first, I used to think we would tend to connect most strongly with the deity spirits of our own cultural heritage and traditions, which in my case is European. However, it has become abundantly clear that those who travel in multiple worlds, with medicines or without, may connect equally strongly with deities of other, remoter cultures, reinforcing the idea that we live many lives and may have connected spiritually with deities of other cultures. So it has been particularly fascinating for me, although I have no genetic or ancestral connection to the Americas, to find a connection with Mesoamerican deities such as Xochipilli, known as the Prince of Flowers [and] god of ecstasy, vision, and poetry; and Kokopelli, the flute-playing seed-carrier whose image adorns countless cave walls in the American Southwest; and Ossaím, one of the Afro-Brazilian *orixas,* the forest-dwelling herbalist, the teaching spirit of healers, chemists, botanists, and pharmacists.

As a result of their psychedelic and other experiences, different people seem to resonate with different spiritual traditions from other parts of the world, perhaps because they were deeply involved in those practices in another life with those teachings and practices. My old colleague and friend Ram Dass connected so strongly to the Hindu tradition, as well as finding a contemporary Hindu guru, that he changed his name and teaches in the devotional bhakti lineage. For myself, the Tibetan Buddhist Vajrayana teachings have been core guiding principles, ever since we worked on *The Tibetan Book of the*

Dead. The Taoist principles of *wu wei,* nonresistance, staying close to the natural flow, have also been and remain cherished teachings. I've always been attracted to and fascinated also with the teachings of the gnostics. These interests were enormously heightened by recent discoveries of long-forgotten gnostic texts dating from the first few centuries of the common era—texts and teachings, including those attributed to Jesus Christ, that were never included in the canonical gospels and forgotten or suppressed for two thousand years.

One of the gnostic texts that was discovered was called *The Song of the Pearl,* describing the search for a hidden pearl of wisdom and remembrance/recognition of our divine origin and destiny. On my CD *Spirit Soundings,* which consists of my spoken-word poetry with music by Kit Walker, "The Song of the Pearl" speaks of the prince (metaphorically, the soul) who ventures forth from the divine palace where he grew up, from his royal parents, the Father of Truth and the Mother of Wisdom, to explore the material world, learn to cope with its challenges, and return to his divine-royal heritage. This tale is a classic myth symbolizing the mystical way as a path of returning to our divine source and origin.

To me one of most profoundly interesting teachings found in several of the gnostic texts is their version of the divine trinity: instead of God as father, son, and Holy Spirit, these gnostic teachings have a trinity of father-god, mother-goddess, and god-child. This gnostic trinitarian doctrine, it seems to me, represents a beautiful and forward-looking updating of Christianity's long-held trinitarian doctrine that supports a patriarchal-dominator ideology, while neglecting the divine feminine.

If you could summarize the basic message of your life in a few words or sentences, what would they be?

RALPH: In my book *The Six Pathways of Destiny,* I describe six major paths in which we express our creative energies in our communities and in our world. Three of these have been the primary fields to which I have devoted most of my time and energy; three others have been paths

I've also pursued and practiced, but more intermittently. The three principals are: one, explorer, scientist, seeker, and pioneer; two, teacher, historian, social scientist, journalist; and three, healer, shaman, therapist, peacemaker. The three secondary pathways, to which I've devoted less time and energy, are four, artist, storyteller, musician, poet; five, warrior, guardian, reformer, activist; and six, builder, organizer, producer, engineer. I expect to change the relative emphasis on one or another of these pathways as my days and years lengthen.

To summarize most succinctly, I could quote Mahatma Gandhi, who said, "My life is my message."

6

Exploring
the Tryptamine
Dimension

An Interview with **Dennis McKenna**

Ethnopharmacologist **Dennis McKenna, Ph.D.,** one of the world's leading experts in tryptamine hallucinogens, has said that ayahuasca and other plant medicines are literally emerging from the jungle, because they have an important message for our species.

McKenna received his doctorate in botanical science in 1984 from the University of British Columbia and was a primary organizer and key scientific collaborator for the Hoasca Project, an international biomedical study of ayahuasca.

McKenna has conducted extensive ethnobotanical fieldwork in the Peruvian, Colombian, and Brazilian Amazon; has helped to develop natural products into medicines; and is the author of more than thirty-five scientific papers.

McKenna also coauthored the books *The Invisible Landscape* and *Psilocybin: Magic Mushroom Grower's Guide* with his brother, Terence, and he is the author of *The Brotherhood of the Screaming Abyss: My Life with Terence McKenna.*

To learn more about McKenna's work, see www.heffter.org/board-mckenna.htm, and to find out more about his new book, see http://brotherhoodofthescreamingabyss.com.

———————————————— ☺ ————————————————

I initially spoke with Dennis on December 29, 2008, to conduct this interview, although Dennis revised it in 2014. I found Dennis to be a gentle soul, thoughtful in his responses, and able to integrate many varied perspectives. It was hard not to be reminded of his older brother, Terence—the first person I ever interviewed—when we spoke.

Their voices sound similar, they shared a lot of early adventures, and the development of their ideas seems intimately connected. We spoke about ecology and psychedelics, his research with ayahuasca, what he thinks of his brother's ideas, and a key from his childhood that he mysteriously manifested one day in the Amazon jungle.

What initially inspired your interest in ethnobotany?

Dennis: I would probably have to say that, like a lot of my contemporaries, I grew up in the sixties. I was a child of the sixties counterculture and all of that. I had some early psychedelic experiences as a teenager that were pretty impressive, but the one that really impressed me the most was my encounter with DMT, which was a very rare thing, even back in those days.

You didn't see it around very much, but it seemed to me, of all the psychedelics that I had had in my limited experience at that time—which was not very many; basically LSD, mescaline, a couple of things like that—DMT seemed by far the most interesting. This was just in terms of the actual experience, and so I was surprised to find that DMT is actually quite widespread in plants, and many of the major South American shamanic medicines ultimately come down to DMT or analogs of DMT.

So this realm of psychedelic experience—loosely defined as the tryptamine dimension—seemed to define the area of interest that I found, at least personally, quite fascinating. And then I was intrigued by the discovery that they were found in many plants. While all this was going on, I became aware of the first book written by Carlos Castaneda, *The Teachings of Don Juan,* which served to place this in context for me.

Castaneda's book created a cultural context for this, which in the sixties we didn't really have. We were hippies. We were in Haight-Ashbury or wherever. We had our own cultural icons, like Timothy Leary and people like that, that were out there talking about it, but most people were not aware that this relates to a cultural tradition that's millennia old.

So I was reassured and fascinated by that discovery, that this is nothing new, that the human encounter with psychedelic states of mind has actually been going on for thousands and thousands of years, and that there is a context for it, that there are cultural practices around it—namely shamanism. And so it was these three things that solidified my interest and got me interested in plants and the uses of plants in indigenous cultures.

This led me to make a resolution that if I were going to seriously pursue the study of these things or the investigation of these things, I had to go talk to the people who knew the most about it, which was the shamans, the people who had been working with it for so many millennia, rather than our own cultural icons. I mean, I didn't disrespect them, but I thought that they weren't really dealing from a place with this tremendous cultural background. So it seemed to make sense to study it in the context of indigenous cultures, and that's what got me into it.

Can you talk a little about how this drew you and your brother, Terence, to the Amazon in the early seventies, and how your experience there helped to influence the course of your research career?

Dennis McKenna

DENNIS: Again, it goes back to DMT. Our experiences with DMT in California were with the synthetic freebase form of DMT, which we thought was totally amazing. But one of the things about it is that it's very quick; the effects pass away extremely rapidly, and there's very little opportunity to integrate or to understand what is going on. By the time you start to worry about those kinds of issues, it's already over, essentially.

So we thought that if you could somehow prolong your state in the DMT dimension, if you want to call it that, for longer than the usual ten minutes, which is pretty much the maximum time you can spend there when you simply smoke the freebase, and if we could spend more time in that place, or something close to it, then we could navigate around better and get a better understanding of what was going on, instead of this overwhelming impression of beauty and bizarre weirdness.

And so, in wondering about how to do that, at about that time, around 1970, we stumbled on a paper by Richard Schultes, the famous Harvard ethnobotanist who everybody in the field of ethnobotany and psychedelics knows about and looks up to.

We stumbled onto a paper he published about *Virola* as an orally active hallucinogen. This paper was published in the Harvard Botanical Museum leaflets, which was the house organ of the botanical museum, of which he was the director. So we stumbled on this article and it talked about *Virola*. *Virola* is a genus of trees in the Nutmeg family, in the Myristicaceae, which is the source of hallucinogenic snuffs that are prepared from the sap of the tree.

There are a number of species involved, but the bottom line is they all contained DMT or 5-methoxy-DMT, or combinations of these two. And they're prepared in the following manner: their sap is extracted, dried down, powdered, prepared as a snuff, and it's taken through the nostrils. So it's not orally active.

But from several tribes—such as the Bora and the Witoto, who were all linguistically related and live in the same areas—there were reports that emerged about that time that they did not use it as a snuff; they used it as an orally active preparation.

They made this resin and they extracted this sap or this resin, and instead of drying it completely down to a powder, they kept it in a pasty form and they took that orally in the form of little *pastillas,* or boluses. And it was said that it lasted longer, and that it was very strong, and so on. So we thought, *A-ha! Maybe this is the long-*

sought, orally active form of DMT that we're seeking. [Laughs.]

So we were determined to go down there and get ahold of this thing, which had various names. The Witoto called it *Oo-koo-he,* roughly.* I can't exactly say it the right way, but that's kind of what it's called. And that's really what led us to La Chorrera, because that was the ancestral home of the Witoto, and that's where these reports said that this cultural practice still survived.

So that's what led us there initially, and when we eventually got to La Chorrera and eventually found the Oo-koo-he, and got someone to prepare it, and so on—which was no easy thing—it proved not to be as interesting as we thought. It wasn't that active. There was a great deal of chemical variability in the preparations. Some were active. Some were not active.

But by that time we had already gotten to La Chorrera, and to our surprise we found that La Chorrera was an ecology where a lot of the land around the mission station, the mission village of La Chorrera, had been cleared and cattle had been brought in. These were zebu cattle, humpback cattle, and the . . . uh, the shit of those cows are the preferred substrate for *Stropharia cubensis* [the name has since been changed to *Psilocybe cubensis*]. So they were everywhere. You literally couldn't walk or cross the pasture of La Chorrera without kicking over huge clumps of these beautiful, large, succulent psilocybin mushrooms.

So we got into that, and that tale has been told many times. It's been told in my brother's book *True Hallucinations* about what went on. I guess the pertinence of this story is that we did find the perfect, orally active form of DMT, but it's not Oo-koo-he; it's psilocybin. Psilocybin and psilocin, the active form of psilocybin, are extremely chemically similar to DMT, and it activates essentially the same receptors. But psilocin and psilocybin are orally active and last much longer than DMT, although in high doses they can get you to pretty much the same place.

---

*Author's note: *Virola theiodora,* a hallucinogenic plant.

What type of relationship do you see between psychedelics and ecology, and do you see psychedelics playing a role to help increase ecological awareness?

DENNIS: I do. I talk about this in my essay on ayahuasca and human destiny. I think that this is what is probably going on, and it's not just with ayahuasca—it's all of these psychedelic plants that are used in shamanic traditions. And rather than use the term *entheogen*, which has one kind of connotation, or *psychedelic,* which has another connotation, I prefer the term *shamanic medicines.* The term *hallucinogen,* again, doesn't fully describe it, and, in fact, kind of misdescribes what they're about. But I like the term *shamanic medicines.*

In a sense, these are plants that are at the core of a set of indigenous practices having to do with deliberately inducing altered states of consciousness in such a way that one can learn from those altered states. Whether, in fact, this actually involves supernatural realms or some sort of superconciousness, I don't know, but that is really what shamanism is about. And I think that what we're seeing in the millennia-old association between shamanic medicines or psychedelic plants and humans is essentially a symbiosis, a form of coevolution.

This is nothing really that unusual in the plant kingdom. Plants and fungi make a large variety of so-called secondary molecules. There's an enormous chemical diversity of these secondary compounds, and they're not essential for life because they don't occur in all species.

But in the species that do make them, they serve a function, and the function that they serve is basically a messenger function. The secondary compounds are a language of plants, in a sense. It's the way that plants communicate with other organisms in their environments and maintain their relationships. In some cases the communication is quite simple. It can be something like a repellent or a defensive compound. But when you're interacting with organisms with complex nervous systems, it gets a little more interesting, a little more complicated, and I think the bottom line on the evolutionary scale is that these plants are teachers.

This isn't really a scientific theory—it's more a personal belief, I suppose—but it's one that is verifiable to an extent. These plants are trying to teach our species about nature, and about how we fit into that. And essentially it's a conduit to, in some ways you could say, a community of species' mind. Or, if you subscribe to the idea of the collectivity of species on the planet is something like Gaia, something like a conscious being, these are the tools that let us communicate directly with Gaia, directly with this consciousness, for all sorts of reasons—but partly, I think, to both understand nature and processes that go on within it. For example, shamans use psychedelic plants all the time to understand the properties of other plants that they may use for curing or other types of activities. So there is a library of information out there, and psychedelic plants are kind of like the operating system that lets you access that and understand it. So I think that's part of the purpose of these things.

I think that the other part of the message—at least in my own personal experiences with psychedelics, and in many other people's—is that Gaia, if you will, is trying to impart to us through these plants, through these substances that seem so close to our neural chemistry, the message for us to wake up, to realize the context in which we inhabit this ecology, and reunderstand that we're part of nature, and that we have to nurture nature. We have to be humble, and, as a species, we're not particularly humble. And we have to understand that we don't own nature, and nature is not there for us to exploit, deplete, and destroy. We have to rediscover a different attitude toward nature, a different way of looking at nature and living in nature.

And I think in indigenous cultures, in which psychedelic shamanism plays a role, they don't really have a problem with this, which is why their cultures can be sustainable and live in natural ecologies for long periods of time without really depleting their resources or spoiling their habitats. I think that the message, in some ways, has gotten more desperate. Or maybe it's our perception that it's more desperate with Western culture, which, essentially, has become estranged from nature. And a lot of very peculiar attitudes have cropped up in Western culture that have now been propagated globally, which I think are very unhealthy and very threatening to the stability of the planet.

So if there exists an intelligence resident in nature that communicates to us through psychedelics, it's getting a little hysterical. It's like, "Hey, pick up the phone and listen! There's important information that you need to hear." So I think that's where the connection comes with ecology, in connecting with this planetary consciousness, for a number of reasons. One of the things that psychedelics do—and this has been well elucidated through neurophysiology and neuroscience—is they activate (or perhaps in some way they suppress) those parts of the limbic system, those parts of the brain, that are involved with defining the boundaries between the self and the world. They dissolve those boundaries, and we invest a lot of time in defining who we are and what separates us from everything else out there—when, in fact, this is an illusion.

We know we are all part of a continuum, and a model that's closer to reality is to realize we are all one. It's not simply a cliché. In some way, that's a more accurate understanding of how we are and how we fit in the world than the idea that we're just individual particles separated by barriers from everything else. And I think one thing that psychedelics teach, as many other spiritual traditions do, is that we're all one and that it's an important lesson to learn, especially at this moment in history.

We're not going to save the planet. We're not going to fundamentally change the way that we relate to nature until we take that lesson, understand it, take it to heart, and try to express that in the way that we live and the way that we think. Psychedelics teach many lessons, but at this historical juncture I think this may be the most important one for our culture and for our society.

I think back in the end of the sixties, two things probably did more to change our perspective as a race, as a species, of who we are and what our place in the universe was. One of them was psychedelics, and the other one was going to the moon. Or, more specifically, that first photograph of the Earth from space. The first time that we were able to look at ourselves, in a sense, from out there and realize what a small planet we are, what a small part of the totality our supposedly very important affairs are, I think that was a very humbling experience, and that helped to put us into perspective—or in some it did, anyway. I really think those two things were what sparked, or initiated, what we might call eco-consciousness.

Can you talk a little about your research with the UDV [União do Vegetal] in Brazil to study the long-term effects of regular aya-huasca use, and what you found?

DENNIS: This grew out of some experiences that I had in the eighties. Terence and I went to La Chorrera in 1971, looking for Oo-koo-he, and we found Oo-koo-he, but what we really found was mushrooms, the end of history, a new theory of time, and all this stuff that is what it is. I went back to Peru in 1981, as a graduate student at the University of British Columbia. I went back to revisit this whole issue of Oo-koo-he and tryptamine-based hallucinogens. The other one that is important in the Amazon is ayahuasca.

When I was a graduate student at UBC, I was studying botany, plant chemistry, and pharmacology. Originally I was studying fungal genetics. I was studying psilocybin and psilocybin biosynthesis. So it was pretty much a lab-based kind of activity, but my supervisor, who was an amazing person—a mentor and a friend for all of my life, who only died a few years ago—offered me a chance to go to Peru for six months and study ayahuasca or whatever I wanted. The projects that I choose were a comparison between the chemistry and pharmacology of Oo-koo-he, this orally active snuff that was a *Virola* preparation, and ayahuasca, which was made from completely different plants but is also an orally active form of DMT. It's made from two plants, one of which contains DMT, which is orally inactive by itself. But the other one contains a group of alkaloids called beta-carbolines, which are very strong monoamine oxidase inhibitors. Monoamine oxidase inside the gut will inactivate the DMT unless you inhibit it. If you inhibit it, or block the action, DMT becomes orally active, and that's the basis of ayahuasca.

So I went back to Peru in 1981. For me, on a personal level, this was somewhat of a personal adventure, because I wanted to prove to myself that I could go down there and, number one, not go crazy [*laughs*], which I'd done before—or some could have interpreted it that way—and also do good ethnobotanical science. I planned to collect specimens, bring them back to the lab, talk to shamans—do the whole ethnobotany shtick—and I did that.

I brought specimens back and studied them. I eventually published my thesis out of it, and so on. Then I went back to Peru in 1985 to do some more collecting with my friend Luis Eduardo Luna, who is an anthropologist that is well known as a scholar of ayahuasca. He also has done a lot of his own practicing.

So we were in Peru in 1985, just collecting plants, collecting ayahuasca, talking to different *ayahuasqueros,* and actually going around the country and taking a lot of ayahuasca. One of the things that kept coming up was that these ayahuasqueros that we were dealing with—and most of them were in their seventies and eighties; some were in their nineties—generally all seemed to be pretty together people.

They were physically and mentally healthy. They were strong. They were impressive in that way. So we were wondering, Is it the ayahuasca? What is it that makes these gentlemen so different from the run-of-the-mill people? We wondered if there is something physiological or biochemical about taking ayahuasca that sets them apart. So we thought it would be very interesting to do some kind of a biomedical study of ayahuasca.

When I got back, I started to write a proposal to the National

Institute on Drug Abuse, and the more I got into writing the proposal, the more I realized that there was no way in hell that the National Institute on Drug Abuse was ever going to fund something like this. So I put that project on a shelf for a few years, actually. I went on and did postdocs—that sort of thing.

Then in 1991, I had just published several articles on ayahuasca for my thesis work and I was invited, along with Eduardo Luna and a number of other researchers in this field, to a conference that was organized by the UDV in Brazil. I had not really been that familiar with the syncretic use of ayahuasca in the context of these religions. All of my experience up to that point had been more or less with *Mestizos,* so not exactly indigenous, but not in the context of a structured religious organization.

But they invited us to come give talks on our research, and they paid the way, so I went down to São Paulo in 1991 and gave my talk. Then it turned out that Eduardo and I decided, "Well, maybe they're interested," because one of the things that dissuaded us from doing the project in Peru, after we had been thinking about them for a while, was simply logistics. It's difficult to go to a culture where witchcraft is very much a part of the cultural context and ask people to give blood samples, donate a little urine, and things like that.

It's culturally very sensitive to ask for these sorts of things. But the people in Brazil didn't really use it within that context; they used it in a religious context. Many of the people who organized the conference and who were members of the UDV were also scientists.

We had psychiatrists, immunologists, neurologists, and people like that. It was a very different sort of socioeconomic slice of people in Brazil that were taking *hoasca*, as they called it, as a sacrament in the context of this religion.

As it turned out—we discussed it with them—that was actually their agenda all along. They wanted to do a biomedical study with hoasca, and that was really the motivation for inviting us down to participate in this conference. So it was a confluence of mutual interests. And we thought it would be interesting to do a biomedical investigation.

They did too, just out of scientific curiosity in some ways, but they also had a political agenda, which was that the Brazilian government at that time was weighing whether they should ban ayahuasca. Was it a dangerous drug? And was this drug abuse, or should they permit it to be used in the context of these religious practices?

So the high mucky-mucks, or whatever you want to call them at the UDV, had this agenda. They wanted to invite international scientists to come in, have a look, conduct a study, and report the results, whether they were good or bad or whatever, but something that they could represent to the government.

So we had these mutual interests. I was able to go back after this conference, and I dug out this old proposal. I finished writing it, and we started soliciting funds, initially through Botanical Dimensions, which was a nonprofit that my brother and his wife, Kathleen, had started, and then through the Heffter Research Institute. Eventually, the Heffter Institute was formed in 1993, so it got in on the tail end of this, but there was some funding that came through them.

I went back in 1993, and we did this study. We went to Brazil, and I enlisted Charlie Grob at UCLA, Chase Callaway at the University of Kuopio in Finland, and other, Brazilian investigators. We went to the oldest nucleo of the UDV in Manaus. I think it was in June or July of 1993, and we did the study.

Could you summarize the results and discuss how it improves the frequency of serotonin 2-A receptors?

DENNIS: We carried out a number of measures; some of them were psychological screening measures, some of them were assessments of the general mental-health status of the volunteers, and some were biochemical measurements.

We published all of this; we generated about six or seven peer-reviewed papers, which have been published out of this. You can go on

PubMed and put in my name or Charlie Grob's name, and it all comes up. But long story short is we found no particular toxicity, evidence of toxicity, brain damage, impaired cognitive function, or anything like that.

These were all men. These were all volunteers, gentlemen who had been taking ayahuasca and been members of the UDV for at least ten years. Some of them much longer than that; some of them over thirty years. So they'd been taking ayahuasca on a regular basis, about once every two weeks, for long periods of time.

We actually compared them to a group of age-matched, controlled volunteers, who were just drawn from the local community. They were relatives or friends of about the same age of the UDV members, but who were not members of the church and didn't take ayahuasca.

We found, on various parameters—memory, cognitive functions, verbal recalls, verbal ability, and that sort of the thing—the UDV members were slightly better than the nondrinkers; the difference was small, but it was statistically significant.

So that was reassuring. Then we conducted very extensive psychiatric life-story interviews with all the subjects. I didn't do it, but Dr. Grob did, using a translator and a fairly structured format, which was basically to get people to tell them what had led them to join the UDV.

They almost all had the story that before they had joined the church they were quite dysfunctional. Usually it was alcoholism, drug abuse, or other types of destructive behaviors. They felt that their lives were out of control, and they were dealing with addiction, domestic violence, other types of crime activities, and just basically not in a balanced state.

Most of them said they were drawn to their initial UDV sessions, that they had a friend or someone urged them to come, or brought them with them, and that their initial experiences were quite unpleasant and rather terrifying, because they found themselves in a self-review process. They could see where they were at, where they were headed, and that it wasn't going to turn out well if they didn't straighten out, basically.

They almost all said that at some point during their initial experiences they had some kind of an epiphany. They had visions of Mestre Gabriel, who was the prophet of the religion, or Jesus, the Virgin Mary, or sometimes all of these figures basically appeared and assured them that it was going to be okay if they changed their ways.

So a lot of them came back and did resolve to change their ways, and as long as they stayed in the church, they stuck with that. It was kind of like a twelve-step program—not unlike, I suppose, the born-again experience that people have in a lot of fundamentalist religious situations.

But then we had this other track, which was we were looking at biochemical changes and all of the expected things, like heart rate and blood pressure, and the acute effects. We did pharmacokinetics of the alkaloids, and measured their absorption, distribution, excretion, and all those other things.

But one of the questions we were looking at, or one of our hypotheses, goes back to our original question in Peru. Finally getting back to that—sorry! Circuitous route. But our initial question in Peru was, Is there a biochemical marker, if you will, that distinguishes drinkers from nondrinkers? What makes these folks so vigorous and so apparently mentally healthy? Is there a biochemical difference that we can identify?

We looked at a number of different parameters. We drew blood samples, and we looked at receptor profiles in blood platelets, which [we] have long thought to be an analog of what's going on in the central nervous system. If you can see it in the platelets, you can figure it's also going on the brain.

So we looked at these different receptor profiles in the platelets, and what we found was serotonin transporters, which are the proteins that mediate the reuptake of serotonin. In other words, serotonin is a neurotransmitter, and in the neuron there's a protein localized in the presynaptic membrane that is a pump. It sucks the serotonin out of the synapse, repackages it, and recycles it.

It's the same membrane structure, or membrane pump, that the selective serotonin reuptake inhibitors work on. So it's the same thing. But the reuptake inhibitors inhibit the reuptake of serotonin. What we found is that long-term use of ayahuasca elevated the density, essentially boosted the abundance, of these transporters, because there's a certain number scattered around in the membrane.

Essentially this created more of them, this induced them to upregulate, which is the technical term. The transporters became upregulated, but we didn't know what that meant. We thought, *Gee, that's interesting.* We looked at it and compared to the nondrinkers. Since serotonin transporters were elevated in density, we were at least able to say, "Well, this is a biochemical difference."

This is a long-term, persistent biochemical difference. It doesn't go away with the effects of the drug. Our measurements were taken two to three weeks after they had stopped taking the drug, and these differences persisted. So what does this mean?

We didn't really know, and then we looked into the literature, and it turns out that there was a whole literature associated with deficits in these receptors. In other words, abnormally low densities of these receptors were associated with things like alcoholism—so-called type-two alcoholism, which is alcoholism with tendencies to violent behavior—as well as to certain types of depression and certain types of suicidal ideation. All of these have been associated with abnormal deficits in the densities of these receptors.

So we were very excited by that, because then we could go back and coordinate that with the life-story interviews of these people, about where they had been at before they started taking ayahuasca.

So we thought, *Gee, this is kind of an interesting fit.* Not only did their experiences motivate them to change their lives in a more positive direction, but maybe the ayahuasca, in some sense, healed them or reversed those biochemical deficits at the level of the nervous system. It seemed like a very neat story in some ways, a rationale for why it might have worked. So that's kind of where it's at. There's a lot of follow-up work one could do on this, but it would take a lot of money. [*Laughs.*]

What are some of the primary areas of psychedelic drug research that you would like to see explored?

DENNIS: The primary areas? Well, I don't know. That's a tall order.

You said previously that you've given up your hope that the FDA would ever approve studies with ayahuasca. However, there's been such great strides that MAPS and the Heffter Institute have made, and MAPS president Rick Doblin told me about a possible Canadian study that you were involved in with ayahuasca.

DENNIS: Yeah, it's not a totally hopeless situation. Ayahuasca is a unique thing, in the sense that it's a plant-based medicine. It's much easier to get FDA approval for a synthetic compound or a pure substance than a plant-based preparation, because with plant-based preparations there's a variability from batch to batch.

Where are you going to get the plants? I mean, there's plenty of ayahuasca available, but the plants have to come from somewhere in order to meet the FDA standards. You have to file what's called an IND, an investigational new drug application. If you want to do a clinical study here in the States, you have to do this, and you have to define the composition of the medicine clearly, in a great deal of detail. You have to say it contains so much DMT, so much of the other alkaloids, and so on.

So the technology exists, certainly, to make a standardized form of ayahuasca from batch to batch, but it does take some special formulation expertise, and it takes an authorized source of ayahuasca. This has been what's held us up to this point. If we import the ayahuasca already made from Brazil or Peru, we could do it that way.

We could probably get permission to import it, but then our quality control goes out the window, because every batch is going to be different. On the other hand, if we try to get it from a domestic source, from growers in Hawaii, for example, then we're faced with the catch-22 that they're not authorized suppliers of a Schedule I controlled substance.

It's essentially no different than medical cannabis. If you want to do research with cannabis in this country, there's only one place you can get it right now: from the National Institute on Drug Abuse, from their pot farm at the University of Mississippi. No other source is authorized.

No one has been authorized, or certified, to grow ayahuasca for government research, as far as I know. So that's one hurdle that we haven't quite gotten around yet. There are other approaches to it; one could develop a combination of pure chemicals. You could develop an ayahuasca analog, which is sometimes called pharmahuasca, which would be a combination of pure DMT with one or more of the beta-carboline alkaloids.

It would be orally active. It would have much of the effect of ayahuasca, but it would lack some of the effects as well, though. The purgative effect being one thing. Some might view that as the good thing, if it doesn't induce vomiting. But on the other hand, the total spectrum of the experience includes vomiting.

If you look at the way the substance is used in a shamanic context, an alternative name for it is *la purga,* and it's thought to be a cleansing thing—that is, necessary to get the full benefit of it. And I think that there might be something to that. There are hurdles to doing this kind of work. There are these technical hurdles that have to be overcome to do such a study in the States.

It's possible it could be done elsewhere. Canada is one of the possibilities. Canada also has prohibitions against these things, but it might be easier to get approval. It may be less of a bureaucratic challenge to get approval in Canada.

There's been work done in Spain by a researcher, Jordi Riba. He's done work with a freeze-dried form of ayahuasca that he's imported from Brazil, and in Spain he's gotten approval and done this work. And, again, he opted to go with a freeze-dried preparation so he could standardize it, so he could quantify the amounts of alkaloids in it, and so on.

But he might have sacrificed an important element of the therapeutic effect, which is that it didn't induce vomiting, and there was no taste involved. And there are important reasons to think that you might need to taste it to get the full benefit. So, for all these reasons, we haven't overcome those yet. I would like to proceed with a biochemical study, with a bigger clinical study of ayahuasca, but these issues on the preparation of the medicine have just kept us from doing it up until now.

I've always found it interesting that many of the ideas that Terence spoke about in his talks and in his books, where actually ideas that he developed from things that you said during the experiment at La Chorrera. In general, what did you think of Terence's ideas about the nature of time, the end of history, and the evolution of novelty—that seemed to originate from ideas that you actually spoke about?

DENNIS: Well, I can't really make that claim. I mean, a lot of Terence's good ideas—I wouldn't say it was me or him necessarily that originated these ideas. It was pretty much a collaboration. But his ideas about the Timewave and the nature and the structure of time, and the connection between the I Ching as a predictive instrument or for something that describes the structure of time . . . I can't really claim any credit for that—or blame, as the case may be.

Because this is something that really emerged when we were both what you might call three sheets to the wind in La Chorrera. I was off doing my own navigation, making discoveries, and Terence was off in another place. Although the nature of—I don't know what you could call it—the simultaneous psychosis, or whatever it was, was that he was hypervigilant. He was very much focused on the environment and kind of on monitoring me so I didn't wander off and do something stupid, although I managed to wander off several times, and did a number of stupid things.

But anyway, he was trying to ride herd on me, and he wasn't sleeping, and he was thinking about a lot of things at the same time. So we were both in a highly altered state, but he was thinking a great deal about time, about cycles, about the I Ching, and the cycles that had defined our coming to La Chorrera. So the initial idea for the Timewave emerged out of these ruminations, and it became increasingly elaborate and refined over time.

I mean, in some ways, I'm a debunker of the Timewave. I think that it's a very interesting idea, and I think that what he did mathematically with the treatment of the I Ching, you can't really take that away because it's there in black and white. And I think that what he actually did, as far as it goes, is he probably rediscovered an ancient Chinese calendar. He rediscovered that you could use the I Ching as a calendar, a thirteen-month lunar calendar. That much is completely defendable, and pretty much there in the mathematics of the Timewave as he constructed it.

I guess where we differ, or over time where I became a skeptic, was around the idea that it describes the structure of time. That time has a structure, and that this wave somehow describes the terrain that time has, time itself—that time is not just a place where you put events, any more than space is a place where you put objects.

I mean, we now know from relativity and other things that space has qualities, that space has structures. So why not time? Well, it's a reasonable enough idea that time itself may put constraints on the types of things that can happen within certain times, things you might call boundary conditions for what is possible. But it's a big leap from there to postulate that this wave describes that structure. So that's a big leap, and there's basically no way to test that hypothesis. The bottom line with his theory of the Timewave is it's not a testable theory; there's no way to disprove it.

There was one date I was actually wondering about. What did Terence's Timewave theory predict for September 11, 2001? Do you know? I asked both Ralph Abraham and Rupert Sheldrake this question, but they didn't know the answer. If Terence's Timewave model predicted a large descent into novelty for that day, it seems like that might be pretty good evidence to support the theory.

DENNIS: That would have been a good validation of something. Well, I don't really know. I can't really tell you at this moment. I'd have to go back and look at it. But the thing is, this was one of the problems with the Timewave, after several mathematical iterations, transformations of the curve, and so on, the wave either goes up or the wave goes down.

You can lay it against a historical sequence of events, and you can say, "Okay, here's September 11, and there's a huge plunge into novelty on September 11." When the wave goes down, when the wave is reduced in value, that was interpreted as an increase in novelty, and when it goes up, when the value goes up, that was interpreted by Terence as a decrease, a diminishing of novelty.

But the thing is, the only person that could really interpret the wave was Terence. There was no objective way to interpret it; there was no quantifiable way to interpret it. You could say it goes up or it goes down. Well, had the wave gone up on September 11 and then it would have fallen again, so you could say, "Well, look. On September 11 the wave was already up here, and then it fell abruptly." So it's sort of like the I Ching itself, or astrology, or many of these other things where you can always find an interpretation that seems to fit.

And that's great as a method of divination, but it's not a scientific theory. There's no way to disprove it. This is the problem: a theory has got to be worthy of that name. A theory has got to state what will disprove it. In other words, this is the way science is supposed to work. Right? You postulate a theory or hypothesis based on observed facts.

You try to put those facts in a framework. Does the theory or the hypothesis explain the observed facts? If it doesn't explain it, or if other information comes in that doesn't fit the hypothesis, then you either have to revise the hypothesis or chuck it completely and come up with a new hypothesis.

But you have to define the criteria that will either prove, or validate, or invalidate the hypothesis. Within the context of the theory of the Timewave idea, that's not defined, so I think that's a fatal flaw.

Having said that, maybe the Timewave is not a precise instrument for predicting the exact moment of the end of history, the collapse of the space-time continuum, and all that, which Terence kind of postulated. But having said that, I think that, in a general sense, he was probably right—in the sense that Alfred North Whitehead's notion was probably right: reality tends to evolve toward novelty, and that novelty ingresses into the continuum over time.

The idea that there's nothing new under the sun would contradict that. What Whitehead said is that there's plenty new under the sun; everyday things happen that have never happened before in the entire history of the cosmos. And there is this slow ingression of novelty into reality. And what Terence's theory and the Timewave theory postulate is that this ingression of novelty is accelerating, that these cycles that are reflected in the Timewave are growing shorter and shorter, and that it's a closing spiral.

So the subjective impression is that things are accelerating, things are getting weirder and weirder, faster and faster, and all you really have to do is open the newspaper [*laughs*] or look around you to be convinced that gee, things sure do seem to be getting weirder and weirder, faster and faster.

So, in some sense, I think he was right. Not so much in the mechanics of the theory, as I think that there's holes in the theoretical framework that are just too big to reconcile—like the fact that you cannot prove or disprove it. With theories in science, you never prove theories or hypotheses. All you can do is say, "Well, at this time, based on what we know, we can't disprove it." But new information may come to light the next day that lets you disprove it. So you can never actually say this theory is definitively proved. You can only say, based on what we know, we cannot invalidate the theory.

Since Terence's death, the idea that the year 2012 would mark a transformation in human evolution—or the end of the world—gained considerable prominence in popular culture. There were many books and films on the subject. I'm curious what you thought of all this, and if you think that anything particularly special occurred on December 21, 2012?

DENNIS: I think that it's not that Terence was entirely responsible for this. I mean, it was a coincidence, or maybe not. It's a bit of a coincidence that the date that he finally settled on for the end of the Timewave was December 21, 2012, which is also the date that the Mayan calendar postulated would be the end of the last great age of humanity. I don't think that those two things were necessarily coincidental.

I mean, you have to know a little bit about the iteration of the Timewave and how it was constructed. When we left La Chorrera, shortly after we came back to the States, Terence came out with a lot of these different cycles that he'd been working on, calendric cycles, and the whole idea went back to the very personal nature of the experience, the so-called experiment that we had done at La Chorrera, which was an attempt to condense, manifest, or materialize this artifact that we claimed that we were going to create out of the voice, mushrooms, time, and all kinds of things. [*Laughs.*] But the elaboration of these cycles became an attempt to nail that down.

When was this object, this transhistorical, transmaterial object, going to appear? Because it obviously hadn't appeared at the end of our experiment. I mean, a lot of things had happened, mainly that we had both gone completely nuts, to the outside observer, at least, for three weeks. But there was no glowing, violet, saucer-shaped artifact appearing. Call it the philosopher's stone, call it the time machine, the UFO, or whatever. All of these things are the same thing on a certain conceptual level. So a lot of the development of these cycles was trying to nail down when was it going to appear.

So there were a number of end dates postulated for the cycles. The first end date was Terence's birthday on November 16, 1971. Well, November 16, 1971, came and went, and nothing happened. Then the next thing, people got excited about the comet Kohoutek, and so we looked at the cycles and we shifted the cycles around, and we thought maybe that is the harbinger of the end of history. I don't know if you remember back that far, but the comet Kohoutek was the most hyped comet in history, other than Halley's comet, but compared to Halley's comet, it was a real disappointment, as you could barely see the damn thing.

So there was an effort made, several dates were postulated, and as Terence looked at the cycles and looked at historical events and historical sequences, he tried to find the best fit for the wave. Where was the best fit? He didn't do this in any statistically rigorous way, which is one of my criticisms. I think that he could have approached it in a much more mathematical way. He didn't really have the tools to do that, and God knows I didn't have the tools.

But I thought he could have approached it from a statistical angle and maybe make it a little more objective, but he didn't. He more or less developed the fit of the wave to history based on his own interpretations of history, and, as it turns out, the fit that came out the best, as far as he was concerned, was one where the end date was set to be December 21, 2012. Of course, he knew about the Mayan calendar and all that, although I'm not sure whether that was a coincidence or not.

I suspect that what happened is that he found an end date that was pretty close to that, and then, knowing about the Mayan calendar, if it's shifted it a little bit this way or a little bit that way, it will coincide, and it won't make that much difference to the fit. So there was this kind of cultural expectation around 2012, and a lot of it had to do with the Mayan calendar and then Terence's interpretation. Terence can claim a lot of credit for getting this idea out there, as a cultural meme, if you will, or sort of raising mass consciousness about this date 2012.

Of course, it became part of apocalyptic expectation of global culture, and how much he had to do with that, I don't know, but probably a fair bit actually. [*Laughs.*] I don't totally dismiss it, in the sense that I say it's not a testable hypothesis.

As 2012 came and went, with nothing much happening, that was a pretty serious disproving of the hypothesis, but I also think that, given the way things are going, it may have been too conservative a prediction. There certainly does seem to be accelerating change. So I'm taking the scientific stance, which is, we don't have enough data, we don't know if this hypothesis was valid or not. I think that in some sense Terence was right, in that we do seem to have entered a period of accelerating change, to such a degree that it even suggests that we are approaching a temporal or historical singularity of some kind. But his hypothesis, that linked it specifically to the December 21, 2012, date, and that asserted that the Time wave was some kind of "map" that described this headlong plunge into novelty, that hypothesis has been shown to be false in its premises. So I would say that his idea or his feeling was correct; like many of us, he had this sense of accelerating change. But the hypothesis, the framework, was clearly not correct, and I think we can consider it disproven at this point.

Dennis, this is a question that I've asked almost every person that I've interviewed for the past twenty-five years, and, in fact, Terence was the very first person who I asked this question to. What do you think happens to consciousness after death?

DENNIS: Oh, boy. Well, what do I personally think happens to consciousness after death? I don't know, and I don't think anybody does. I think that's the only honest answer anybody can give. No matter what they may claim, or whether they claim to know or not, the bottom line is nobody really knows.

Now, I can speculate a lot, as I think a lot about the answer to that question. The basis for speculation is the question of whether consciousness is something that resides in the brain. Whether consciousness is something that is generated mainly by the brain, and the neural activity of the brain, or whether consciousness is something more like the ether, and something that permeates space-time, permeates the continuum.

If the latter is true, then the brain is more of a detector than a generator. It would be like radio antennae, essentially, and by changing the channel, you change the frequency of the radio antennae, and you pick up different stations.

It could be that the brain is more like that, more like a radio tuner for something that's kind of everywhere in the continuum. And I think if that's what consciousness is, then the idea that it persists after death is certainly much more plausible—and that's not even the way to interpret that anymore, as it's not that it persists after death. It would be more like asking, Does the electromagnetic spectrum persist after you break the radio and send it to the ash heap?

Of course it does. It has nothing to do with the individual radio receiver. It's still out there. So in that sense, if you choose to believe that, and I don't think we really know yet what it is, then I think there's every possibility that, in some sense, consciousness does persist after death, or some nucleus or a kernel of individual consciousness reemerges into the universal mind, or whatever you want to call it.

Certainly this is many people's experiences on psychedelics, that they have this type of experience, and that convinces them that that's what happens after death. I think that if there's a pharmacological analog for the death experience, I think psychedelics are it, and especially DMT. Rick Strassman's work very strongly suggests this about DMT.

We know that DMT exists in the human brain, and that it may have important functions at certain stages of development—one of them being at the moment of death, when the stressors that are expressed on the organism and on the brain at the moment of death may cause a massive release of DMT, and other neural chemicals in the brain, that, in some sense, simulates the near-death experiences or actually is the near-death experience.

Do you pass through the doorway and get beyond that to some sort of Pleroma, where all minds are merged together? I mean, hell. I don't know, but it's not an implausible idea.

What is your perspective on the concept of God?

DENNIS: Well, again—God! These are huge and inappropriate terms to throw around. I do tend toward the notion that consciousness is a quality of matter, that they're not separate, that it is a force or quality that does permeate space-time. It's inseparable from space-time.

And so to the extent that I believe in God, God for me is not a personal entity that looks over my shoulder and makes sure that I'm behaving myself and not jacking off, or whatever. It's not like the super–Santa Claus notion of God . . . God is a force that's intrinsic in the universe, that leads toward a net increase in consciousness. I guess the glib way to put it is, God is the universe in the process of waking up to itself, becoming consciousness of itself. That's what I would say.

This is a question that other people have probably asked you, but I've never heard your answer and have long wondered about this. In True Hallucinations, ***Terence talks about an experience that you had in the Amazon together.***

According to Terence, at one point you supposedly physically manifested a key to a box from your childhood in your hand. I've wanted to ask you this for a long time: Do you have a recollection of this actually happening, and, if so, what do you make of this experience?

DENNIS: I have a recollection of it. I have a recollection of many things that happened in La Chorrera, but there's no sequence; there's no chronology. It's like they're vignettes that I remember. I can't really put it into sequence, only roughly say, "Well, first this happened, then that happened, and then the next thing happened."

So I remember this incident, but I have no idea where that key came from or how it got there. I mean, I know what the key was. It was the key to a box that my grandfather had given us, a wooden box with a secret compartment, and you needed the key to unlock it. And he'd given us the box, he'd given us the key, years and years before.

Why I would have taken that key with me to the Amazon, I haven't the foggiest idea. [*Laughs.*] So I can't even vouch that the key that I produced was this key, or what would have led me to stick it in my luggage.

You know, I had no voice saying, "When you're completely ape-shit lost in the jungle, if you want to really surprise somebody, and come up with this key . . ." [*Laughs.*] I can't answer the question. I don't know how it manifested, but we're pretty sure it was the key.

Wow, that's really fascinating. Dennis, what are you currently working on?

DENNIS: I'm working on a number of different things. I moved back from British Columbia in August. I was working at BC Institute of Technology there for the last two years, and now I'm back at the University of Minnesota. So I'm teaching, which is what I did here before—ethnopharmacology and ethnobotany, or, rather, botanical medicines.

I'm teaching two courses. I just got approval to teach a course next semester called Culture, Drugs, and Society, which should be pretty interesting. So the basic gig that pays the bills and puts food on the table is teaching. Fortunately, I was able to come back here and pretty much get my old job back.

I actually do a lot of teaching in South America. I teach a summer field ethnobotany course for Arizona State University in Ecuador—at least I did last summer—and I'll probably do that this summer. So a lot of teaching, this is what I do, what I can do, and what I enjoy.

Then I'm trying to get some more research going. I had a grant before I left Minnesota from a private foundation, to look into Amazonian ethnomedicines, different ethnomedicines, looking for new compounds that could be used potentially for the treatment of schizophrenia.

That grant is almost done with now and is winding down, but we have got some interesting results from that. I don't think we have the next blockbuster schizophrenia drug, but we do have some interesting results. What I'm trying to do is build on that, actually, and continue the collaboration I've developed with my colleagues in Peru while doing this project. They're the same colleagues I had originally hooked up with when I was a graduate student, so we go way back.

My own personal contribution, if you will, or passion, as the way to save the rain forests, the way to save the planet, is to provide economic incentives to develop the rain forest in a sustainable way. We know that burning the rain forest, deforestation, and other types of unsustainable land-use practices in the Amazon contribute between 20 and 30 percent of the total global carbon emissions into the atmosphere.

So one obvious way to help cut that down is to provide indigenous people or to provide these countries with high biodiversity, with the motivation to stop burning the rain forest, to stop clearing it.

And one of the most direct ways to do that is to show that it's a source of new medicines. This is commonly talked about, that the drugs of the future will come from the forest primeval, which is what R. E. Schultes said years ago, and I believe that. So I'm trying to work on developing a sustainable, long-term infrastructure in the form of a collaboration between the University of Minnesota and the university in Iquitos, Peru, where I've worked off and on over the years.

They have some good scientists, some good capabilities, and we have some up here. I just submitted a grant to a place here called the Institute on the Environment. It's a new center that the university set up. They have some money to support research projects that will benefit the environment.

I think we have a very good chance. We have a good story to tell, so I'm hoping they'll look favorably upon that and decide to fund that project. If they do, that will be the basis for a long-term, sustained collaboration that can ultimately help the university in Peru develop their own research and direct-discovery capabilities.

That's exciting. Well, those are the questions that I had for you, Dennis. Is there anything that we haven't discussed that you would like to add?

DENNIS: I think we pretty well covered it. I think we could go on for hours. [*Laughs.*] But I really think, in terms of the ecology thing, I think in some ways these plants are tools for changing people's consciousness and changing people's understanding of their relationship to nature.

As we've said earlier in the interview, this is what they've always done. This is one reason why they are so threatening to the sort of power hegemonies that run the global economy, which is mainly governments and religions, which are not really separate, in my opinion. At least Western governments, Western political institutions, grew historically out of ecclesiastical and religious institutions.

I think one of the great disservices that Christianity, in its institutional format, has done to humanity, is the notion that this world doesn't matter. In other words, one should reject the things of this world—reject the flesh, reject physical embodiment, and, essentially, reject biology. This is why sex and drugs are so threatening to the religious hegemonies, because they are all about being biological entities in the context of a biosphere, and the whole notion of Catholicism, Protestantism, and the Western religious traditions is that you should not value the things of this world, that your reward comes in Heaven, after you're dead. Right? You must just have faith that your reward will come.

There, of course, is not a shred of evidence for any of this, but that's the nature of faith. To tell someone to have faith is essentially to ask them to believe something without any evidence. So it's an antiscientific kind of thing, and I think it's very dangerous.

I think this is why these plants, these drugs, are so heavily censored, made illegal, persecuted, and vilified, because they don't require faith, and they present people with another way of looking at things.

They cause people to ask questions, and questions are dangerous. As Terence liked to say, "They give you funny ideas." That's the point that he made, that they make you have funny ideas, and funny ideas are always threatening to the authorities.

So that's the thing, I think, in terms of their ecological significance or helping people understand. It's just the fact that you don't have to have faith. Any individual can have these experiences and make of it what they will. They don't need a priest or anybody else to interpret it.

They can come to their own conclusions, and that's very dangerous. But I think it's very important and necessary, in this historical juncture, for us to be asking our own questions, to be questioning authorities, and to not necessarily believe what we're told.

Examine it and decide for yourself. That's what these things do. They can actually change hearts and minds, and if we don't change hearts and minds on a global scale—especially about nature and how we're going to live with it—I think we're probably doomed. So these plants are important tools to try to escape that, and foster the transformation into a more sustainable way of life.

7
Ayahuasca, DNA, and Decoding the Cosmic Serpent

An Interview with **Jeremy Narby**

Anthropologist **Jeremy Narby, Ph.D.,** is the author of *The Cosmic Serpent* and *Intelligence in Nature* and is the coeditor of *Shamans through Time*. He received his doctorate in anthropology from Stanford University and spent several years living with the Asháninka in the Peruvian Amazon, cataloging indigenous uses of rainforest resources to help combat ecological destruction.

Narby sponsored an expedition to the rain forest for biologists and other scientists to examine indigenous knowledge systems, and the utility of ayahuasca in gaining knowledge. He has said that the information that shamans access "has a stunning correspondence with molecular biology" and that one might be able to gain biomolecular information in ayahuasca visions.

Since 1989, Narby has been working as the Amazonian projects director for the Swiss NGO Nouvelle Planète. Narby's *The Cosmic Serpent* is one of my all-time favorite books. It's a revelation-after-revelation, *aha!*-filled scientific adventure/detective story about why the image of the serpent appears so commonly in shamanic traditions around the world and why this relates to the double-helix structure of the DNA molecule.

———————————————————— ◎ ————————————————————

I interviewed Jeremy on December 18, 2008. He is unusually articulate, and he maintains a good balance of open-mindedness and skepticism. He has a quick, analytical mind and appears to enjoy debating intellectual ideas. We spoke about the relationship between ecology and ayahuasca use by indigenous peoples in the Amazon, intelligence in nature, and what he has learned from his experience with ayahuasca.

What originally inspired your interest in anthropology?

JEREMY: I suppose the real answer is a psychoanalytical one. I grew up in a family with a culturally mixed background—with Irish, Egyptian, English blood—in the suburbs of Montreal, in a French-speaking neighborhood, but with an English-speaking family. Then, when I was ten, we moved to Switzerland, to another bilingual town. I became a foreigner at that point, and have been since.

I grew up as an English-speaking Quebecer in French-speaking Switzerland, right on the frontier with German-speaking Switzerland. By the time I got to be eighteen I could feel a lot of cultural diversity inside me, and I suppose that I was drawn to anthropology, which studies cultural diversity, first and foremost to understand myself and how I stood in the world. In other words, Was I Canadian, Swiss, Irish, or Egyptian? So that's what I think drove me toward studying anthropology.

Can you talk a little about what originally drew you to the Amazon as a doctoral student, and about your anthropological work and ecological projects there?

JEREMY: Thank you for asking that, because it allows me to add the political dimension to the psychoanalytical. It's true that by the time I became a doctoral student in anthropology I was interested in one

Jeremy Narby

overarching question, which is, Why are there rich people and poor people in the world? There seems to be enough material wealth to go around for everybody. So that led me to be interested in what was called third world development, and a professor of anthropology at Stanford pointed out that indigenous peoples were the Achilles' heel of all the different theories of development—be they capitalist, socialist, or communist.

This was back in the 1980s, when there still was Communism. So, in other words, if one really wanted to understand third world development, and understand the relations between rich and poor countries, it was important to look at a case where development was being carried out in territories of indigenous peoples, because this is where the contradictions would be greatest. So it was for theoretical reasons, and also for a desire to critique Western theories of development. World Bank–financed visions of development in those days—in the seventies and eighties, in places like the Amazon, for example— consisted of building roads into the rain forests, which they called jungle at that point.

They confiscated the territories of the indigenous people that had lived there for a long time, saying that they didn't know how to use their resources rationally, and then gave the land to individuals with a market mentality, so that they could cut down the trees and do cattle ranching. This was actually deforestation, but they called it development. Not only was it not socially appropriate and grossly violated the rights of the indigenous people who were there, but it was even ecologically and economically inappropriate. Cutting the rain forest down on that scale was simply a recipe for creating sterile savannas. So there was enough there that called for a politically engaged anthropology, and that's what took me to the Peruvian Amazon in 1984.

What type of relationship do you see between psychedelics and ecology? Do you see psychedelics playing a role to help increase ecological awareness?

JEREMY: In the spirit of dialogue, I would quibble with the question a little bit, because I think that in as much as psychedelics have a relation with ecology, it's via people. So people are lacking in the question. Then I think that psychedelics have different effects on different people. So the short answer to your question is that it depends, and if you could make your question more precise, I could advance with it. I don't just think that psychedelics—as a group of substances—are any sort of instant ecology-awareness pills.

Perhaps you could talk a little about the relationship between ayahuasca use in the Amazon and how this effects the ecological relationships there.

JEREMY: Okay, that's getting a bit more precise. But, once again, I think that by asking the question that way it does omit who is taking the ayahuasca, what ayahuasca it is, and where they are taking it. I think that the ayahuasca experience is also a function of who's doing it, where they're doing it, and how they're doing it—beyond set and setting, which is just obvious.

So, in other words, who are we talking about? For example, the indigenous people of the Amazon and what we know about them historically, or how ayahuasca has impacted their eco-cosmologies? That could be a subject of a whole book, but it's certainly a precise question. You want me to talk about that precise question?

Yes, and maybe you could also talk a bit about the worldwide ecology movement, and whether you think that's in any way related to people who have used psychedelics? A lot of people think that psychedelic experiences have been an important part of the inspiration for the ecology movement.

JEREMY: Yes, it's true that one runs in to quite a few people in the broad ecology movement who say that their engagement has been souped up by ayahuasca, and I guess I would include myself in that bunch.

So maybe you could also address a little bit about the use of ayahuasca by indigenous people in the Amazon, and how that affected their relationship with their environment.

JEREMY: I think the way that they look at it is like this: there is a level of reality that is parallel to our own, but that we don't see with our, let's say, normal eyes, but in certain states of mind you can see it. Ayahuasca is known by the people who use it to make the invisible visible, and first and foremost you take ayahuasca to see, and to see what you normally don't see. So in their view, one could say that ayahuasca is an important tool for knowing the world, as microscopes have been for biologists. It's an absolutely central tool in approaching an otherwise invisible level of nature.

So in their view, ayahuasca—but also other plant teachers like tobacco—have enabled them to have an ongoing conversation with the powers in nature, entities or essences corresponding to the different species. For them, ayahuasca is the telephone, but the person on the other end is the whole assembly of nature. So what's important is not the telephone; it's the conversation that you have with the other species. It would seem that these indigenous societies have been dialoguing—at least in the visions of their shamans—with the essences of plants, animals, and ecosystems for millennia. And they view nature not as an object, but as a subject or a series of subjects with whom you negotiate if you want game and health.

So, yes, ayahuasca is central to the eco-cosmology of many indigenous Amazonian peoples. It is that which enables communication, but that doesn't mean that it needs to be worshipped. Once again, the importance of the conversation, in their view, is because nature really is a bunch of subjectivities, and it really is important to communicate with them, because we're on the same planet as them. So how the human community negotiates its relation with other species is precisely what shamans negotiate traditionally in their visions attained using these plants. That's why these plants are central to their eco-cosmology.

But I guess the reason why I object to the general nature of the question about psychedelics and ecology is that it's like the question about psychedelics and creativity. If only it sufficed to take psychedelics and everybody could play the guitar like Jimi Hendrix, but it doesn't happen that way. Some people have taken psychedelics and have done terrible things. Likewise, there are a lot of people in the ayahuasca movement, and they may talk about this and that, but some of them lead pretty unecological lifestyles, it seems to me. Unfortunately, there are Westerners that are demonstrating that it's possible to turn ayahuasca into a kind of a drug, really. So if only everyone who was guzzling ayahuasca became an ecological activist, at least it would be easy to answer the question.

I was just wondering whether you've seen a pattern of any kind. It seems to me like psychedelics, in general, are basically boundary-dissolving, nonspecific brain amplifiers.

JEREMY: Exactly. So if somebody's got an ecological sensitivity, then it will amplify it. But if they're power-hungry, then it will amplify that too. So depicting ayahuasca as this magical thing that draws people to understand nature better and then to become healing-oriented would actually be misleading. It's way more complicated than that. One of the loops that's missing is that it depends entirely on the individuals, and there's a lot of variation in the individuals out there.

Another thing that I would like to say about this is that the more I've been able to get into the ayahuasca realm with indigenous Amazonian shamans guiding me, the deeper my respect for their knowledge has gotten. So, obviously, the more you really respect people and actually look up to them, the more it enhances, well, at least my desire to be useful to them. In other words, it galvanizes me as an activist.

Is what you're describing, what you think is the most important thing that Western civilization can learn from indigenous shamanism?

JEREMY: Well, that's speculative. I'm enjoying arguing with your questions; that's what I think questions are for. I don't know what Western society can learn. I mean, for the moment, it's had a hooligan, vampire-like behavior, and it's sucked out what it wanted to suck out—mainly for material benefit—and just spat out the rest. Look at what it did to the Inca temples. It just melted them into gold. And look at how it's treated shamanism for the last five centuries. It said it was the devil's work or balderdash, and then went on to label shamans as psychotics. We've taken the shamanic plants like tobacco, and look at what we do with them: we turn them into drugs that cause harm to health and create addiction. Look at what we've done to coca: turned it into a nasty drug.

So there's been this sort of, I don't know, ghoulish mercantile touch to what Western cultures have done to indigenous cultures. Yes, it's about time it changed, but let's see some action. I don't want to sit here speculating on the sidelines as to what we could learn. I want to incarnate learning. I want to see more people learning, and I don't want to be there saying, "Oh, if only we could do this, then maybe we could all change," and so forth. Enough already of this telling Western people what they could benefit even more from! Let's start thinking about reciprocity. Let's become lucid about the last five hundred years of history, and what we've imposed. Let's break with it, denounce our own behavior, and show something different.

What are some of the primary things that you think people should be focusing on to help restore ecological balance on our planet?

JEREMY: I'm not any kind of expert on how to re-equilibrate Western lifestyles; there's a whole bunch of people who talk about that. But I think that the more that we can move away from using hydrocarbons and the smaller our personal imprints can be, the better. The less light-bulbs and everything else that we use, the better. But, nevertheless, here we are having a conversation over a telephone, using tape recorders. The very existence of this conversation in text is the fruit of the electric world. Because our world seems irremediably electric, there aren't any easy solutions.

But I think that the more of us that can sit with, let's say, both forms of knowledge, the better. In other words, technological knowledge, and let's call the other shamanic knowledge, for telegraphic sake. We're not going to be throwing out the baby with the bathwater. We're not going to get rid of science and technology. On the contrary, it's too good to throw out. But, obviously, it needs complementing. It needs critiquing and controlling, let's say.

I think that, for example, one thing that's also really clear for me—but it's also a matter of opinion—is the view that nature is just an object, or a bunch of commodities that we can just exploit as we wish, has led us to the ecological situation that we're in. I think that it's been a powerful way of coming to dominate nature, treating all those different beings as if they were objects. One can hold that gaze for 2,300 years, and that's what we've just done, but that doesn't mean that it's right. You can treat beings like objects, because, actually, beings are objects, but they're more than just objects, and treating them like just objects is nixing a whole, important part of their existence.

So I think that getting away from the objective view of nature and moving toward a deeper understanding of the other beings with whom we share the planet would probably be a good move. And that would precisely be a combination of knowledges, using science and shamanism. I mean, in as much as you accept that shamans have some kind of dialogue in their visions with entities that represent other species on this planet, one could consider including them on bioethics committees.

Why do you think that nature is intelligent, and do you see any teleology in the evolutionary process?

JEREMY: That's two questions.

You don't think there's a link between the two? This is in contrast to the blind-chance view of evolution as a random process, which most evolutionary biologists adhere to.

JEREMY: One question at a time. Why do I feel that nature is intelligent? Well, by asking the question, it implies that you may feel that nature is not intelligent, right? I've written a whole book about this particular subject. [*Intelligence in Nature,* Tarcher, 2006.] You've got to examine or unpack the concept of intelligence. It turns out that most of the definitions of intelligence have been given in exclusively human terms, and so, by definition, you can't apply the term to other species. So *intelligence in nature* is actually a contradiction in terms, if you're strict with words, because nature is defined in opposition to the human, and intelligence is defined as exclusively human.

But that just shows that we have concepts that separate us from nature, and it's not so much nature that lacks intelligence, but our own concepts. So you say, "Okay, there are so many different definitions because Western cultures have been obsessed with putting a line between human beings and other species, and one of the properties that was supposed to separate us from other species was intelligence." It was supposed to be one of the exclusively human traits, along with tool making, abstraction, and so forth. And so, as such, it was supposed to be one of the human treasures. It became this very political thing, and that's why there are so many definitions—because people fought for decades over how to define this human treasure called intelligence.

So here we are. But now, through recent biology, we are beginning to realize just how stunningly similar we are—at least on a physical-chemical level, down to the gene sequences, down to how the brains are constructed—to all these other species, and that it's really true that we have a kinship with bacteria, amoebas, and so forth. When you look into a blade of grass—which is what we've been able to do for the last ten to twenty years—we see that, as it goes about its business being a blade of grass, it integrates information from the outside world. It transduces this external information into electrochemical information, and there are signaled conversations between the cells as the plant integrates the information, makes decisions, and then enacts them.

Then, if you intercept these molecular signals that go between vegetal cells in the blade of grass, you see that many of them are identical to the molecular signals used by our own neurons. So a plant may not have a brain, but it acts like one. If you look at the etymology of the word *intelligence* you find that it comes from *inter* and *legere,* which means to "choose between," and this implies the capacity to make decisions. Well, it turns out that if you look at how biologists describe how individual cells behave, they are forever integrating information, making decisions, communicating, and acting according to the information received.

So if you use a simple definition of intelligence, you can find intelligence all the way down to the behavior of individual proteins, and this is what scientists have been discovering in their labs over the last ten or twenty years. We're even talking about single-celled organisms, like slime molds and amoebas, and also simple invertebrates like bees. Bees are capable of abstraction. They have small brains of about one million neurons, but it's been demonstrated that they can handle abstract concepts. I mean, it just goes on and on. The list of characteristics that are supposed to be exclusive to humans have more or less melted like snow in the sun. So, meanwhile, we know that we've evolved and are part of nature. So how could nature just be a bunch of stupid objects or machines, if we ourselves are intelligent? On the contrary, it would seem that the whole edifice of biological life here in the biosphere is infused with intelligence—and we're part of it.

So, now, do you want me to move on to teleology from there?

Yes, I'm curious how you view the evolutionary process from this perspective.

JEREMY: See, you may have noted that in this whole discourse I'm trying to stick to the facts that have been established. So what's going on inside of a blade of grass is what researchers have discovered and published in peer-reviewed journals over the last ten to fifteen years. The fact that we have many genetic sequences that are identical to those found in the bacterium or the banana has been known for ten years.

So there's no teleology in my discourse about intelligence in nature; I'm just sticking to what science is generating, as far as data. You can put a single-celled slime mold in a maze and it can solve it. That's a fact. We don't know how it does that. It doesn't have a brain; it only has one cell. But we can see through its behavior that it can figure out a maze. Now, let's say that we are detecting intelligence in nature, depending on how we define the world *intelligence*, but we're detecting more than a mechanical thermostat-like behavior, we are detecting plasticity and foresight. Well, okay, so does that mean there's a goal in nature? Well, that's another question.

I see.

JEREMY: Doing teleology is doing theology. I think there are parts of the neo-Darwinian approach that are actually quite theological. Some people, without realizing it, go on to theological terrain.

I don't think that teleology implies theology.

JEREMY: Well, teleology implies a goal, and so as soon as you start talking about a goal, I think that you are crossing a line and are stepping onto theological territory. That's why I don't go there. I'm an agnostic, and I am interested in dealing with what can be known. So, for example, take the question of the origin of life. There are at least a hundred thousand scenarios possible, none of them testable. Any certitude about how life started is a belief. You can talk about Stanley Miller and his test tubes, or any of the different RNA worlds, or whatever. All of that, for the moment, is of the order of belief. It's not of the order of demonstrable knowledge. But there are a lot of people in the scientific world who don't seem to be aware of this. This is actually an epistemological question.

If somebody says, "I believe that life began on Earth by chance, in a spark collision, in a wet pool 3.5 billion years ago," that's fine, but that's a belief. You're welcome to believe it, like you're also welcome to believe that a guy with a gray beard did it. But as an agnostic I know that I don't know, so I don't even go there. There's a lot of other business at hand in the . . . let's say, verifiable world.

What are some of the most important lessons that you've personally learned from your ayahuasca experiences?

JEREMY: Well, heck, the whole thing! I guess the first thing was that when I was a twenty-five-year-old whippersnapper from the suburbs, who had studied chemistry in high school and thought I knew what reality was, the ayahuasca experience opened my eyes to the fact that there was a whole level of reality that one didn't normally see, that there was something that seemed associated with plants, animals, and the forest world, that had a mind-boggling, well, intelligence about it. It taught me things, and showed me how stupid I was. It showed me how anthropocentric I was. In French, one says to *deniaisé,* which means that it made me less stupid—fast.

It also made me see that there was something there that the materialist-rationalist perspective, which thinks it's so smart, actually didn't get and couldn't get. That kind of defined it, and that made me listen to the indigenous people even more. I just knew there was something there that flew in the face of our categories, and that needed more investigating. And by investigating ayahuasca, one was clearly investigating the indigenous approach to knowledge—but also plants and animals themselves, or nature. In other words, thinking about what it is to be a human being, and what it is to be a human being in the rain forest, is to be immersed in this breathing, hooting, scratching environment that's clearly alive. I mean, if you think nature is stupid, all you've got to do is go into the rain forest at night and listen. It sounds like a bunch of loud electronic musicians.

What do you think happens to consciousness after death?

JEREMY: In brief, I don't know, but I hope to see you at the bar.

What are you currently working on?

JEREMY: I'm continuing to study the world, and it's not getting any less crazy.

8
DMT Research and Nonhuman-Entity Contact

An Interview with **Rick Strassman**

Rick Strassman, M.D., is a medical researcher who conducted the first U.S.-government-approved and -funded clinical research with psychedelic drugs after a twenty-year, worldwide ban. These studies, which took place between 1990 and 1995, investigated the effects of DMT (N,N-dimethyltryptamine), a powerful, naturally occurring psychedelic.

During the project's five-year duration, Strassman administered approximately four hundred doses of DMT to fifty-five human volunteers. This research took place at the University of New Mexico School of Medicine in Albuquerque, where he was a tenured associate professor of psychiatry.

Strassman received the Sandoz Award for outstanding graduating resident in 1981, and he spent ten years as a tenured professor at the University of New Mexico, performing clinical research investigating the function of the pineal gland hormone melatonin; during this time his research group documented the first-known role of melatonin in humans.

Strassman has published dozens of peer-reviewed scientific papers and has served as a reviewer for several medical and psychiatric research journals. He has been a consultant to the U.S. Food and Drug Administration, National Institute on Drug Abuse, Veterans Health Administration hospitals, Social Security Administration, and other state and local agencies.

In 1984, Strassman received lay ordination in a Western Buddhist order. He cofounded, and for several years administered, a lay Buddhist meditation group associated with the same order. Strassman currently lives in Gallup, New Mexico, and is a clinical associate professor of psychiatry in the University of New Mexico School of Medicine, as well as president and cofounder of the Cottonwood Research Foundation.

Strassman is the author of the popular book *DMT: The Spirit Molecule,* which is a compelling and fascinating account of his research with DMT. In the book he discusses how DMT may be involved in near-death experiences, alien-abduction encounters, and mystical experiences.

As the book unfolds, what begins as a study to explore the pharmacology and phenomenology of DMT becomes a science fiction–like journey into a hyperdimensional reality inhabited by intelligent alien creatures. A popular documentary hosted by Joe Rogan—also titled *DMT: The Spirit Molecule*—was made by director Mitch Schultz about Strassman's DMT study.

Strassman's more recent book, *DMT and the Soul of Prophecy,* is about how the Hebrew Bible offers a spiritual model for understanding the DMT experience. Strassman argues that the states of consciousness associated with prophetic experience in the Hebrew Bible result from our interactions with God's intermediaries and that these reported interactions offer a more inclusive model for understanding DMT experiences—and the commonly reported encounters with nonhuman entities in hyperspace—than either Buddhism or Latin American shamanism.

Buddhism, Strassman points out, interprets DMT experiences as illusory, and shamanism lacks a centralized deity. I think that Strassman's ideas are really interesting and worth considering. To find out more about Strassman's work visit his website, www.rickstrassman.com.

I interviewed Rick twice, on September 28, 2004, and then again on February 22, 2014. The following chapter contains the revised material from both interviews. Rick and I discussed how Buddhism helped to guide his medical research, the potential therapeutic value of psychedelic drugs, the reality of nonhuman-entity contact, and different models for understanding the DMT experience.

How did you become interested in medicine, and what led you to study psychiatry?

RICK: In college, I actually didn't quite know what I wanted to do. I began as a chemistry major, because of my keen interest in fireworks, which I indulged in more or less safely in high school. I had hoped to start my own fireworks business. Funny, in retrospect, how I switched from an interest in outside-world fireworks to ones more internal.

Nobody I knew really was that encouraging about the fireworks idea, so I switched to a zoology/biology major, but didn't think much about medical school at the time. During the summer between my third and fourth year of college at Stanford, I read much of the material for the upcoming year's classes: Early Buddhism, Sleep and Dreams, The Psychology of Consciousness, Physiological Psychology.

I had an epiphany of sorts that summer, deciding I'd like to combine my interest in psychedelics with Eastern religions and psychoanalytic theory and practice, all in a sort of unified theory of consciousness that related to integrating what I saw as a biological basis for spiritual experience—the pineal, endogenous DMT, et cetera—with what I believed was the most comprehensive system of psychological defenses, psychoanalysis, with what I thought was the most sophisticated view of human mental mechanics, Buddhism.

This was a little ambitious for my medical school applications, and I had a hard time toning it down enough to fit into the format required for those applications. And my mentor at Stanford thought I had lost my mind, telling me to keep my mouth shut. Most medical-school interviews ended badly when they asked why I wanted to go to medical school.

The only ones I got into were those where the interviews were short, and I didn't have a chance to launch into my reasons. Right before starting medical school, I was offered a research position in an outstanding physiological psychology laboratory at Stanford with Karl Pribram, and arranged to delay entrance into medical school for a year. However, when it turned out there was no funding for the research position, I decided to start medical school on schedule.

I maintained this idealistic, somewhat manic, view during my first year of medical school, and was sorely disappointed. I got depressed, dropped out, ended up at the Zen monastery with which I was ultimately to have a twenty-plus-year relationship. There at the monastery I learned to get back to basics, and returned to medical school, got into my own psychoanalytic psychotherapy, and put the whole psychedelic-research idea on the back burner.

When it came time to decide what specialty to pursue, I chose psychiatry for several reasons: the hours were good; I liked the patients; I liked the reading material; I liked other psychiatrists; I admired my psychiatrist, who had helped me a lot. Last but not least, I thought if ever I were to do psychedelic research, psychiatry would be the field in which to do it.

What inspired your interest in altered states of consciousness in general, and what led you to study the effects of DMT and psilocybin?

RICK: I was very curious about how similar were states of consciousness brought on by psychedelics and those described by mystics and seasoned meditators throughout the ages, across all cultures, as well as descriptions by those having the recently discovered near-death experiences. Later I saw some of the overlap between psychedelic consciousness and psychosis. And against my better judgment, I began seeing some overlap between the abduction experience and the psychedelic one, at least with respect to those of our DMT volunteers.

Once I was finally positioned to begin psychedelic research, almost

Rick Strassman

twenty years after the original epiphany, DMT was a natural choice to begin such research anew. It had been used in humans in previously published research; was endogenous, that is, naturally produced, which made it a great candidate for eliciting spontaneous psychedelic experience; it was short-acting, which I knew would be helpful on an aversive research unit; and was relatively obscure, thus less likely to draw the sort of attention that an LSD study might.

Psilocybin is chemically very similar to DMT, but is orally active and longer-acting. I thought it might produce a more easily studied and managed state, both for phenomenological research, as well as for therapeutic work, than did DMT, which was so mind-shatteringly short-acting.

How has your interest in Buddhism helped to guide your medical research?

RICK: I was first drawn to Buddhism because of its unabashed manner of describing rather exotic and lofty states of consciousness in a relatively objective manner. The techniques and concepts of the mind, as defined and affected by meditation, appealed to me; it seemed that even the most outrageous states of consciousness could be held, described, even objectified.

Particularly, the Buddhist Abhidharma—the canon of psychology in Buddhism—approach to mind as a composite of a small number of mental functions appealed to me as a facile means of developing a rating scale, a tool for measuring the states of consciousness I anticipated finding in our psychedelic research.

This rating scale has been a legacy of the DMT research, and has been translated into several languages, used to measure effects of several different drugs, and has held up well in comparison to some of the other, more traditional ways of measuring drug effects.

Later on, when I actually started practicing Zen meditation, I found it very grounding and powerful, and the state of active passivity, so to speak, or alert quietness, was useful as a means of holding the DMT sessions themselves, on my end. I also saw that some of the principles I had learned about meditation, and from teaching it, were useful in coaching the volunteers on how to deal with the things they encountered, or might encounter, during their sessions.

One of the most fascinating things about DMT is that it is found naturally in the brain. What function do you think endogenous DMT plays in the human brain?

RICK: I think it plays several roles. It may help mediate some of the more profound mental experiences people undergo: near-death, mystical states, psychosis. This was one of my hypotheses beginning the research: that endogenous DMT mediated these states of consciousness. Thus if by giving exogenous DMT we saw features found in those states, that would support our theory that elevated levels of endogenous DMT were involved.

Also, the brain brings endogenous DMT into its confines, across the blood-brain barrier, using energy—something that it does for very few compounds, such as glucose, certain amino acids. Thus it seems as if endogenous DMT is necessary for normal brain—read: perceptual—function. Something like the internally generated Matrix.

Do you think that DMT experiences can have therapeutic value? What about other psychedelics?

RICK: Intravenous DMT is so overwhelming that the most one can hope for is to hold on and try to remember as much as one can, at least for a single, isolated session. We found that people could work through things much more, though, psychologically, spiritually, when given repeated doses in the course of a morning, which we did in our attempt to develop tolerance to closely spaced, repeated DMT injections.

This is probably somewhat akin to what happens with ayahuasca, which is an orally active preparation of DMT—two plants: one contains DMT, and one contains an inhibitor of the enzyme that normally breaks DMT down in the gut—which lasts about four to six hours, and is much more workable.

Other psychedelics may be therapeutic to the extent that they elicit processes that are known to be useful in a therapeutic context: transference reactions and working through them, enhanced symbolism and imagery, increased suggestibility, increased contact between emotions and ideations, controlled regression, et cetera. This all depends, though, on set and setting. These same properties could also be turned to very negative experiences, if the support and expectation for a beneficial experience aren't there.

In your book you expressed some doubt as to whether DMT use might have any spiritual value. What are your thoughts on this now? Do you think that DMT has any entheogenic potential?

RICK: I still don't think psychedelics, including DMT, have intrinsically good or bad values. It all depends upon how they're used and taken. Sort of like the very trite and overused analogy of a hammer: it can be used to break things apart or build things up.

Do you think that there is an objective reality to the worlds visited by people when they're under the influence of DMT? And do you think that the entities that so many people have encountered on DMT actually have an independent existence?

RICK: I myself think so. My colleagues think I've gone woolly brained over this, but I think it's as good a working hypothesis as any other. I tried all other hypotheses with our volunteers, and with myself. The "this is your brain on drugs" model, the Freudian "this is your unconscious playing out repressed wishes and fears," the Jungian "these are archetypal images symbolizing your unmet potential," the "this is a dream," et cetera.

Volunteers had powerful objections to all of these explanatory models—and they were a very sophisticated group of volunteers, with decades of psychotherapy, spiritual practice, and previous psychedelic experiences.

I tried a thought experiment, asking myself, "What if these were real worlds and real entities? Where would they reside, and why would they care to interact with us?" This led me to some interesting speculations about parallel universes, dark matter, et cetera. All because we can't prove these ideas right now, lacking the proper technology, doesn't mean they should be dismissed out of hand as incorrect.

How do you think the DMT experience is related to the near-death experience and the alien-abduction experience?

RICK: I hypothesize that DMT levels rise with the stress associated with near-death experiences, and mediate some of the more psychedelic features of this state. I think that, based upon what many of our volunteers experienced viz entity contact, high levels of DMT could break down the subjective/objective membrane separating us from other levels of reality, in which perhaps some of these entities reside.

I've been criticized by the abduction community because of the lack of objective evidence of encounters in our volunteers—for example, stigmata, metal objects, et cetera. In response to these concerns, it might be worth considering a spectrum of encounters—from the purely material (about which I withhold all judgment), to the purely consciousness-to-consciousness contact experience that may usefully describe what our volunteers underwent.

Were there any times during your DMT research where you witnessed something that you couldn't explain in terms of conventional science, such as a form of psychic phenomena?

RICK: I didn't see much in the way of psychic phenomena. The reports people came back with, though, were the things I had a difficult time conceptualizing, such as the entity-contact thing.

Do you think that the study of psychedelics might provide us with some insight into psychic or paranormal phenomena?

RICK: I'm not sure what you mean by paranormal. And, I'm not too interested in, say, psi or clairvoyance or telepathy. Those don't seem necessarily a more enlightened way of viewing our lives and our society. However, the concept of consciousness existing without a body, and the implications this might have on our behavior, ethics, ecology, interpersonal relationships—these hold more interest to me.

How has your study of DMT affected your understanding of the nature of consciousness?

RICK: I think we're mighty small. But I think what we're connected to is mighty big, and through our connection can affect it.

What kind of an influence did Terence McKenna's explorations and ideas have on your DMT research?

RICK: He introduced me to DMT. He and I had some long conversations about how to formulate a research agenda that would both fly with the traditional scientific community and would address our deeper questions about consciousness. He was a friend too.

My friend Cliff Pickover, the popular-science writer, told me that he once corresponded with you about his hypothesis that DMT in the pineal glands of biblical prophets may have "given God to humanity, and let ordinary humans perceive parallel universes." His idea is that if our human ancestors produced more endogenous DMT than we do today, then certain states of consciousness, or certain kinds of visions, would have been more likely. He suggests that many of the ancient Bible stories describe prophets who seem to have had DMT-like experiences. Cliff told me that you said to him, "If indeed we made more DMT in the past, this may have to do with the increase in artificial light that has come upon us in the past thousand years or so." Do you think this is a possibility?

RICK: Well, this relates to my theory about the pineal and DMT, which is basically that the pineal is a source of endogenous DMT production. I marshal a lot of circumstantial evidence for this, but there are no hard data yet. Nevertheless, the stress model of increased DMT production is established in humans and lower animals, as it is well established that brain, lung, and blood all make DMT, and that in lower animals and humans, endogenous levels rise with stress.

With respect to the pineal, pineal activity increases in darkness and during winter, and decreases in increased light and in summer. Even relatively dim artificial light, indoors, has a suppressive effect on pineal function, and it may be that if generic pineal activity were related to

DMT production, decreased activity through the aegis of increased ambient light during hours which were previously dark may have something to do with decreased normative DMT levels.

What kind of potential do you see for future research with psychedelics?

RICK: I don't think organized religion can handle them, because of the threat to their turf. I also don't think science can handle them because of the nature of what they reveal—at least mainstream science. Any mainstream scientist doing research into the true, real, hardcore psychedelic experience is so hamstrung by political correctness that they cannot discuss what they really have seen in their research, and what they think and feel about it.

Thus for the foreseeable future, psychedelics will exist in some sort of limbo, waiting for the proper discipline to be developed that can approach the experience through the relatively objective tools of the scientific method, and the context and wisdom of perennial religious teachings. In some ways, this is unfortunate, because much of this work is now going on underground, with no peer-review and general aboveboard forum for discussion, quality control, and the like, which occurs in the nonunderground world.

What has your own personal experience with DMT been like, and how have psychedelics affected you?

RICK: I don't answer anything about my use or nonuse of psychedelics. If I say I've used them, people accuse me of being a drug-addled zealot. If I say I've never used them, people accuse me of not knowing what I'm talking about.

What do you think happens to consciousness after death?

RICK: I think it continues, but in some unknown form. I think a lot depends upon the nature of our consciousness during our lives—how attached to various levels of consensus reality it is. My late, former Zen teacher used to use the analogy of a lightbulb, with electric current passing through it. The lightbulb goes out, but the current continues, changed, in a way, for its experience in the bulb.

He also referred to like gravitating toward like in terms of the idea of the need for certain aspects of consciousness to develop further, before it can return to its source. That is, doglike aspects of our consciousness end up in a dog, humanlike aspects get worked through in another human, plantlike aspects into plants, and so on.

What is your perspective on the concept of God?

RICK: I'm working on it. Put simply, I think God is the creator and sustainer of this whole scene. And the creator and sustainer of cause and effect, which for many Buddhists is equivalent to God, but by not believing in God, they get to sidestep the whole issue of a beginning or an end—which, I believe, is extraordinarily important.

I spend much of my time studying Jewish scripture and commentary, from as conservative and medieval an approach as I can. I'm interested in the Jewish conception of God, as that's my own biological/genetic/social background, and also in the Jewish mystics'/sages' ideas about no-corporeal existences. They draw from those ideas (God, and spiritual realities) a very profound ethical-moral system. And such a system must be incorporated into any truly psychedelic view of reality, consciousness, and society.

How do you think that the Hebrew Bible can help us to better understand the relational aspects of the DMT experience?

RICK: The DMT experience is usually highly interactive. That is, one maintains a sense of self while relating to the DMT world and, in particular, with its inhabitants. This type of experience is quite different than a unitive, formless, selfless one that is the goal of Buddhist enlightenment and the Western union with God. I had been expecting enlightenment-like experiences due to my approaching my research through the lens of a long-standing Buddhist practice.

The other current model for the contemporary Western psychedelic experience is Latin American shamanism. This system posits the external reality of the DMT world as experienced through ayahuasca and also is highly interactive. One meets up with beings quite similar to those described by the DMT volunteers. However, the worldview of Latin American shamanism is not native to the modern West.

The Hebrew Bible posits the external reality of spiritual worlds, is replete with accounts of contacts with beings in the spiritual world, and has the advantage—or disadvantage—of being the foundational spiritual text of the Western world. In fact, one half of the world's population belongs to a religion in which the Hebrew Bible plays a prominent, or the prominent, role. Secular Western culture can be traced to notions articulated in the text: our economy, philosophy, science, theology, law, art have all been influenced by the narratives, laws, poetry, imagery, and wisdom literature of the Hebrew Bible.

That is why I think it is worth considering the Hebrew Bible as a key to deciphering the contemporary Western psychedelic drug experience. The biggest problem I see regarding contemporary psychedelic use is its lack of a cogent spiritual matrix through which to view, understand, and apply it in our daily lives. The Hebrew Bible may provide such a matrix.

A familiarity with the Hebrew Bible may help us gain a familiarity with the nature and function of the beings found in the DMT state, as well as availing ourselves better regarding the informational content of the experience. Can we express in words what we apprehend under the influence of DMT? Learning the vocabulary, concepts, and imagery of the prophetic state might thus be transferable to the DMT one.

If the beings that one encounters during a DMT experience have a genuinely independent, freestanding existence outside of our minds, then do you think one day in the future we may be able to establish more sophisticated communication channels with them?

RICK: Maybe one day we will develop a dark-matter or parallel-universe camera, take pictures of what we see there, and then compare it to what a DMT subject witnesses in his or her altered state. That way we would establish the objective existence of the beings and their world. Even if we do establish their objective existence, however, then what? This is where it's good to ask them, "To whom do you pray?"

Even if the beings exist solely within our own mind-brain complex, they still exert a profound influence upon us and we need to determine their nature and function. To the extent that they exist outside of us, perceived not generated, it is even more challenging to consider the implications of such a finding. Again, this is where the Hebrew Bible provides quite interesting and practical guidelines for communicating and relating to the beings in spiritual states. One of the chapters in my new book deals with the relatedness occurring between the beings and those who observe them in both altered states. The degree of articulation of the relationship in the prophetic state is vastly more developed compared to the DMT one.

In your discussion of ayahuasca, in DMT and the Soul of Prophecy, *you mention that DMT is consumed with beta-carbolines (such as harmaline) in the shamanic brew, which block MAO production in the gut and thus make the compound orally active. However, you didn't mention how these MAO inhibitors also radically change the nature of the DMT experience, by significantly slowing it down and stretching it out, so that it becomes more digestible and comprehensible to the person experiencing it. Because this is the way that indigenous people have used it traditionally for at least thousands of years, I've wondered whether there might be something natural about our use of this botanical combination. Could you speculate about this idea and share any thoughts that you may have?*

RICK: I think that the prolonged experience of ayahuasca is much more manageable than smoked or injected DMT. The beta-carbolines in ayahuasca also exert psychological and physical effects by themselves and synergistically with the DMT. There also is a culture built around the ayahuasca experience, and that of contemporary Western DMT use has not been worked out to anywhere near the extent. That's not to say that injected DMT, because of the rapidity of action, lacks potential benefit. The optimal set and setting have yet to be determined.

In what ways do you think that the results from your previous study may have differed if the subjects had been prepped with MAO-inhibiting harmaline two hours prior to being administered DMT?

RICK: If people were pretreated with an MAO inhibitor, harmaline or the synthetic MAO inhibitors that are prescribed in Western medicine, two effects would be noted. A much lower dose of DMT would be effective. In addition, the effect of DMT would be prolonged.

Another future DMT study might involve a constant infusion of the psychedelic blood level. A German study was published in the English literature in 2005 comparing a constant infusion of DMT with a constant infusion of ketamine for hours. They published no narratives of subjective experience, and I was unable to obtain any more information than that which is in the article. It might be valuable to repeat a study like that, but focus on the subjective effects to a much greater extent, and publish them.

How do you think that your study at the University of New Mexico might have differed had you used 5-methoxy-DMT instead of N,N-DMT?

RICK: The logistics of the study would be the same if we used 5-methoxy-DMT. I think we may have gotten more unitive, formless, ego-dissolving, white-light types of experiences in such a study. There is a concept in the Hebrew Bible called God's glory, which is anomalous as a prophetic experience because of its formless—fiery and cloudlike at most—unitive, inchoate characteristics.

I have wondered whether this phenomenon relates more to endogenous 5-methoxy-DMT than DMT, as the latter compound usually produces the more typical interactive, being-filled state. It's also worth considering the role of endogenous 5-methoxy-DMT in the state of Buddhist enlightenment and the states attained by certain Western mystics. It may also be the case that there are ethnic and/or racial differences in the ratio of DMT to 5-methoxy-DMT, sensitivity to or metabolism of the compounds, et cetera.

Why do you think that the shamanic use of ayahuasca is associated with so many reports of people being healed from various illnesses?

RICK: That's an amazingly interesting phenomenon. Beyond the purely biological, pharmacological, physiological explanations—for example, antibacterial, anti-helminthic, immune modifying, and psychological effects—it's important to speculate regarding the spiritual mechanisms that might be at play. By *spiritual,* I mean either affected by outside influences that we normally cannot see or interact with, but in the DMT or ayahuasca state we can.

What are the beings in this case, and how do they heal? Are they activating latent tendencies or potentials within us, or are they bringing in something entirely outside of us? Or is there some interaction? Which of the beings are the most helpful, and which are the least? How do we optimize our relationship with healing beings? At the same time, the Hebrew Bible reminds us not to lose sight of God: the creator, sustainer, and director of all of these beings, angels, or forces.

9
Psychedelic Warfare? Exploring the Potential of Psychoactive Weapons

An Interview with **James Ketchum**

James Ketchum, M.D., is a retired Army colonel, a board-certified psychiatrist, and an assistant clinical professor of psychiatry at UCLA. He received his M.D. from Weill Medical College at Cornell University and is the author of the book *Chemical Warfare Secrets Almost Forgotten.*

During the 1960s, Ketchum was a research director for the Army's Chemical Center at Edgewood Arsenal in Maryland, where thousands of U.S. soldiers served as volunteers for the secret testing of psychedelic and deliriant drugs as incapacitating agents. The goal was to develop nonlethal military weapons, which could be used to temporarily knock people out without necessarily hurting them.

I found Ketchum's book, *Chemical Warfare Secrets Almost Forgotten,* to be absolutely fascinating and difficult to put down. It's a treasure chest of rare information, compiled from a massive amount of research of which I was largely unaware. The book is filled with many interesting personal photographs and humorous anecdotes, and it is compulsively readable.

Most important, it fills a vital historical gap in the archives of psychedelic drug research. From 1955 to 1975 several thousand U.S. soldiers served as volunteer test subjects for psychedelic drugs (such as LSD and strong cannabis derivatives) and deliriant drugs (such as BZ and other belladonnoid compounds). The soldiers were administered a battery of physical and cognitive performance tests to see how well they could perform under the drugs' influence.

While reading Ketchum's book I was struck by the strange historical irony that some of the very drugs that were associated in the 1960s with the counterculture's antiwar movement in America were at the very same time being researched as secret military weapons.

While the thought of government-funded experiments into chemical-warfare agents may give you the chills, Ketchum maintains that his research was motivated by the desire to save human lives and develop more humane, nonlethal weapons. Part of his motivation for writing his book was to clear up the misconceptions that many people in the media have about the Army's all-volunteer research program, often confused with the CIA's notorious and nefarious MK-ULTRA mind-control program, which sometimes even administered LSD to ordinary, unwitting U.S. citizens.

Ketchum is a difficult man to pigeonhole as he has always been somewhat of a maverick. In 1966 he was granted two years off from his research at Edgewood Arsenal to become a postdoc in neuropsychology with Karl Pribram at Stanford University. While in California he spent time documenting on film the psychedelic subculture in the Bay Area and volunteered time as a physician at the Haight Ashbury Free Clinic in San Francisco.

Ketchum also supports research into the potential therapeutic benefits of cannabis and psychedelics; he served for several years as a member of the National Organization for the Reform of Marijuana Laws (NORML) and is still active in MAPS.

Ketchum's book contains a foreword by the legendary psychedelic chemist Alexander Shulgin. Popular cyberculture commentator Ken Goffman (a.k.a. R. U. Sirius, founder of *Mondo 2000*) helped with the editing of the book. In 2007, Ketchum even lectured at the Burning Man festival in Nevada, so he's demonstrated a rare ability to communicate across some pretty varied subcultures.

———————————————— ☺ ————————————————

I spoke with James Ketchum on September 8, 2008. I found Jim to be very gracious, and he appears to have a lot of integrity when he talks about his research. We discussed his studies at Edgewood Arsenal, why chemical warfare agents may be more humane than traditional weapons, the future of chemical warfare, and the possible therapeutic potential of psychedelics.

How did you become interested in psychiatry?

JIM: When I was eight years old I wrote a composition in class that stated I wanted to be a scientist when I grew up and "help struggling humanity." So when I entered college I started as a premed student. Then I shifted briefly to a philosophy major. I left it to major in clinical psychology, and finally reverted to premed. I focused my eye on psychiatry when I got through all this switching around. I got the necessary training in medicine at Cornell University's medical school, but then entered the Army for my internship and residency training. It was only near the end of my residency that the story starts, as far as chemical warfare goes.

When you graduated from medical school, what was your initial reaction when you were first approached by the military to do secret research into incapacitating agents?

JIM: The invitation came more than four years after completing medical school, and was actually somewhat of a happenstance. The Edgewood Arsenal program of research into chemical weapons had started to focus on incapacitating agents—which is to say nonlethality, or low-lethality agents. No psychiatrist had been assigned to the medical labs, and a disturbing psychiatric reaction had occurred in one of their studies. My mentor at Walter Reed, Dr. David Rioch, called me in and said a psychiatrist was needed at Edgewood Arsenal, and would I be interested in such an assignment? I grabbed at it, because it seemed challenging and really interesting.

What were some of the chemical agents that you studied at Edgewood, and what did you learn about them?

JIM: Before my arrival LSD was the only agent that had been studied in some detail. My predecessor, Dr. Van Sim, initiated and supervised most of the human research prior to 1961. But a new and different agent was provided to the Army a few months before I arrived. Over time it was referred to by a number of names, but finally was called simply BZ. I spent the better part of three years studying it intensively and eventually writing up a detailed summary. I also did, however, some additional work with LSD, and with a variant of THC—tetrahydrocannabinol—provided by Harry Pars, a chemist at A.D. Little, with some technical guidance by Dr. Alexander Shulgin, primarily known, then and now, for his creative synthesis of psychedelic drugs.

It was evident that this variant of THC had several times the potency of THC found in marijuana, so there was speculation that it might be powerful enough to be useful as an incapacitating agent. It certainly was predicted to be safe, much like the marijuana to which it was related, but it lacked sufficient intoxicating effects in the dose range we studied. It was obvious that it wouldn't be a practical agent, so after a brief trial with the volunteer subjects, I turned my attention almost entirely to BZ, whose effects I thereafter studied in detail with the help of more than three hundred highly cooperative enlisted soldiers.

Convinced of its effectiveness and safety, BZ was actually adopted by higher Army echelons as the first, and only, standard incapacitating agent. It was produced in quantity and loaded into volleyball-size bomblets for delivery as an aerosol from overhead aircraft. I had very little to do with this phase, nor was I particularly interested in the dispersal aspects.

Meanwhile, we continued to study additional compounds of similar type, which is to say the belladonnoid category, since their effects were qualitatively very much like atropine, a drug approved for use for many centuries. Some people may be familiar with atropine, used as a preanesthetic to reduce salivation.

BZ differs from atropine in that it is about twenty times as potent and up to twenty times longer lasting than atropine. The dose required by injection or inhalation is only about half a milligram, enough to produce an incapacitating delirium lasting forty-eight to ninety-six hours, followed by full recovery.

The other compounds that came under scrutiny after BZ were often even better. Some acted relatively more on the central nervous system, with very little effect on heart rate or blood pressure. Such physiological effects were more characteristic of atropine and BZ. We guessed that some similar agents might even be better from a safety standpoint. Thus we went on to study about a dozen different compounds that were structural relatives of BZ—either shorter acting, longer acting, more potent, more predominantly central in action, and so forth. But meanwhile the Army seemed to lose interest in these compounds as a group and put them aside, perhaps primarily for political reasons related to the unpopular war in Vietnam and the growing protest against chemical weapons of all types.

Why do you think that chemical-warfare agents may be more humane than traditional weapons? And can you talk a little about what inspired you to write the book Chemical Warfare Secrets Almost Forgotten?

JIM: It seemed obvious to me that chemical weapons that could produce nonlethal temporary incapacitation would be more humane than conventional deadly weapons. You have to go back in time and change your mind-set a little to understand what I mean. Back to the early 1960s the idea of developing a nonlethal chemical weapon was generally accepted and even encouraged. The notion started out with chief

Photo by Judy Ketchum

James Ketchum

of the Chemical Corps, Major General William Creasy, who had developed the somewhat idealistic belief that LSD might be such a weapon. He became wildly enthusiastic about it and presented his arguments to Congress. As I try to point out in my book, harm reduction was just as important to the Army then as it is among civilians today in relation to drug problems.

Congress, in 1955, was wildly enthusiastic about Creasy's vision of a city being temporarily neutralized with LSD in order to carry out a military mission with minimal loss of life. They voted, with only one naysayer, to triple the Chemical Corps budget, as requested, and they gave their blessing to further LSD research. I shared the enthusiasm expressed by Congress and felt I was working toward a very noble goal. My feelings haven't changed in that regard, but after I left Edgewood in 1971, I went on to other assignments and left the whole program behind me.

After 1970, I knew the Army was winding down this research, and that I had done all I had set out to do with incapacitating agents. I let the subject slip to the back of my mind, since I had many other new things to do. After most of the documents from the 1960s were declassified, most of the physicians involved had gone their separate ways and had no further interest in such work. But I believed that perhaps I should be putting all this together in some form, because no one else had done it. I had such an intention for quite a while, but my various other assignments—substance-abuse treatment, drug education, and so on—prevented me from finding time to do it.

But it recently has become obvious that there is a reticence on the part of the government to talk much about what went on in the 1960s. Gradually it all seemed to fade from collective memory, and the reports were relegated mostly to seldom-opened file cabinets.

Some people didn't even know that there had been a program. One of the chemical officers was asked two decades later, "What about that volunteer program back in the sixties?" And his response was, "What program? There was no volunteer program." The Army, of course, had not denied its existence, but it spent very little time telling anyone the details of what research had been done. I became upset, because I felt that the experimental work was extensive, detailed, and important scientifically for the medical and pharmacological community to know about.

What pushed me past the edge of indecision, ultimately, was the September 11 disaster, which soon led to a marked increase in public concern about chemical weapons as well as with other so-called weapons of mass destruction. By the way, I make a point in my book that it's really not accurate to refer to chemicals as weapons of mass destruction. In practical terms, only a small area could be effectively blanketed by an airborne chemical fog—certainly not a city or any large number of people, unless in a closed facility, such as a domed stadium.

I finally sat down and started working on my book in 2002, at the age of seventy. It took me about four years to get it all together, and I decided to publish it myself. Since then, although I've sent out less than a thousand copies, it's been purchased by readers in sixteen or seventeen countries, the latest being Russia.

Many people in the media have confused the Army Chemical Center's research into psychedelics and deliriants in human volunteers, for use as nonlethal weapons, with the CIA's MK-ULTRA project. Would you like to clarify the difference between these two programs?

JIM: They were entirely separate, and that was another stimulus to me to write this book. The public had acquired the notion that the CIA operations back in the 1950s—when they actually gave LSD to unwitting citizens—was somehow tied to the research that we did at Edgewood Arsenal with the same compound. In fact, it was not. The program that the CIA ran was so secret that most of the other members of the CIA didn't know much about it. When it finally came to light, its leader, Dr. Gottlieb, arranged to destroy all the records, so it is no longer possible to know who actually received it surreptitiously.

Edgewood, on the other hand, had a fully transparent program that was approved by the Surgeon General, the Secretary of the Army, and the Secretary of Defense, so the program was not any kind of secret. Furthermore, the MK-ULTRA program conducted by the CIA was aimed at seeking drugs that could produce actual changes in behavior. They thought that perhaps they could give LSD to someone and make him confess to something he was holding back, or carry out some mission he had been told to carry out while under the drug's influence. None of this was achieved, fortunately, and while these illegal experiments were in progress, our laboratories at Edgewood began a totally different approach to the development of chemicals that could temporarily incapacitate without any lasting effects. They would be used only for short-term military purposes, and there was no thought of changing personalities or getting people to do anything they wouldn't otherwise do.

In short, I wanted to articulate that these two programs were completely different, and I went to some length in my book to do so. I hope I succeeded because, really, I still feel quite proud of what we did while working for the Chemical Corps. As you can tell, I didn't feel very good about the CIA work. A few years ago, in fact, I testified against the CIA in federal court as the sole expert witness for the prosecution. Much time was required before the trial writing reports and rebuttals on behalf of a former Deputy U.S. Marshal. In my opinion, he was one of the "ordinary American citizens" who were given LSD covertly in the late 1950s, at the same time other black CIA operations were being carried out close to his place of work.

Although there were several other factors that pointed definitively to the covert use of LSD in that case, the judge, unfortunately, didn't buy it. She said it was possible but not fully proven, and the hearing was ended prematurely. His attorney took it to the Appeals Court and tried unsuccessfully to bring it to the Supreme Court, but so far has been unsuccessful. This poor guy's life was ruined as a result of his erratic behavior after consuming the drug in a drink at a Christmas party. In short, he was an unwitting victim of the CIA's unethical behavior, in my opinion, and experienced something he didn't understand and couldn't handle. That sort of deception is really the differentiation I have tried to make between the CIA activities and the Army's later bona fide research with LSD.

What sort of reactions have you received from government officials and others who have read your book?

JIM: It's interesting. Somehow, I seem to have managed to walk a line that didn't require me to be a strong advocate in any particular direction. I wasn't arguing for or against these incapacitating agents. But I thought we should be talking about them, and I thought the public ought to know what we did back there in the 1960s. My book is really a truthful story, supported by pharmacological data, and it was well received by the Chemical Corps people when they learned about it. A number of them bought copies and, surprisingly, I was even invited back to Edgewood Arsenal after thirty years to give a keynote address at a major international science conference. It must have been favorably received, because I was invited back the next year to give a similar presentation.

So from the Chemical Corps' perspective, my revelations of previously unpublished data seemed to present no problem. It was reviewed positively in military publications. It caught the eye of Steven Aftergood, who publishes *Secrecy News*. *USA Today*, in turn, chose to write an illustrated article about me and the book. This was followed by a number of published reviews, mostly positive in tone.

The counterculture, on the other hand, which you might think would be skeptical of anything the Army approved of, also liked the book. I think that this was because of the informative content, including the details of the effects of LSD, THC, and other compounds that weren't available anywhere else. A number of them have written me letters of congratulations and thanks and have told me that I've preserved a bit of history.

Of course I feel good about it. And this may sound funny, but I've also had no crank phone calls, no letters of protest. I've had very few negative comments about the book. There were some reservations expressed by some reviewers, mostly on the matter of informed consent. I argue, however, in some detail, that we really provided more informed consent than many research programs did in those days, but some people think that because we didn't reveal the name of the drug, these weren't truly ethical studies.

However, with regard to informed consent, subjects rarely felt they had been insufficiently informed. We created several hoops to jump through before even being invited to spend two months with us, and consent forms were required not only on arrival, but before each and every test. Many volunteers were not averse to receiving two or more different agents. Some even agreed to undergo a high-dose BZ test twice, to permit double-blind procedures.

Much preparation—in the form of baseline testing, preliminary discussion with the responsible physician, and, if films or TV recordings were to be used, an additional consent in writing—was required. Subjects spent a full day and the night before each procedure, during which they were familiarized with the test environment and the performance and physiological measures required to establish reliable baselines. Thus they had an extended opportunity to get to know the nurses and technicians who would be with them during the actual testing.

Although we adhered to the Nuremberg Code, if you read it carefully, it doesn't really address the subject of testing drugs. There are two provisions that either require the responsible doctor to discontinue the experiment if it appears that it may be producing adverse effects, or to stop it immediately if the subject does not feel able to continue. If you give someone a drug, especially when you have no effective antidote available, there is no way to stop it until the drug itself wears off. So, obviously, the drafters of those provisions of the Nuremberg Code weren't thinking about drug testing, but more probably of a physical procedure, such as isolation or tolerance to extreme cold—procedures that can indeed be interrupted at any time at the discretion of the physician or the subject.

While the general nature and duration of each test were explained in some detail, we were not allowed to reveal the name of the drug for security reasons—although subjects often figured out among themselves whether they were on a BZ or an LSD test. There was much paranoia about the Soviet Union learning from our experiments, so we used classified numbers to identify the agents being tested. Most of them had no ordinary names, so knowing their number or even their structure would be of no practical value if medical attention were required in the future.

We usually ended up with three to four times the number of volunteers that we could accept for any given two-month assignment. Then, after they arrived, we examined and interviewed the subjects and classified them into one of four levels. Only the group A individuals were considered eligible for the higher doses of psychoactive drugs. These would be soldiers who appeared to be unusually stable, based on their personal histories, MMPI profiles, lab tests, and psychiatric interviews. We avoided volunteers who had a history of drug abuse or any criminal behavior. Overall, we had really superior subjects, with above-average IQs, and half of them had at least a year of college education. In summary, they certainly weren't unwitting guinea pigs, as so often described by the media.

One of the things that you hinted at in your book, just briefly, was that one of the LSD subjects might have experienced some sort of therapeutic benefit in one of your studies. What sort of therapeutic value do you think that psychedelic agents might have?

JIM: That's a big subject. Actually, we weren't looking for therapeutic effects. We weren't trying to treat anyone. Nevertheless, I observed one subject who seemed to undergo a therapeutic experience, as I detailed in a chapter. You might call his improved social behavior an unanticipated beneficial consequence.

In general, I think that the field of psychedelic drugs is a very fascinating one, and that such drugs ought to be studied with respect to their beneficial potential, rather than dishonestly outlawed as dangerous. It's strange to me how vehement and irrational the prohibitory sanctions have become. With governmental approval, I think that some of the synthetic psychedelic drugs might indeed be useful medications. Actually, that's starting to be recognized, in the case of MDMA—the drug called Ecstasy, which Alexander Shulgin introduced to the public—and now a few, limited therapeutic studies with LSD are also being carried out. LSD was, of course, widely studied and used as an aid to psychotherapy until it was made illegal in 1965.

That put a stop to what was a promising avenue of research into the psychological and, some would say, spiritual potential of psychedelics. The draconian prohibitions and penalties our own government has established are both outrageous and, in the opinion of many, including myself, unconstitutional. These drugs are not addicting. Psychedelics are certainly not to be compared to cocaine, heroin, amphetamines, morphine, or even alcohol, as far as addiction potential and medical harm are concerned.

Psychedelic drugs do seem to have the ability to open up an individual's awareness of many surprising things that are actually hiding in their heads. Major insights can occur, and people are often astonished at what's in there. Sometimes the world appears in a totally new and propitious light. Bad feelings that they've had about themselves, for example, can often be alleviated by realizing that we're all part of one universe and one family of human beings. And these insights often seem to carry over, long after the drug effects are gone.

Many people have described LSD in particular, and perhaps some of the other psychedelic drugs that haven't been tried in more than a few people, as having these unique properties. Some really treasure the experience, and believe that it reshapes their life in some way. LSD has even been found to alleviate the suffering of dying individuals. Aldous Huxley was one of the first to advocate its use for this purpose.

LSD given to patients during the final weeks or months of their illness often seems to provide a much more serene feeling about death. The dying patient can see that death is part of the life cycle and that he or she will somehow continue on as part of the universe, even after death. One can only hope the government will eventually allow scientists to continue research with psychedelic drugs and allow their appropriate use by physicians and qualified therapists!

What was your personal experience with LSD like, and how did it affect your perspective on the research that you were doing at Edgewood?

JIM: I have to say that it was somewhat anticlimactic. I took it because at a conference I attended in 1965, it seemed that everyone working with LSD had taken it one or more times. So I thought, *Gee, I've never even tried it. I guess I ought to.* And, with a little bit of trepidation, I took a relatively small dose—80 micrograms—which wouldn't be considered in the incapacitating range by our testing criteria. I took it under the same conditions that I required of the volunteers—namely, being in a padded cubicle; doing arithmetic tests every hour or so; having to Draw-a-Man periodically; fill in checklists; and have my blood pressure, temperature, pupil size, respiration, and heart rate checked by the nurses at frequent intervals.

So although I was more of a witting guinea pig, if you will, not much occurred in the way of new insights. In fact, I didn't even have any marked perceptual distortions. At a higher dose, however, such effects would no doubt have been more prominent. So, personally, I was a bit disappointed in my trip. It did not, however, influence my overall view of the research we were doing. In fact, it reassured me that an LSD trip was something that one could actually go through and emerge intact. It helped corroborate my beliefs about the safety of the drugs that we were studying. They weren't harming anyone, as far as we could tell, and we were learning much of value from testing them.

Did any of the subjects who were given LSD at Edgewood ever have anything resembling a mystical experience?

JIM: In this setting, I don't recall hearing anyone say he did. The men certainly had a variety of experiences, but I'm not sure that the term *mystical* would apply. We used fairly low doses, for one thing. As I described in the book, the responses varied from being highly amused to being fascinated with the amazing otherworldly colors that they saw. Subjects did sometimes become irritated with the routine questions being asked, and sometimes they became paranoid about the whole situation. But I don't recall any so-called mystical or spiritual enlightenment experiences. I think a lot depends on the setting and the intent of the study. If you give a drug to see how people will perform under the influence, then you mainly tend to ask, "How well can you perform under the influence?"

If you give LSD to someone in a therapeutic setting—as with Cary Grant, who took it more than a hundred times as an adjunct to psycho-therapy, as did many other luminaries in that era—then you tend to get more reports of a spiritual nature. Some degree of suggestion may play a part, by the way, but I don't want to pour cold water on the notion that these drugs can indeed be very enlightening. LSD, for example, doesn't *always* produce a mystical result, but frequently it does, as testified to by many users.

Some report it provides a new view of the world—a sense of belonging to a larger system. Some even believe they have been able to be briefly in touch with God or, for that matter, the entire universe. These are undoubtedly very memorable experiences. Although it doesn't always happen, I do believe such an epiphany happens often enough to justify responsible use of such drugs. These drugs may also provide an enhanced basis for psychotherapy. But, of course, one can't expect them to answer all of one's psychological needs.

How do you envision the future of chemical warfare?

JIM: Oh, boy. I don't know. As mentioned, there's strong opposition to chemical-warfare agents in any form, including the incapacitating agents. In 1966, I exchanged letters with Matthew Meselson, a leading anti-proliferationist. His opinions haven't changed much—he presents pretty much the same point of view now as he did then. We did have a cordial exchange. He argued that incapacitating agents might be okay in themselves, but he feared they would open the door to the use of more destructive chemicals. This is basically the familiar slippery-slope argument so frequently invoked to discredit some new strategy. It was used by a Republican administration to justify the Vietnam War, for example. Recently, however, I did seem to succeed in per-suading a few people active in the anti-proliferation movement that incapacitating agents perhaps could be used safely and could possibly save lives.

Ironically, this was clearly demonstrated by the Russian successful use of a fentanyl-type gas in November 2002, which enabled them to rescue more than 80 percent of the eight hundred members of a Moscow theater audience taken over by Chechen terrorists. Gas was apparently delivered through the air-conditioning system and through holes in the floor and roof, putting everyone into a narcotized, unconscious state. Then, thirty to forty minutes later, special troops entered and started bringing people out. The doctors used naloxone, the favorite antidote for morphinelike compounds, to reverse the narcosis. I think that over-all it was a marvelous result, but, unfortunately, it's been looked at by some skeptics as a kind of a tragedy. They say, "Look—a hundred thirty people died." Well, I think that 130 is better than 800, and it's also better, as a secondary consideration, not to have to blow up a beautiful theater.

Whether this dramatic use of an incapacitating agent is going to be picked up by anyone, including the United States, is difficult to predict, because we've signed—somewhat foolishly, I believe—the 1993 chemical-warfare convention treaty. The treaty outlaws the use of any chemical weapon during any aggressive military action.

Unfortunately, perhaps for political reasons, we were allowed to tie our own hands. Even tear gas, for example, is a forbidden chemical weapon, except when used for police actions in one's own territory. I believe that has to be changed. Either we have to draw ourselves out of the treaty, which would necessarily take quite a bit of guts, or we have to persuade the world that some chemical agents are less lethal than conventional weapons, and that people can be spared death through their proper use in selected circumstances. I'd certainly like to see it go that way.

Colonel John Alexander, an unconventional weapons consultant to the Department of Defense, has long been arguing forcefully for the use of incapacitating agents. He read my book and told me, "You're on the right track." Alexander, of course, is primarily an expert in physical incapacitating agents, such as sticky foam, bright lights, snares, nets, and other devices that can control crowds or stop vehicles. He suggests many ways to neutralize enemy troops without killing them. Since he's not a physician or pharmacologist, he claims less expertise in chemical weapons.

John has proven to be an ally, supporting my views in writing, hoping to promote my book. But he represents a small minority among decision makers in Washington. There is still a great deal of reluctance to talk about or underwrite further research with chemical incapacitating agents. Even if there were a renaissance of such an effort, there is, alas, no longer a volunteer program, and no longer any proper facility in which to do the required testing.

The latest pharmacological proposals that have being advanced are kind of ridiculous, because the drugs suggested are generally far more lethal than the ones we studied, at least in terms of safety margins. But it's sort of been decreed that we can't go back to what was done in the sixties. A white paper—written under contract by three university pharmacologists—contains almost no reference to anything done in the 1960s, other than a passing mention of BZ.

These professors are younger than I am and perhaps have little familiarity with work accomplished forty to fifty years ago. The chemicals they suggest just don't make practical sense. They include Prozac, Valium, or perhaps some enzyme or hormone in the brain that might reduce the tendency to fight. None appear to be feasible, and I doubt any of them will ever become acceptable agents.

So I think there would have to be a return to a more rational approach. I hope my book can stimulate reconsideration of the drugs we abandoned in 1973, despite their impressive safety and effectiveness. Whether this will ever happen, who knows?

Do you think that the human species will ever learn to live in peace, without war?

JIM: It's not likely, based on history. Aggression seems to be built into the human condition, as some innate defensive response to those who try to either hurt us or take what we own. It's built into the biology of the people in this world, and will remain there until we can find some way of modifying that biology. I'm speaking now not just about pharmacology. Perhaps through genetic engineering we may be able to reduce aggressive tendencies and help people become less inclined to kill, hurt, steal power, or take territory from other people. It's only a possibility. But to me, it's science that offers the one shining hope for the future of mankind. Just how that will evolve is very difficult to say.

In general, are you optimistic about the future, or do you think that the human species is doomed to extinction?

JIM: I'm optimistic. I think that there will be an increasing number of new technologies coming along in the near future. They're coming now at a very rapid pace, enabling us to look into the brain more closely, for example, and better understand what's going on. And perhaps we will eventually be able to connect up those events with behavior and mental attitudes. I'm not as pessimistic as many scientists are. I think, yeah, we might blow ourselves up, but we might also find a way to calm down and live peacefully. That's my hope—through science.

What do you personally think happens to consciousness after death, and what is your perspective on the concept of God?

JIM: I don't know how to answer that. I definitely have a personal belief in God. It's not within a particular religious framework, although I grew up in a religious family. I feel a personal connection with God that I don't understand. I've met people who express similar thoughts. They sense a higher power, but they can't really describe it. The idea that there may be a creative intelligence in our universe gives me some hope that maybe, as one person put it, "God invented the universe to discover his own identity." That's a challenging and difficult concept, I suppose, but it appeals to me.

What are you currently working on?

JIM: Right now, I am in a state of suspended animation. My book is out there, and it's selling to some extent. I hope for sufficient energy to promote it, but I'm not emotionally tied to it. I have other interests, totally unrelated to science. I like to do video editing and have a vast collection of pictures and films, so I'm not expecting to write anything significant in the near future. I'm willing to talk at a few meetings, and I still get invitations. I'm very happy to accept them, but I don't foresee myself as an agent of change beyond what I've done in the form of a book.

10
Cultivating Compassion and Fearlessness in the Presence of Death

An Interview with **Roshi Joan Halifax**

Roshi Joan Halifax, Ph.D.—medical anthropologist, Zen priest, hospice caregiver, civil rights activist, ecologist, and renowned author—has an unusual talent for integrating scientific and spiritual disciplines. Halifax has done extensive work with the dying for more than forty years. In 1994 she founded the Project on Being with Dying, which has trained hundreds of health care professionals in the contemplative care of dying people.

Halifax served on the faculty of Columbia University, the University of Miami Miller School of Medicine, the New School for Social Research, and Naropa University, and she has lectured at many other academic institutions, including Harvard Divinity School and Harvard Medical School. She is the founder of the Ojai Foundation, an educational and interfaith center in Southern California, which she led from 1979 to 1989. Halifax currently serves as abbot and guiding teacher of Upaya Zen Center in Santa Fe, New Mexico, a Zen peacemaker community that she founded in 1990.

In the 1970s, Halifax and her ex-husband, Stanislav Grof, collaborated on a landmark LSD research project with terminally ill cancer patients at the Spring Grove Hospital Center in Maryland, which we discuss in the following interview.

Halifax is the author or coauthor of seven books, including *Being with Dying, Shaman: The Wounded Healer,* and *The Fruitful Darkness. Being with Dying* is the best book I've ever read about caring for people who are dying, and I can't recommend it more highly. It's a book that I think every human being should read. Halifax also coauthored *The Human Encounter with Death* with Grof. This important book discusses their LSD research and describes a number of psychedelic experiences that in some ways resemble reports of near-death experiences. (*The Human Encounter with Death* has recently been revised and updated by Grof and was republished by MAPS as *The Ultimate Journey.*)

Halifax is a Zen Buddhist roshi. She has received dharma transmissions from both Bernard Glassman and Thich Nhat Hanh and previously studied under the Korean master Seung Sahn. The procedure of dharma transmission refers to the manner in which the teachings of Zen Buddhism are passed down from a Zen master to his or her disciple and heir. It establishes the disciple as a transmitting teacher and successor in an unbroken line of teachers and disciples, a spiritual bloodline, so to speak, that is said to be traced back to the Buddha himself.

I interviewed Joan on December 16, 2009. I felt a lot of gratitude that she took time from her busy schedule to speak with me, and she was very kind and gracious. We spoke about her work with people who are dying, some of the most important lessons that she learned from this work, and how the LSD research that she participated in during the early seventies helped to motivate her to do more work with dying people.

How did your experience with your grandmother's death as a child influence your motivation to work with dying people?

JOAN: One of the people that I was closest to as a child was my grandmother, who worked as a sculptor carving tombstones for local people in Savannah. She was a remarkable woman who often served her community as someone comfortable around illness and death, someone who would sit with dying friends. And yet when she herself became ill, her own family could not offer her the same compassionate presence. When my grandmother suffered first from cancer and then had a stroke, she was put into a nursing home and then left largely alone. Her death was long and hard. When she finally died, I felt deep ambivalence—both sorrow and relief. As I stood there looking at her gentle, peaceful face in a coffin at the funeral home, I made the commitment to practice being there for others as they died.

What other factors led to your interest in helping to care for people who are dying, and how do you think that caregiving can be viewed as a spiritual path?

JOAN: We all are facing our mortality. Plato clearly said the bedrock for spiritual experience is understanding death. And it is a very profound experience to contemplate one's own mortality, as is the experience of actually caring for a dying person.

Can you talk a little about the LSD research that you did with Stan Grof, and how this affected your perspective on death and dying?

JOAN: Stan and I worked with dying people at the Maryland Psychiatric Research Center [in Spring Grove Hospital]. Prior to this, I had been at the University of Miami [Miller] School of Medicine, where I saw that the most marginalized people in that medical setting were individuals who were dying. The physicians would say that medicine and drugs are about saving lives. So when Stan and I got married and I moved up to the Baltimore area, I joined him in his project, working with dying people.

It was a very extraordinary project. It was really a contemporary rite

Joan Halifax

of passage. I had studied rites of passage as an anthropologist, and to engage in such a powerful one was very interesting. So he and I worked with a number of people who were dying of cancer. Subjects were referred to the project by social workers and physicians.

There was one patient, a doctor who had referred himself to the group. He was dying of pancreatic cancer. And through that work I had to opportunity to have a real experience in seeing that the human spirit, the human psyche, is profoundly underestimated. LSD is referred to as a nonspecific amplifier of the psyche, and I felt very privileged to sit for many hours with a person dying of cancer and share his or her psyche in the most intimate way—aspects of which were, in general, not normally accessible in a nonaltered state of consciousness.

How did this affect your perspective on death and dying?

JOAN: It inspired me to continue the work. I began this work in 1970, feeling very concerned about dying people. Prior to that I'd been inspired by my grandmother, who was taking care of dying people, and then herself had a very difficult death. I made a vow that I would try to make a difference. Then I saw that the work with LSD was so effective in facilitating a deep psychological process for people who were dying, that actually it enhanced the quality of their life and their relationships. It enhanced their experience of dying and of death.

How do you think a psychedelic experience is similar to and different from the natural dying process or a near-death experience?

JOAN: I think that you can't really say. At least I can't say, although maybe Stan can. But the unbinding process that individuals go through on physiological and psychological levels in the process of dying can be very powerful. From my point of view, sitting with many dying people over the years has basically been a psychedelic experience. We had at least one patient tell us that he died, went through a near-death experience, and came back. He reported that he experienced what had happened to him in the LSD therapy. He didn't die in the end. Well, he died in the end, but in the middle he didn't die. However, he went through a clinical death experience, came back, and said it really transformed his view of death. In the end he was much more accepting of his mortality as his death drew near.

How has your Buddhist perspective been helpful in working with people who are dying?

JOAN: Buddhism has many important perspectives on the truth of impermanence, the realization of the absence of an inherent self, or the experience of meditation and letting go, and on bearing witness to suffering, and the experience of compassion. Quite frankly, I think that if our patients at the Maryland Psychiatric Research Center had had more of a Buddhist orientation, or Buddhist practice, they would have gotten a lot more out of their LSD experiences. It's not to say that their LSD experiences were not profound, but sometimes it's very hard for people to let go. That's just not what happens in our Western culture; Buddhism is about accepting and letting go. So it certainly has a profound parallel to what we had hoped to see happen in LSD experience when we were working with dying people.

How do you think the prevailing Western attitudes about death hinder our ability to properly care for, and learn from, people who are dying?

JOAN: I think that we have not reconciled ourselves with the experience of dying, because people in Western cultures fear death so much. But I feel that Western cultures are coming along, in part through their insight from psychedelic experiences, and also through Buddhist forms of meditation.

What would you say are some of the most important lessons that you've learned from working with people who are dying?

JOAN: As you can imagine, there are so many. I'd say read my book *Being with Dying*. But, in essence, I think that the most important part of working with dying people is about encountering the sanctity of life—to see life in all of it's richness in the present moment, to appreciate one's life, and share the fundamental joy of being alive and helping others. I think that it's really important to ask ourselves on a daily level: How do we serve people? And this is one of the frequent outcomes of people who have had the LSD experience. Stan and I often found that the psychedelic experience was a source of profound inspiration, which motivated people to want to be of service in the world, even if they were facing the end of their life.

What do you personally think happens to consciousness after death?

JOAN: I have no idea.

Have you ever speculated or thought about what might happen?

JOAN: No. I stay away from speculation.

So are you saying that you value not knowing?

JOAN: It's not a matter of "not knowing." I really don't know! It's not theoretical; it's just pragmatic. I don't know what happens after death. When people ask me, I say "I don't know." And when a dying person asks me, I say, "I don't know. But what do you think happens after death?" I listen and learn from their perspectives, which I value. But from my own experience, I have no idea.

What do you think is the best preparation for death?

JOAN: Meditation. No question about it.

I heard that years ago you had spoken with Laura Huxley about developing a concept called dying healthy, which was about dying in a healthy and balanced way. Is this a concept that you could expand upon?

JOAN: I feel that the work that I'm doing, and we're doing, in all these dimensions to better the care of the dying is, in a certain way, very much in accord with what Laura was trying to establish at that time. My own work in the field of death and dying now, and for many decades, has been in the training of clinicians, in bringing more presence, more compassion, and more wisdom in their care of dying people.

Can you talk about the Project on Being with Dying, and what you're currently working on?

JOAN: I've been working on a big project for many years that is engaged with training clinicians in compassionate and contemplative care of the dying. We work in three transformational areas: transforming the experience of the clinician, transforming the experience of the patient, and transforming the institutions that serve dying people. We do an intensive training program annually. We're also working on the development of regional projects throughout the country, where I teach in medical schools and medical settings.

Is there anything that we haven't spoken about that you would like to add?

JOAN: Just that I feel very grateful for having met Stan, and having had the opportunity to engage in the LSD project at Spring Grove. It was a pivotal process in my life, where I saw a very deep kind of therapy, which was also a sacred therapy. It was a rite of passage, guiding individuals in the experience of living and dying. So my gratitude for working with Stan and having that opportunity, which opened up new doorways for me, is really profound.

11

The Near-Death Experience, Parapsychology, and Psychedelics

*An Interview with **Charles Tart***

Charles Tart, Ph.D., is a psychologist and parapsychological researcher. He is best known as one of the founders of the field of transpersonal psychology, for his psychological work on the nature of consciousness—particularly altered states of consciousness—and for his scientific research into psychic phenomena.

Tart earned his Ph.D. in psychology from the University of North Carolina at Chapel Hill in 1963. His books *Altered States of Consciousness* and *Transpersonal Psychologies* have been widely used as academic texts, and they were instrumental in allowing these areas to become part of modern psychology. Some of Tart's other popular books include *States of Consciousness, On Being Stoned: A Psychological Study of Marijuana Intoxication,* and *Mind Science: Meditation Training for Practical People.*

Tart's most recent book, *The End of Materialism: How Evidence of the Paranormal Is Bringing Science and Spirit Together,* is the best book that I've read about integrating science and spirituality. Tart clearly and patiently demonstrates precisely how new scientific evidence is breaking down outdated paradigms, and he believes that the scientific evidence for psychic phenomena is helping to bring science and spirit back together.

Tart says that his primary goal is to "build bridges between the scientific and spiritual communities, and to help bring about a refinement and integration of Western and Eastern approaches for knowing the world and for personal and social growth."

Tart is currently a core faculty member at the Institute of Transpersonal Psychology, a senior research fellow at the Institute of Noetic Sciences, emeritus member of the Monroe Institute board of advisors, and professor emeritus of psychology at the University of California–Davis, where he has served for twenty-eight years. To find out more about Tart's work, see www.paradigm-sys.com.

I interviewed Charles on December 16, 2009. Charles is a very eloquent speaker, and he speaks about anomalous phenomena with great precision. We discussed near-death experiences, out-of-body experiences, and how psychedelic experiences and other altered states of consciousness are similar to and different from a typical near-death experience.

How did you become interested in studying altered states of consciousness?

CHARLES: I think that part of it was just curiosity. Ever since I was a child I've wondered how my mind worked.

Can you describe what a near-death experience is commonly like?

CHARLES: I can always refer people to Raymond Moody's list of fifteen characteristics that are important in every near-death experience (NDE). But to sum it up in a shorter fashion than that, it happens like this: You think that you're dying. There are periods of unconsciousness, and commonly—but not universally—you find yourself floating up above your body, which may be in an operating room. You go through the very powerful psychological shock of hearing your doctor pronounce you dead.

Charles Tart

That's quite a heavy psychological proclamation. [*Laughs.*] Then, if the experience develops further, I'd call it an out-of-body experience (OBE), because during an OBE you're fully conscious. Then the NDE goes on to become an altered state of consciousness, not just a feeling of being outside your body. Now, of course, in real life there are times when it's hard to decide whether an experience is an NDE or just an OBE, but those are the ideal cases.

I thought that an OBE usually implied an altered state of consciousness.

CHARLES: No, the typical thing about an OBE is that a person feels like their mind is perfectly normal, and therefore the situation that they find themselves in is ridiculous and impossible. This is different from being in a dream, for example, where you're—from our waking perspective—out of your body all the time.

When you're dreaming, you don't know that you're not occupying your physical body in a normal way. You're in dream consciousness. And it's the clarity of consciousness in an OBE that causes people to think that this simply cannot be really happening. People generally feel perfectly awake, perfectly conscious, and yet they're floating up to the damn ceiling. So they automatically think, this just can't be happening!

I've had OBE-type experiences with psychedelics—such as DMT and ketamine—but I was unquestionably in an altered state of consciousness at the time, and it seemed more like going into other dimensions of reality, which I guess is closer to dreaming than the type of OBEs that you're describing. With all my psychedelic use, I've never had an experience where it felt like my normal mind was just floating above my body. I find that absolutely astonishing that people have that experience.

CHARLES: Yes, that's the archetypal OBE; the mind remains clear. There are a lot of psychedelic experiences where the concept of what it means to be in a body can get pretty hazy. We call that an OBE, but I think that can be confusing. I like to get clarity in the descriptions that we're talking about, and that's why I say that this feeling of your consciousness being clear, normal, and logical is characteristic of the OBE.

How is an NDE similar to and different from a psychedelic experience?

CHARLES: I wish that I could say we have a lot of studies that have made detailed phenomenological comparisons, but of course we haven't.

The NDE is, of course, centered on the fact that you think that you've died, which is a pretty powerful centering device. It usually includes the feeling of moving through a tunnel, toward a light; contact with other beings; and a quick life review. A psychedelic experience may not have all of these characteristics. Some of the characteristics may be present, but certain details of the NDE may be missing, like the quick life review or the speedy return to normal consciousness.

Now, this is interesting. This is one of the very vivid differences between psychedelic experiences and NDEs. With NDEs you can feel like you're way out there somewhere, and then "they" say that you have to go back, and bang! You're back in your body and everything is normal again. With psychedelics, of course, you come down more slowly, and don't usually experience a condensed life review. So that's what the major difference is. But psychedelic experiences also reach over a far wider terrain of possibilities.

Let me tell you something about the life review. It's extremely common in NDEs for persons to undergo a life review, where they feel as if they remember at least every important event in their life, and often they say every single event in their life. Sometimes it even expands out into not only remembering and reliving every single event in their life, but also into knowing psychically the reactions of other people to all their actions. For some it must be horrible, because it seems that you would really experience their pain. I very seldom hear people say anything about a life review on psychedelics. Yeah, occasionally past memories have come up, but not this dramatic review of a person's whole life.

Do you see any similarity in the consequences or the aftereffects of an NDE and a psychedelic experience? Do they have any similar consequences, or long-lasting effects for people?

CHARLES: There are sometimes consequences that overlap and are mutual, but I would say that the NDE is more powerful. It's more powerful in the sense that a person may make more drastic changes in their lifestyle or in their community if they try to integrate the acceptance of the NDE and make sense out of it. It's also more powerful in the sense that it's more liable to cause more lasting changes.

A psychedelic experience can also have powerful, life-changing effects. But let's face it: some people can pretty much forget their psychedelic experience afterward, much less alter their lives. It can simulate certain aspects of the NDE, but it doesn't carry the same force that the typical NDE does.

This actually rings true with my own experience. My psychedelic experiences were pale compared to the time that my car went over a cliff.

CHARLES: Ah, okay. I didn't know that you had an NDE.

For about a year the experience allowed me to appreciate life in a completely new and joyous way, and it eliminated my fear of just about everything, including death. However, this new state of perception faded away after about a year. I'm wondering what sort of biological value or psychological function you think that NDEs have?

CHARLES: To the people who have them, they usually feel that they've gotten profound insight into the way that their life ought to be, just from that one experience. With psychedelics, again, there's a wide range of experiences. It can range from a low sensory-enhancement level—where you see a lot of pretty colors and images, and afterward you just say, "Now let's go out and get back to work"—up to really deep levels of insight into the nature of one's mind. So there's a very wide range of experiences that are possible with psychedelics.

But with NDEs there is the feeling of being absolutely beyond one's life experience. This raises interesting possibilities then, because not everybody who comes near death reports having had an NDE. Could there be a lot of NDEs that are psychologically repressed? Does this happen sometimes?

It's an interesting discussion I've been having with some of my colleagues. If you do or don't recover a memory of this state, how do you know if it's something that really happened or not? It's possible that our minds might make something up, or repress certain experiences, so it's tricky. But it's also quite interesting that some people come close to death and don't report having an NDE.

What sort of relationship do you see between the NDE and various altered states of consciousness?

CHARLES: [*Laughs.*] You're asking me about my life's work, David. My really active research has been on altered states of consciousness. I began my research on dreams and hypnosis, and it was very fascinating stuff. I loved the laboratory work that I was doing, but I slowly became aware that there were a lot of other methods for altering consciousness, and a lot of different altered states.

So I had to stop specializing so much, and tried to get a feeling for that whole spectrum, including psychedelics, and learned about methods like meditation. We also included emotional states of consciousness. So your question is almost like asking, What's the relationship of life to life? You've got to narrow it down more specifically. [*Laughs.*]

I guess I was just looking to see if there were any aspects of an NDE that are common in other altered states of consciousness, or whether you think there's something really unique about an NDE.

CHARLES: Oh, I think it's pretty unique. Very few people have had a near-death experience and say, "Well, there was a little element of this and a little element of that."

I've heard of some situations where people had hellish NDEs.

CHARLES: Yes, there are a few like that. The fact that there are only a few is disappointing to right-wing Christians, who think the majority of people should get a taste of hell, because that's what they deserve. But it's very rarely reported. The rarity of reports might be because they actually are very rare. Or it might mean that a lot of cases, if you look at them more closely, are partially forgotten or not reported quite accurately.

An NDE could also be very scary to some people who are really afraid of OBEs or altered states of consciousness. Or it might be that they are much more common than we think, but people just don't report them. Can you imagine someone saying, "I almost died, and God told me that I was going to hell." That's not a very good way to enter a social relationship. [*Laughs.*]

No, I guess not. Charles, what do you personally think happens to consciousness after death?

CHARLES: After doing more than fifty years of professional work with consciousness now, one of the things that's really been interesting to me is that it's become more and more clear that there's an aspect of consciousness that appears to transcend physical or material reality. At the same time, it's also clear to me that a lot of our ordinary consciousness is very dependent on being shaped by the nature of our bodies, or at least by our brains. Clearly, that shaping is completely gone from one's reality after death.

I was once asked what I thought about the evidence for survival after death, and I summed it up by saying this: When I die, I expect that I'll probably be unconscious for a bit—but I expect to recover from it. On the other hand, I'm not quite sure that the *I* that will recover from death will be the same *I* who dies. I think that there's going to be some major changes in whatever survives, and this is a gross generalization.

There is a very large body of literature about the possibility that consciousness survives death, and I've been running a discussion group with many of the world's experts about this for years. The commonality of the NDE helped to decrease my bias against what I thought was an impossibility. However, I think that although consciousness probably survives death, it probably doesn't survive in quite the same form as we're used to. However, if people merely believe in an afterlife it may influence their interpretation of the evidence.

I think that it's just so fascinating that, depending on how one looks at the situation, there's an abundance of evidence both for and against the survival of consciousness after death. Like psychic phenomena, I think that a big part of what people usually believe about what happens to consciousness after death is based more on their spiritual or philosophical assumptions than on an examination of the scientific evidence.

CHARLES: I should also add here too that I'm one of the few people who tried to say, "Let's rationally look at the phenomena that might suggest survival, and try to make sense of it"—with a little proviso that ordinary rationality is not the only way to understand something. That was very hard to do, and very few people, I think, are anywhere near objectively looking at the evidence at all. Most people form a belief, stubbornly try to protect it, and don't want to look at anything that might challenge that belief.

Earlier in this conversation I said that I'd like to see a fair, evidence-based comparison between the NDE and other states of consciousness, but I discovered that people, even doctors, aren't usually interested in asking questions that challenge their beliefs. But this is not science. To me, everything is open to examination. Everything. Now, this doesn't mean we can really see everything, but we have to look at everything—even those areas where we have a lot of emotional investment.

12
The Sacred
Secrets of
Salvia divinorum

*An Interview with **Daniel Siebert***

Daniel Siebert is one of the world's experts on the subject of *Salvia divinorum*, an unusually potent, hallucinogenic plant that grows in central Mexico and that has been used for centuries by the Mazatec Indians as a shamanistic healing tool.

Although he wasn't the first to chemically isolate the compound, Siebert is the person who discovered the powerful psychedelic effects of the plant's primary psychoactive component, salvinorin A.

This unique substance isn't active when consumed through the digestive tract, and must be taken sublingually or smoked to be experienced. This discovery had eluded even celebrated chemists Albert Hofmann and Alexander Shulgin, who couldn't determine what the primary psychoactive component of the plant was. It is because of Siebert's discovery that many people in the West are now experiencing states of consciousness that were previously known only to a handful of Indians in central Mexico.

To find out more information about Siebert's work and about *Salvia divinorum*, visit his website, www.sagewisdom.org.

———————————————————— ☙ ————————————————————

I interviewed Daniel on November 9, 2008, and he fully revised the interview in April 2014. We spoke about how the Mazatec Indians have traditionally used salvia, how he discovered the psychoactive properties of salvinorin A, the medical potential of salvinorin A, the sentience of everything, and the possibilities of otherworldly entity contact and encountering parallel universes.

How did you first become interested in Salvia divinorum, and can you describe how you discovered the psychoactive properties of salvinorin A?

DANIEL: It was a long chain of events that led to my increasing interest in *Salvia divinorum,* and, ultimately, to isolating salvinorin A and testing it on myself. I had a general interest in medicinal plants, and a particular interest in mind-altering plants. In the reading that I did on the subject, which was fairly extensive, I occasionally came across descriptions of *Salvia divinorum.* It was reportedly used as a mild hallucinogen by the Mazatec Indians, as an alternative to mushrooms when the mushrooms were out of season. But at the time when I first came across it in the literature, there was a lot of uncertainty about whether or not it was actually hallucinogenic.

Aside from Mazatec shamans and some of their clients, few people had experimented with it. Live specimens first entered the United States in 1962. Eventually that material was propagated and the plant became increasingly available. Sometime in the late 1980s I obtained a plant. At that time it was still quite rare and obscure. I was an avid plant collector and had a fairly large collection of unusual medicinal plants.

One day, at a Terence McKenna lecture, a stranger gave me a cutting of *Salvia divinorum* as a gift. At the time, I wasn't particularly interested in trying it myself, because what I had heard about it gave me the impression it did not produce worthwhile effects or may be entirely inactive. It is often the case that properties traditionally attributed to plants used in folk medicine are nonexistent when

Daniel Siebert

scientifically studied. I was also cautious about experimenting with poorly studied herbs because some have toxic properties and can be quite dangerous.

I grew that *Salvia divinorum* plant in a pot for about a year, mainly as a botanical curiosity. One day, when I was moving the pot to a different location, the top-heavy plant leaned over and the main stem broke off at the base. I salvaged a few cuttings to reestablish new plants from, but most of the plant ended up in my compost heap. It seemed a shame to throw away all this material, so I decided to save some of the leaves for future experimentation.

Back then, it was generally believed that the leaves had to be used fresh, that they lost their activity when dried. So I stored them in a plastic bag and kept them hydrated in the refrigerator. About a week later I got together with my girlfriend and another friend, and the three of us ingested the leaves. We took them in the traditional Mazatec fashion, which is to consume them orally. We sat out on my friend's patio one evening around dusk, and we each chewed twenty-six large leaves.

I had read pretty much everything that was available to read about *Salvia divinorum* at that time, which wasn't much. Most reports suggested that its effects were subtle to nonexistent. Some reports described the effects as being so mild that one would only experience them in a dark and silent environment, free of distractions.

I knew of only one case of someone experiencing dramatic effects from the leaves. Kat Harrison and Terence McKenna had told me about an anthropologist they knew named Bret Blosser. He had taken *Salvia divinorum* with a Mazatec shaman whom he had met while traveling through the Mazatec region on a caving expedition. He claimed to have had an extremely intense visionary experience. Kat had grown the plant and tried the leaves herself, but said that the effects were so subtle that she wasn't really 100 percent sure she really felt anything.

Blosser's report intrigued me, and I thought, *Well, whatever he did, we should do it the same way, and maybe it will work.* I didn't know Bret at the time. Kat and Terence told me that he was told to take twenty-six large leaves, bundle them up in the shape of a cigar, and just chew away at the bundle until he got to the end of it. We copied that procedure.

Since his experience seemed inconsistent with all the other reports I had heard of people experimenting with the leaf and not experiencing much of an effect, I was skeptical that it really would do anything. So

I was not prepared for much to happen. Previously, I'd experimented with other plants that were in a similar category of iffy hallucinogens and been disappointed. I was expecting this to be another thing like that.

But, as it turned out, just about when I thought this, and was chewing my way through my pile of leaves, I suddenly started feeling a slight shift in spatial awareness. It was a subtle thing, and I thought, *Well, maybe if I get up and try to move around I'll be able to determine whether there is really anything going on here.* So I got out the chair I was sitting in and took a few steps. Then I noticed a glow surrounding objects in the environment, almost like an aura.

So I said to my two companions, "I'm definitely feeling something." And one of them said, "I don't feel anything." And, actually, before he finished his sentence, before he finished the word *anything,* he suddenly fell out of the chaise longue he was sitting on, onto the ground. He started laughing uncontrollably.

I wasn't as affected as he was. I was still able to talk, and I asked him, "Are you okay?" He wasn't able to reply because he couldn't stop laughing, so I kept asking him, "Are you okay? Are you okay?"

Finally, after a couple of minutes of not being able to get a word out, because this laughter had gripped him so thoroughly, he finally said, "Are you in it?" I didn't know what he meant. So I said, "What do you mean?" He just repeated himself, several times. "Are you in it?"

Later, after the effects subsided, I asked him again what he meant by that. He explained what had happened. Just when he was replying that he wasn't feeling anything, he suddenly fell through a hole in the ground and found himself in an underground cavern. That's what he was asking; he was wondering if we were in the same place he was. Were we in that cavern too? He had been transported.

In my own case, the effects did develop further, and I did have a fairly intense experience, but not quite as intense as my friend. I still retained some awareness of my actual surroundings, although my surroundings appeared dramatically altered. I still perceived the environment around me, but was seeing things that are not ordinarily there. We were on a patio outside a house perched on a hillside, surrounded by chaparral. There were no actual houses in the hills above us, just wild vegetation. But I saw little houses nestled in the hillside. And they weren't like ordinary houses. They were clearly built into the hillside, and I could see little windows sticking out. There was light coming from the inside of them, and some of them had smoke coming out of little chimneys. There was something very hobbitlike about them.

At the time, I sensed that these were the homes of nature spirits that lived in the hills, and that they were there all the time. But ordinarily I am not able to perceive them there. It seemed totally real at the time, as if that is just the way it always is.

It was an interesting experience. I felt awestruck by the power of this plant and its extraordinary visionary effects. The duration of the experience seemed ideal. We felt the first effects about fifteen minutes after we began ingesting the leaves. The effects were strong for about an hour and a half, and then tapered off over another hour and a half—about three hours from beginning to end.

Many other hallucinogens require a much longer time commitment. The effects of LSD and mescaline, for example, typically last at least ten hours. After a few hours on those drugs I often feel like I have had enough and wish the effects would subside. I feel like I've done enough introspection and am ready to rest. Sometimes I find myself going around in mental loops, just rehashing the same material over and over. This did not happen with salvia.

The other thing I found really intriguing about it was how natural it felt. It didn't feel like I had taken a drug. It felt like I had somehow opened up a part of my psyche that was always there, but that I was not ordinarily conscious of. It felt like a completely natural way of seeing things. I didn't feel any physiological reaction to the drug, just a purely mental shift, almost like what happens when people go to sleep at night and dream—just a natural shift of awareness. I felt completely comfortable with it. Afterward, I felt revitalized and renewed. That experience made a big impression on me, and it inspired me to study *Salvia divinorum* intensively for many years.

Could you speak about how this led to your discovery of the psychoactive effects of salvinorin A?

DANIEL: Because I found the experience intriguing, I subsequently repeated it several times, once I got the plants growing again from the cuttings I'd saved. I tried eating the leaves again a few months after that first experience, but I didn't get any effect, or almost no effect. It seemed like I got some very vague effect, but it was disappointing, and I wondered, *What's going on? I ate the same number of leaves, but not much happened.* I took it with a friend that time, and he didn't get much of an effect either.

So when my plants produced enough leaves, I did it again, a few months later, only that time I took an even larger number of leaves. I wanted to make sure that I would get an effect comparable to my first experience. But yet again, almost nothing happened. I did this a few more times, over the course of about a year, but was not able to get much of an effect. I could see why many people had the impression that this plant might be inactive.

There was a persistent question in my mind: Why did this plant work so well the first time I tried it, but not the other times? My curiosity, and my desire to repeat the type of experience I had the first time, led me to produce extracts.

I had tried increasing the number of leaves I was ingesting to get an effect, and had gotten to a point where I just couldn't physically consume a larger number of leaves. Even twenty-six large leaves is a pretty big bundle. Also, the leaves are bitter, and as you chew them it becomes increasingly difficult to keep swallowing them. The gag reflex starts protesting after a while, and you just can't keep swallowing the leaves.

So I had hit this wall of not being able to increase the dose any further, not getting effects, and getting fed up with the whole thing.

So I decided to try concentrating a larger volume of leaf material into an extract. That would be a way to increase the dose and get it down. I made some simple, crude extracts and tested them on myself. I did not detect any effects after swallowing these extracts, even though they were equivalent to very large doses of leaves.

I tried a few different approaches to making extracts. Initially, I made an alcohol extract and evaporated the alcohol off to leave a tarlike residue. I used heat to evaporate the alcohol off. I thought maybe the heat destroyed the active constituent of the plant. So I decided to make another extract that didn't use heat. I put the leaves through a wheatgrass juicer. Then I put the juice in a lyophilizer, a freeze-drier. So I freeze-dried this leaf juice, and I tried swallowing that. Again nothing at all happened.

I was puzzled and frustrated that my efforts seemed to be leading nowhere. But I did not give up. I decided to make another extract, following the initial extraction procedure utilized by Jerry Valdez, who had published a paper describing two compounds he had isolated from the plant. Valdez initially called these divinorin A and divinorin B, but later learned that a Mexican chemist, Alfredo Ortega, had isolated the first of these and given it the name salvinorin. Since Ortega's paper was published first, Valdez later revised the names to salvinorin A and salvinorin B.

But there was no indication that these compounds were hallucinogens. Many people doubted that they could be responsible for the effects of the plant. Mainly, I think, because they are diterpenes and are chemically unrelated to other hallucinogens, most of which are alkaloids.

I wondered if one or both of these compounds might be responsible for the effects of the plant. They had never been tested in humans. Valdez had tested them in mice. In those tests salvinorin A produced a sedative-like effect at high doses, while salvinorin B was inactive. In any case, I decided to proceed as if they might be psychoactive, and so I followed the initial extraction procedure that Valdez had outlined in his paper.

I planned to only do the preliminary extract workup he had done. I didn't have the expensive lab equipment required to completely isolate and purify the compounds as he had done. After I performed the initial extraction procedure I was going to evaporate off the solvent to leave a crude extract, which I intended to test on myself. However, I noticed that the solvent mixture had an odd iridescent quality about it. I thought it was very unusual. I had made extracts from many different plants in the past, and had never seen this iridescent quality in a solution before. I thought, *Perhaps there are tiny crystals floating around in there, causing the iridescence.*

So I looked at the solution with a magnifying glass, and sure enough, it was full of tiny crystals. I thought they were probably crystals of some inorganic mineral salt that had come out of solution—probably nothing worth bothering with. I figured I should filter off the crystals and remove them from my extract, thus making the remaining extract that much more concentrated.

So I filtered out the crystals and was just about to toss them in a trash can, when I had a second thought: *Maybe I should try a little, just in case it might have some activity.* So that's what I did. I tested a bit. I put a couple of milligrams on a piece of aluminum foil and heated the foil from below with a small torch to vaporize the crystals.

Did you say you put a couple of milligrams of it?

DANIEL: Yes.

Isn't it usually measured in microgram doses?

DANIEL: Yeah, well, I didn't know at the time how potent it was. I thought I was being pretty conservative, just doing a couple of milligrams. And whatever it was, I could tell it wasn't a pure compound. Clearly there was a lot of chlorophyll trapped in the crystals, which gave them a greenish color. Actually, I first put only 1 milligram on the foil, but when I tried to vaporize the crystals, I got the flame a little too close to the foil and it melted a hole in it. I tried to inhale some of the vapors anyway, but didn't get any effect at all. Initially I thought, *Yeah, just as I thought; this stuff isn't anything interesting.* But then I thought, *Well, maybe I'd damaged the material when I melted the foil.* I thought, *Well, I'll give it one more try, and 1 milligram isn't very much anyway. Maybe I should do a little more.*

So I put a little bit more on the scale. It measured 2.6 milligrams. I thought, *Well, I'll try that.* So I did it again, being careful not to get the flame too close to the foil. This time I clearly saw the crystals melt and then vaporize. And I inhaled all the vapors. I waited a little while. It seemed like enough time to wait, although it really wasn't very long, probably about 30 seconds. I was already thinking, *This isn't going to do anything.* Then, suddenly, almost instantly, I found myself in a disembodied state of awareness. I had lost all contact with the physical world and my physical body. I had no memory of how I had gotten into this state. I didn't remember that I had just smoked something. Suddenly I was someplace else, with no knowledge of how I got there.

I did have some vague sense that I was supposed to be some other place and I should be trying to get back to that place. So I started trying to remember: *Where is it that I am supposed to be? Where was I before I was here?* As these thoughts were going through my mind, I tried to search my memory for clues, any memory that might connect me with where I was supposed to be. I made a huge effort.

Then I started panicking about the situation, because I knew something was very wrong and things were not as they should be. I searched and searched, but could not find a memory of having ever been anyplace else. Then I realized that perhaps there was no other place, that this disembodied state was all there was. Perhaps I had only imagined that there was some other place before. At that point I gave up the idea that I was supposed to be someplace else, or had ever had some other existence in the past. I was resigning myself to this disembodied state of awareness. Then I thought, *Where am I supposed to go from here?* I felt very confused, because I didn't really know what was going on.

Then, suddenly, my eyes opened, and I found myself back in my body, back in physical reality. I looked around and felt greatly relieved. But then, a moment later, as everything came into focus, I realized that I wasn't in the right place, temporarily or physically. I found myself standing in a familiar place: it was the home of my maternal grandparents, but it was as it was when I was a small child. This alarmed me, because I knew it wasn't right. I had somehow stepped out of this disembodied state, seemingly into the wrong place in my personal history. It didn't feel at all like a vivid memory; it felt like I had literally stepped back into time in the wrong spot.

Everything seemed completely real in the environment around me, and that frightened me. I panicked and somehow returned to a disembodied state, unaware of any physical reality. Then it happened again. I suddenly snapped out of it and opened my eyes. I looked around, and once again I was in the wrong place. I was at a friend's house. It was familiar to me, but it wasn't where I was supposed to be. This cycle repeated several times, returning again to a disembodied state, regaining awareness of physical reality, and finding myself in the wrong place.

Eventually the effects truly did subside, and I did end up where I was supposed to be. My memory slowly returned, and I remembered experimenting with the crystalline material I had isolated. Suddenly it all made sense.

When I pieced together what had happened, I realized that I had stumbled on a significant discovery. I felt euphoric. I had isolated the psychoactive principle of *Salvia divinorum*. I was amazed by its potency. Even when I chewed the leaves the first time and had such an interesting experience, it didn't really prepare me for what I just experienced.

Obviously, it was a question of dosage, primarily, and method of ingestion. My first experience with *Salvia divinorum* gave me the impression that it was a very easy-to-handle herb—an herb that could only produce pleasant experiences (either that or no experience). But this recent experience was alarming, somewhat frightening, and hard to manage. Prior to this experience, I had no idea that the plant contained anything so powerful. I won't go into the details here, but it is important to mention that with further analysis I was able to determine that the compound I isolated was salvinorin A. Interestingly, it is the most potent naturally occurring hallucinogen thus far discovered.

What type of healing properties or medical applications do you think Salvia divinorum or its derivatives may possibly have?

DANIEL: There has been a lot of interest in salvinorin A in the pharmacological world. We now know that it selectively targets a particular type of opioid receptor called the kappa-opioid receptor. This receptor has interested pharmacologists for many years. Several synthetic drugs that target this receptor have been developed, and some have even gone through clinical trials.

There are three main types of opioid receptors—the mu-, delta-, and kappa-opioid receptors. These are all involved in regulating pain perception. Morphine, codeine, and many closely related opioid drugs act primarily on mu- and delta-opioid receptors. Some of these also affect kappa-opioid receptors, to a minor extent.

These drugs are valuable pain medications, but it's long been known that they also produce unwanted side effects. They are highly addictive, they produce constipation, and they slow respiration. This last side effect is the most serious, because people stop breathing if they take too high a dose. This is why heroin users die of overdoses. People also develop tolerance to these drugs fairly quickly. This means that people who take these medications on a regular basis (people who suffer from chronic pain, for example) have to take increasingly larger doses over time to obtain the level of pain relief that they're seeking. These undesirable side effects are due to the fact that these drugs activate mu- and delta-opioid receptors.

Interestingly, drugs that selectively activate kappa-opioid receptors reduce pain perception but don't produce these unwanted side effects. Consequently, pharmacologists have been studying kappa-opioid-receptor-selective compounds, hoping to develop safer pain medications. Unfortunately, these drugs do have a side effect that makes them impractical for use as pain medications: they alter consciousness. Many of the subjects who had been given these drugs experimentally experienced mind-altering effects that made them uncomfortable.

Obviously, this is also true of salvinorin A. Nevertheless, since salvinorin A is structurally quite different from other opioid receptor ligands, pharmacologists hope that it could lead to the development of a whole new chemical class of potentially useful drugs.

By altering the structure of salvinorin A, it might be possible to create nonaddictive pain medications that do not have the hallucinogenic property of the parent compound. There are other potential applications for salvinorin A and its derivatives. For example, there is some indication that salvinorin A has an antidepressant effect. There are a lot of anecdotal reports describing this effect. This is something that needs to be looked into further. There are also indications that such compounds could be useful for treating many other conditions, things as diverse as HIV and some types of stroke.

What kind of research into Salvia divinorum would you like to see done?

DANIEL: That's a good question. To a large extent it's already being done. There are a number of different labs investigating salvinorin A and its derivatives and looking for useful medical applications. For example, Thomas Prisinzano, at the University of Kansas, thinks that some of these compounds may be useful for treating addiction to dopaminergic stimulants, such as cocaine and amphetamines. His research is based on previous animal studies with other kappa-opioid-receptor-agonist drugs, which show that they can reduce addiction to these stimulants. In animal studies, these drugs reduce the frequency of self-dosing with cocaine and amphetamines. So there's a possibility that humans might be similarly affected.

I want to point out that most of this research is focused on trying to find medically useful derivatives of salvinorin A that do not produce a significant mind-altering effect. The mind-altering effect of salvinorin A is considered an unwanted side effect. And this is why several kappa-opioid-agonist drugs were rejected after primarily clinical trials, because they produced mind-altering effects that were considered unacceptable. But I think some of these researchers are missing something important here. This is actually a property that can be tremendously valuable, in psychotherapeutic applications, for example. I am convinced that salvinorin A can be extremely useful as a tool for introspection and for gaining access to parts of the psyche that aren't ordinarily accessible. In the 1950s and early 1960s there was a lot of research with LSD, psilocybin, and other hallucinogens, and much of it was focused on the use of these things as psychotherapeutic tools. I don't see anyone doing that with salvinorin A.

That's too bad, because it's legal right now, and it would be easy to do. MAPS president Rick Doblin told me that he "would be surprised if salvinorin A is eventually shown to have medical applications. It's too short and too weird for psychedelic psychotherapy." What do you think about Rick's statement?

DANIEL: I would agree that it is too short when it is smoked, generally speaking, and unfortunately this is the way most people outside the Mazatec region are taking salvia these days. But when taken orally, which is how the Mazatecs take it, the duration of its effects is ideal, in my opinion.

When it's smoked the effects are extremely brief; the main peak of the effects only lasts five or six minutes, and then it tapers off over another twenty or thirty minutes. There is only a small window of time to do any self-exploration with it. And the onset of effects is often so sudden and disorientating that most of that time gets used up just trying to get a handle on what's happening.

However, when it's taken orally the effects last quite a bit longer.

Typically, the peak effects last between forty-five and ninety minutes. Then it gradually tapers off over another hour or two. I'd say there are at least two hours of productive time available for soul searching, meditation, interacting with a therapist, or whatever one wants to use it for.

Could you talk a little about how Salvia divinorum has been used traditionally by the Mazatec Indians in central Mexico?

DANIEL: They take it ceremonially as a tool for gaining access to the supernatural world, or what they believe to be the realm of divine beings and supernatural entities. That's the primary way they use it.

They also use it as a remedial medication. They take low doses to treat arthritis and headaches, to promote urination, reduce abdominal swelling, and stop diarrhea. Sometimes it is applied externally to burns to promote healing. When used for these purposes, it does not produce mind-altering effects.

When it's taken in a ceremonial context, they take a larger dose of leaves, and the objective is to produce a profound visionary state of awareness. For them, such visions are not hallucinations. They believe they are real. They believe that they can make contact and communicate with divine beings, often a particular saint or the Virgin Mary, who might aid them with a problem or illness.

The Mazatec are a rather superstitious people. They often believe that bad things are the result of spells or curses put on them by a bad witch, an envious neighbor, and things like that. So, consequently, they seek to remedy those problems by going into the supernatural realm to discover what caused the problem, remove a curse, get a blessing from the Virgin Mary, and so forth. It's basically a tool for accessing supernatural realms and petitioning aid from divine entities.

What type of spiritual potential do you think Salvia divinorum has?

DANIEL: That's a tough question. I don't even know where to start with that one. It depends on what you mean by the term *spiritual*.

I think that is a very individual thing that depends on a person's own worldview. Certainly that's true for any psychedelic drug, because these drugs really reflect the mind back on itself. They are all about mind and psyche. They reflect back on you your own beliefs and ways of interpreting things in the world.

So, for example, the Mazatecs are a very religious people. They are sincere Catholics, for the most part. But they also retain a lot of animistic beliefs from their past, from their pre-Catholic history, when they believed in supernatural beings that inhabit caves, elves in springs that make thunder and lightning, and things like that. So for them, in their worldview, they interpret the salvia experience in that context, and it all has meaning that fits with the way they see things.

Naturally, people from different cultures and with different beliefs experience and interpret salvia experiences differently. Some people who consider themselves to be spiritually oriented people interpret their experience with salvia in a spiritual context, and they find all kinds of personal meaning that fits with their particular worldview, whereas other people who don't have that spiritual orientation often don't see it that way. They just see it as an interesting mental phenomenon, and they don't particularly give it any more meaning than they give the dreams they have at night.

Now, that's not to imply that dreams are not meaningful. Actually, there are a lot of parallels between salvia visions and sleep dreams. Sometimes dreams are meaningful in obvious ways. They bring up material that we sometimes avoid facing head-on in our lives, and sometimes we get useful insights from our dreams. This also happens with salvia, even if you're not reading meaning into the visions; sometimes they are meaningful in obvious ways. Meaningful insights often emerge out of the experience. You might see something about yourself or the way you've been thinking about things, something you were not aware of before. This is something that I find particularly helpful about salvia. It has been tremendously useful to me over the years, for helping me to understand myself better.

What other potential do you think that Salvia divinorum *has, such as to help foster psychological insight or creativity?*

DANIEL: Many people find that they are inspired in some way by the material that comes up during a salvia experience. The imagery, for example, can be inspiring. Often creative people experience visionary imagery during salvia experiences that they try to reproduce in drawings, paintings, or poems, so it can certainly be a source of inspiration. I don't know that it particularly has the ability to increase creativity in any way, but it can certainly be a creative inspiration for some people.

I think that the greatest potential of *Salvia divinorum* lies in its ability to foster psychological insight. It has this property. Obviously, the Mazatecs identified this characteristic of *Salvia divinorum,* probably hundreds of years ago, because that is primarily how they use it. They interpret the experience in terms of their spiritual/mystical/religious beliefs. But it's clear to me that they too are delving into their psyches to find useful information about themselves, their relationship to their community, and so forth. Because that is what salvia does.

I also want to point out that visions can distract from the kind of psychological self-exploration that people can do with salvia. This is something that Mazatec shamans are very aware of. When you take salvia with them, they try not to give you an excessively strong dose. This is so you can have a manageable experience, and also so the dose isn't so strong that you lose track of the reason you took it in the first place. When the effects are too strong, the visions totally overwhelm the person and take control of the experience, to the point where it's like the experience has its own agenda. That can sometimes be worthwhile, but it often takes one off on a journey that one is unable to navigate or direct.

When people take high doses, they often forget they took salvia or that they even took a drug, let alone that they wanted to contemplate their life, relationships, or whatever. The ideal dose for self-exploration is one that allows a person greater access to the inner recesses of their psyche but also allows one to retain the ability to think clearly about things.

The visions, even when they're not totally overwhelming, can be distracting. It is easy to be amazed by some extraordinary spectacle that's appearing before you. But that can distract from any introspective work one might have intended to do.

Mazatec salvia ceremonies are serious occasions. You're there to do serious work, not to fool around and have fun. Laughter is strongly discouraged. They use salvia to do important work. From that perspective, it's understandable that they consider it inappropriate to laugh and giggle during the experience. If you get caught up in a hallucinatory realm that doesn't have anything to do with the purpose of the session, the concern you're there to address, the shaman will try to bring your attention back and help you focus on that purpose. Certainly us non-Mazatec people can use it in a similar way. I'm not saying it's the only way it should be used, but I do want to emphasize the fact that salvia is a tremendously valuable tool when used this way.

I appreciate the fact that intense psychedelic experiences are fascinating and worthwhile in their own right, whether or not one is seeking valuable personal insights. Provided that one takes proper safety precautions, I think that curiosity is as good a reason as any to take a psychedelic drug. I think that most people can benefit from such an experience, under the right circumstances. They can make one realize that there is more than one way to perceive reality, and that ordinary perception is largely influenced by one's own history and habits. Psychedelic drugs provide opportunities to step outside of habitual ways of seeing reality. They allow one the opportunity to see the world with fresh eyes.

Do you think that Salvia divinorum *helps to increase ecological awareness and one's connection to nature?*

DANIEL: In some sense. When salvia is taken at moderate doses, people often feel an extraordinary sense of connection with the natural world. Often people comment about what a wonderful feeling that is. People often describe it as an expanded sense of self. They feel that the ordinary boundaries dividing their sense of self from the world-at-large dissolve.

People often say that they feel at one with the natural world, especially when they take it outdoors, in a natural setting. There's a tremendous connection with the natural world. Birds fly by, and you feel like you understand what it feels like to be a bird—things like that. Often people feel a connection with life in the natural world that they were unaware of before. Sometimes such feelings extend beyond living things, to where rocks, mountains, clouds, and everything in the natural world seem like living entities. So, in that sense, yes, salvia does foster a connection with the natural world and, I think, a greater appreciation for it. But it does not do this reliably for everybody. This type of experience is partly dose related, in that it occurs most often at the lower end of the active dosage spectrum.

Unfortunately, I think most people experimenting with salvia these days are taking excessively high doses. Many people are smoking highly concentrated extracts, which are widely available commercially, and are having very brief, extraordinarily intense, disorientating experiences. At high doses, people lose all awareness of their physical environment. When people take such high doses, I don't think they connect with the natural world outside themselves, just the internal world of their own mind.

When used to connect with the natural world, I think it best to take salvia orally, at moderate doses, outdoors, surrounded by nature.

How does Salvia divinorum's future legal status look to you?

DANIEL: Pretty bleak. In the United States there are about a dozen states that have declared salvia illegal, and it looks like more will soon follow. Some of these states impose severe penalties on people caught using or possessing salvia. A few states just prohibit selling salvia to minors. The DEA is quite aware of salvia, is studying it, and is trying to decide whether or not something should be done about it at the federal level. Actually, I think the federal government has been very rational in considering this. They haven't decided to make salvia illegal simply because it is a hallucinogen. They're actually watching it closely to see if it causes significant harm or becomes a serious problem, whereas several states have had a knee-jerk reaction and decided to ban salvia without good reason.

Do you think that these misguided laws may interfere with future scientific research?

DANIEL: Yes, they can definitely get in the way of future scientific research. Several states have classified *Salvia divinorum* and salvinorin A as Schedule I controlled substances. Drugs that are in Schedule I are extremely difficult for scientists to work with; they have to jump over numerous hurdles to work with them. It's not impossible, but such obstacles certainly hinder research in a serious way. When LSD, psilocybin, and many other hallucinogens were made illegal in the 1960s, research on those substances quickly ground to a halt. The research that did continue was mostly in a forensic context, because these drugs were now illegal. Human research on the potential benefits of these drugs completely dried up. Only recently have a few scientists made the extra effort needed to meet government requirements to gain access to these drugs for scientific research.

What are your thoughts about the nonhuman-entity contact that many people experience on Salvia divinorum? And do you think that the plant itself is attempting to intelligently communicate with people?

DANIEL: That's a good question. Well, I used to think that it was, but I don't believe that anymore. I think that a lot of people do have contact with nonhuman entities during salvia experiences, but also people have experiences with human entities, or what appear to be human entities. Also, people frequently experience visions from their past. Often childhood memories and familiar people from their life appear in these visions. So there are lots of different entities that may appear, but you're asking specifically about nonhuman entities, and that can really vary all over the place. Sometimes people see elfish beings, sometimes giants, sometimes intelligent animal-like creatures that communicate. Often entities are just present in the visions and don't communicate with the viewer, but other times they clearly are communicating information. Sometimes they're acting as guides, taking a person on a journey, pointing things out, and imparting some kind of knowledge to them.

The Mazatecs regard *Salvia divinorum* as an incarnation of the Virgin Mary. They believe that the plant provides access to her. They blend the Virgin Mary from Christianity with a feminine, caregiving spirit that resides in rivers and is associated with water—probably a divine entity worshipped before the Spanish brought Catholicism to the region. They regard this plant as an embodiment of this feminine entity, and when they take salvia, they often seek that contact. Interestingly enough, a lot of non-Mazatec people also find that they have experiences in which they encounter a powerful feminine entity. In some cases, that might just be because they read something about the history of the plant and know that it's traditionally associated with this feminine entity. But many people who don't know that also report this kind of experience. It's intriguing that that would happen, and I don't know what's going on with that. Maybe there is some kind of spirit in the plant that people contact. I'm skeptical of that personally, but a lot of people do believe that is the case. Perhaps there is something about the nature of salvia's effects that tends to bring up archetypal feminine imagery.

Didn't I read that when you were in the process of discovering the psychoactive properties of salvinorin A that you felt guided by the plant spirit?

DANIEL: That is true. I did. But that was years ago, and I've reconsidered what I think about that now. I'm not totally closed off to that possibility, but I don't think it likely.

Albert Hofmann and Alexander Shulgin are both prominent chemists with extensive experience investigating psychoactive compounds. They both worked on the plant independently, but were unable to isolate its active constituent. And I just stumbled on it almost by accident. At the time I thought that was too easy. I felt as if I had been led to that discovery.

I had an interesting experience when I was preparing the leaves for the extraction that led to my isolation of salvinorin A. I had a large number of leaves that I had harvested, a grocery bag full, and I wanted to dry them quickly. So I decided to stick them in a tumble dryer, the one I ordinarily use for laundry. I thought this was a clever idea. After the leaves had been drying for an hour, I went to check on them. I opened the door of the dryer and discovered that the leaves had gotten so bruised up from the tumbling action that they turned completely black. I was horrified. I thought the rough treatment had probably destroyed the active constituent of the leaves. At that time it was thought that the active constituent was quite labile, since it had eluded prior detection. I decided to test some of these leaves to see if they had any activity, before I put any effort into extraction. So I smoked some, and had a vision of flowerlike entities. They were flowers with faces, and they were saying to me, "Keep on going; you're on the right track. Keep on going." Something like that.

Then later, as I proceeded further with the extraction, crystals came out of the solution, and it turned out that these crystals are responsible for the effects of the plant. So I put all of this together in my mind, and somehow concluded that I had been led along this path of experimentation, and that isolating salvinorin A, testing it, and finding out that it was responsible for the effects of the plant were all guided by the plant spirit. Back then, I was much more mystically oriented than I am now, and I interpreted a lot of things in terms of mystical entities, unseen forces, and so forth.

Do you think that experiences with Salvia divinorum *could possibly lead to any new insights in physics, other dimensions, dark matter, or parallel universes?*

DANIEL: I don't know if parallel universes exist, but if salvia provides some kind of portal into such places, that would be extraordinary. When people have these experiences, they often feel they are, in fact, gaining access to real places that exist independently from their own minds, and they often seem so unfamiliar and different from ordinary reality that they feel convinced that they've entered another dimension or some other reality. Often these experiences feel convincingly real.

I suspect that the reason people have these kinds of experiences on salvinorin A is because it alters neurochemistry in parts of the brain involved in modeling reality. So the brain in this altered state constructs or models reality in a different manner than it ordinarily does—in a way that's not bound to real-time sensory information, as it ordinarily is. This produces very different impressions of reality. I don't think people actually travel to other independently existing realms, except in their own mind.

What would you say are some of the most important things that you have personally learned from your experiences with Salvia divinorum?

DANIEL: It's kind of ironic. My experiences with salvia have made me more of a skeptic. I think these experiences demonstrate that the brain constructs our sense of self and constructs internal models of reality in our mind, which we perceive as external reality. Ordinarily, these models represent reality with enough accuracy that we can interact with the real world and function effectively in it. This is because that modeling is reflexively generated from sensory information, which is a reflection of physical reality. Hallucinogens alter sensory information processing. They also interfere with normal processes of reality testing, which are largely based on real-time sensory information. The fact that a chemical such as salvinorin A can so radically alter the fabric of consciousness strongly implies that consciousness is chemistry based.

I used to be a dualist. I thought that people have an immaterial spirit separate from their physical self—an immortal soul. This idea implies that we never really die. It is a powerfully attractive idea, and once it has been embraced, it is a hard one to let go of. I now think that notion is based on wishful thinking, and that it was something I picked up from other people when I was very young, impressionable, and did not have good critical-thinking skills. My salvia experiences have made me more materialistic, which seems to be the opposite effect of what a lot of people say about their own salvia experiences.

That's very interesting. I've gone back and forth with those two perspectives my whole life, so I understand very well. What do you think happens to consciousness after death, and what is your personal perspective on the concept of God?

DANIEL: I am convinced that consciousness is produced by brains and therefore does not persist after death. Regarding the concept of God, I equate theology with mythology. I am an atheist.

What are you currently working on?

DANIEL: I am finishing up a book about salvia, which I began writing about eleven years ago.

I've been eagerly awaiting that book.

DANIEL: It's almost ready for publication. Actually, it has been almost done for a long time. I just haven't found time to finish it. I have been busy with higher-priority projects, like making a living and parenting. My wife and I had a baby recently. I also had an encounter with cancer, and was in treatment for many months. That was a huge interruption.

Who's going to be publishing it?

DANIEL: I've been planning to self-publish it. I think that I'm still going to go with that. Although sometimes I am tempted to have someone else publish it, just because I think it would get done faster.

I'll bet that Inner Traditions would jump on it.

DANIEL: Yeah, that would be an obvious choice. But I am reluctant to hand my book over to a publisher. I would like to maintain complete control of it. I have heard many discouraging stories from authors who were disappointed by the way publishers edit and market their books.

I've personally used your sublingual salvia extract, the Sage Goddess Emerald Essence. It's absolutely wonderful; one of my favorite herbal extracts in the world.

DANIEL: That is how I usually take salvia, using that extract. It is a tincture. The effects and duration of the experience are similar to that of chewing the leaves, but it is easier to ingest and much more convenient to use.

Curiously, some people are unable to experience strong effects when taking salvia orally, even when they take it in a way that optimizes sublingual absorption. Perhaps these people have higher levels of salvinorin A–deactivating enzymes in their saliva, or in the tissues it has to permeate before it enters the bloodstream. Fortunately, smoking salvia usually does work for these people.

I think that people probably have very different distributions of kappa-opioid receptors.

DANIEL: Yeah, that is probably true.

Some people seem to have powerful experiences with doses that other people get little effect from.

DANIEL: There is quite a wide range of sensitivity amongst different people to salvinorin A. Certainly, with any drug, people vary in sensitivity, but it's particularly noticeable with salvinorin A, more so than with most other psychedelic drugs. And, yeah, that might be due to individual differences in distribution and concentration of kappa-opioid receptors. It is also possible that some people might metabolize it more rapidly than others.

13

The Future of Psychedelic Drug Medical Research

*An Interview with **Rick Doblin***

Rick Doblin, Ph.D., is the president of the Multidisciplinary Association for Psychedelic Studies (MAPS), an organization that he founded in 1986 to support research into the therapeutic potential of cannabis and psychedelic drugs.

MAPS has been designing and funding research studies into using MDMA to treat post-traumatic stress disorder, social anxiety in autistic adults, and end-of-life anxiety, as well as LSD for end-of-life anxiety and ibogaine and ayahuasca to treat drug addiction, with the goal of turning these substances into prescription medicines. The National Institute on Drug Abuse (NIDA) approved MAPS to do the first study into medical marijuana as a potential medicine for PTSD.

Doblin earned his Ph.D. in public policy from the Kennedy School of Government, Harvard University, in 2001, and he served on the board of the National Organization for the Reform of Marijuana Laws for fourteen years. Doblin was also in Stan and Christina Grof's first training group to receive certification as a Holotropic Breathwork practitioner.

I was happy to work with Rick for five years, while I was the guest editor of MAPS, periodically writing their newsletters and editing their theme bulletins. Rick has an unusually energetic personality, coupled with the admirable ability to easily and effectively communicate with people at many different levels of society.

Although this interview with Doblin was originally conducted in 2008, when I first began working with MAPS, it was thoroughly updated by Doblin in 2014. Rick spoke with me about how he founded MAPS, the research that MAPS is currently involved with, and what his dreams for the future of psychedelic drug research are.

How did you become interested in psychedelics, and what initially inspired you to found MAPS?

RICK: I was born in 1953 into a Jewish family, and was a child of the Holocaust. As I was growing up, I was just very much aware of the mind, and in particular of scapegoating, projections, and cultural insanity. That was presented to me as I was growing up as the big threat to my personal existence, that there's all these other aspects of survival having to do with making enough money to eat, making enough money to have a place to stay, and the normal career kind of stuff.

But I was raised in this political awareness of the power of the unconscious, and the power of the unconscious in a way to be harnessed toward destructive ends. So I was interested in psychotherapy and the unconscious, and was trying to figure out how to make it so that the Holocaust would never happen again, but I wasn't really that interested in psychedelics. In fact, as I was growing up and in high school, I had this education that taught me that psychedelics made you crazy, particularly LSD. And I believed it.

The way that I broke that mind-set was through literature, initially. I was very interested in the Vietnam War and the antiwar movement. I became a draft resister, and so I was widely read in Tolstoy and others about nonviolence.

I was learning about the Other. So in high school, I studied Russian.

It was the late sixties, early seventies. So we're at the height of the cold war—the nuclear arms race, and all this kind of stuff going on—so I studied Russian. I wanted learn about what the Russians were like. There was this kid in my Russian class who was the class clown. He was really funny, and he sat next to me. He was a friend of mine, but we weren't that close, and the rumor, though, was that he had taken LSD.

So I was constantly looking at him for when he would betray this fundamental insanity that he had in some deep portion of his brain. He was nuts because he tried LSD and he'd ruined his life. So I kept looking for signs of this, and I never really saw them. Then one day he gave me this book he was reading, *One Flew over the Cuckoo's Nest* by Ken Kesey. He said it was a great book and I should read it, so he loaned it to me when he was done with it.

Well, I just loved it. I read it, and then when I handed it back to him, he was like, "Some of that was written while the author was on LSD." And I'm like, "That can't be. I mean, it just doesn't work that way. LSD makes you go crazy." But he convinced me that that was true, and that was the crack in the propaganda for me, about the negative potentials of LSD, and to help me understand more about the positive.

But I still was not a drug user. I didn't smoke pot in high school. I didn't do any of that. But I was studying psychology. I had a class on Jung in high school, and was getting into Jungian psychology and transpersonal psychology. When I went to college at New College in Sarasota, Florida, that's when I decided to try LSD. The first time that I tried it, it moved me at these deep levels. I made this link between my bar mitzvah, which was this rite of passage that I had thought would turn me into a man but didn't, and LSD.

Even though I didn't handle it well, because I wasn't emotionally very open, and it was a very difficult, scary experience, I felt that it was touching me at those levels of a rite of passage, of the deep unconscious. And that, if I were to work with it, I could learn a lot about myself.

It seemed to me that this extremely abbreviated theory that was in the air at the time—that LSD equals mystical experience, which equals

Photo courtesy of the Multidisciplinary Association for Psychedelic Studies (MAPS)

Rick Doblin

social change—basically symbolized a breaking down of the barriers
between an understanding that comes out of fundamental unity, deeper
than our religion, our race, and gender and our nationality, political
perspective, and all of those things. If you had an appreciation for the
diversity you'd be less likely to be snared into this scapegoating and
negative projection, which I also saw going on in a way to justify the
Vietnam War.

So the LSD really touched me as a potential tool, and I couldn't handle it, but I felt it was necessary. So I kept doing LSD, and I kept having these difficult experiences. Finally I went to the guidance counselor at New College in 1972, and to my utter good fortune, he handed me a copy of Stan Grof's manuscript of *Realms of the Human Unconscious*. Everything came together for me when I was reading that, and understanding that there was this spiritual experience that did have implications for personality change and behavior change.

Additionally, the whole thing could be studied in a scientific way, and that's where I really developed this whole focus on psychedelic psychotherapy. So at age eighteen, in 1972, is when I decided to be an underground psychedelic therapist. That's how it came together, because also, as I said, as draft resistor I expected to go to jail. I expected that I would not be a licensed professional in anything, but that the one profession I looked forward to that wouldn't require a license would be an underground psychedelic therapist.

What led to founding MAPS?

RICK: Keep in mind that in 1972, as I'm awakening to the potential of LSD, it's exactly when things were being shut down, so I felt that because of my age and emotional insecurities I woke up late to the psychedelic revolution, just as it was being shut down. I actually wrote to Stan Grof in 1972 and he responded. I have the letter from him, which is amazing.

I almost went to Hollywood Hospital in Vancouver, as I had all of the application forms for going through therapy up there completed, but it was five hundred dollars and that was too expensive. I didn't realize the value of a sitter, and I thought I could do it all, so there was this feeling that I woke up just as it was being shut down.

Then in 1982, I discovered MDMA, and I realized that even though I thought this psychedelic movement had been crushed, there was this underground flourishing with the therapeutic use of MDMA, and I felt like, *Now here's a chance for me to get back involved before it's all smashed.*

I recognized as I got more and more in touch with various people involved in the psychedelic therapy movement, and got more interested in politically protecting MDMA, that history was going to repeat itself inevitably. There was going to be a social movement, a social reaction, against MDMA, and the DEA was going to come down and try to criminalize it. In 1984, Debbie Harlow, Lee Fagar, and I started Earth Metabolic Design Lab, which was the first nonprofit organization that was designed to sponsor research with MDMA, and would be kept private until the DEA moved to criminalize it.

That was to become the vehicle that we would use to sue the DEA and block the eventual criminalization. Earth Metabolic Design Lab involved everybody and anybody who was in the field, or on this incredibly illustrious board of advisors. And we did use that to launch the DEA lawsuits. We were eventually able to prevail in court with our witnesses, many of whom we had been contacted in explicit preparation for this, like Lester Grinspoon and others at Harvard Medical School.

We won the lawsuit—meaning that the judge recommended to the DEA that MDMA continue to be made available as a prescription medicine for therapeutic use. However, the political overlay came in. The head of the DEA, John C. Lawn at the time, rejected the recommendation. So we sued him again, based upon the fact that his rationale was that the DEA could not reschedule the drug, that only the FDA could do that. That's not what the statute says. We sued them and went to the D.C. Circuit Court of Appeals. The D.C. Circuit Court of Appeals agreed with us, sent it back to the DEA, but they just came up with a new rationale.

Eventually, by 1986, it was clear to me that we won the battle but lost the war, and that MDMA was going to stay illegal, and there were just two ways to bring it back. One was to end the drug war, which, at the time, didn't seem very likely. Even at this point, nearly thirty years later, the drug war continues. The other way was to try to move MDMA through the FDA system—do the research and show it has therapeutic potential.

MAPS was created in 1986 as a nonprofit pharmaceutical company, with the goal to develop MDMA, other psychedelics, and marijuana into the category of FDA-approved prescription medicines.

Can you talk a little about the studies that are looking into MDMA as an adjunct to psychotherapy in the treatment of post-traumatic stress disorder?

RICK: Yes. Let me back up to the early 1980s, when I had a chance to work with a woman who had been brutally raped by her dad. She was suicidal. She ended up thinking she was going to need to commit suicide, and she was sure. She was a friend of a friend, and he referred her to me. We ended up working first with MDMA, and then with an MDMA and LSD combination.

I saw with my own eyes how these drugs could be really helpful. That was in 1984 or 1985, and now she's married, has a child, and is a therapist. So it's lasted for all these years. That was some of the early motivation for MDMA for PTSD.

The other condition that we were considering was using MDMA for people with anxiety around end-of-life issues. When it came time to try to really do our first clinical study, I was hoping to work with Charlie Grob. I had been working with Grob on the phase 1 safety study, and then we were working on a study with pancreatic-cancer patients. We were studying MDMA for anxiety associated with pancreatic cancer, and we got pretty far down the road with the FDA.

In 2001, I went to a conference on ayahuasca in San Francisco, and Michael Mithoefer was there. Michael was a member of MAPS, primarily. I didn't really know him, but he was a member because he had done breathwork with Stan Grof. Michael is a psychiatrist and a board-certified emergency-room doctor. He said he wanted to consider setting up an offshore clinic to do some psychedelic therapy or to do some research somewhere else. This was before we really had psychedelic psychotherapy research in the U.S.

So I said to him, "I don't think that it makes sense to do foreign research or to set up a foreign clinic. I think that we can do the most good by trying to work within the U.S. context, so that any progress we make with the FDA would radiate around the world."

Then he indicated that he had focused quite a lot on PTSD with his patients, and that he would be interested in trying to do an MDMA for PTSD study in the U.S. So I said, "That sounds perfect. I know from the past that there are great potentials here." And he had both medical and breathwork experience. He and his wife would be a male-female cotherapist team, as she's a psychiatric nurse. So we started on this road that was way more difficult and extended than we had intended.

Ironically, the problem was not with the FDA; the FDA said yes. But we had to spend years trying to find an institutional review board that had the courage that the FDA did to let us do the study. Then we had to do a lot of political work to pressure the DEA to finally get the license. It took years, but today we have a sequence of drug-development studies on MDMA for PTSD, for social anxiety in autistic adults, and for end-of-life anxiety.

The first U.S. PTSD study in Charleston, South Carolina, cost us 1.2 million dollars. Much of this money has gone to protocol development and the approval process, extended over a really long time. Then some went toward what now looks to be unnecessary safety procedures. Our current Charleston study has cost us 1.4 million dollars, and we only have sixteen of twenty-four subjects enrolled.

We've spent over forty thousand dollars just buying insurance for the IRB. They wanted a one-million-dollar insurance policy to indemnify them, in case one of the subjects sued the IRB, which is almost unheard of. We also had to spend over fifty thousand dollars on an ER doctor and a nurse, sitting in the next room, for every MDMA and placebo session—and they've never been called once—because we're doing the therapy at a clinic and not at a hospital. We had to be better than a hospital setting, and we were in a clinic, so we had to have a rapid medical response available right there. There were thousands of dollars sitting there for every subject in that study. We've spent another forty or fifty thousand dollars on travel expenses, just bringing in subjects. The most important thing to say is that the study is the key aspect of what MAPS is doing. It's the cornerstone of our work, and the results so far are dramatic and very promising. At several different stages over the years, we've been able to negotiate with the FDA to expand the protocol design to increase therapeutic efficacy, in ways that might be considered a risk increase, and both the FDA and the IRB have seen the risk/benefit ratio our way every single time.

Initially, it began with two sessions of MDMA, each using 125 milligrams or inactive placebo, and there were going to be twelve MDMA subjects and eight placebo subjects. This is a standard experimental drug design, but I realized that you don't always need this 50/50 division between experimental group and control group, so we tilted it a little more toward the 60/40 percent. But that's how we began, after we did the first five subjects.

Several of them had MDMA, and of the ones that had MDMA some had dramatic reductions in their scores on CAPS, which is the outcome measure on the Clinician-Administered PTSD Scale. So what we then did is, we went to the FDA, and we started each time asking for some different kind of expansion with the study.

The first thing that we did is we asked if we could give a supplemental dose of half the initial dose of MDMA after two and a half hours, which is a common practice in underground MDMA therapy. If you give half the initial dose after two and a half hours it extends the plateau of the peak therapeutic opportunity, and then you can get a lot more work done. The FDA said yes to that.

Then we said, "What we want to do, at the end of their two-month follow up, is offer all of the placebo subjects the opportunity to enroll open label with MDMA in the same study, repeat it exactly. But this time everyone knows they're going to get MDMA." This was because, sadly and unfortunately, we were finding that our nondrug therapy was having some effect, but not much.

The FDA said yes to that. So now we have a control group of subjects that are not only compared to experimental subjects, but are also their own controls before MDMA and after. This means that we're getting a tremendous level of scientific data.

Then we went to the FDA and said there are some subjects for whom their trauma is very deep. We phrased it this way: One of the lessons from the 1960s for us was that there was this unrealistic hope that psychedelics represented the one-dose miracle-cure model. That was the high-dose LSD for alcoholism model, the high-dose LSD for cancer patients with anxiety. We've since learned that not only is that unrealistic, but it underemphasizes the whole focus on preparation and integration, and that there's a lot that can be done—but that this is like other things, and that deep-seated personality traits require a fair amount of work.

So we said we wanted to do a third session, instead of two, and the FDA said yes to that. So now our treatment model has three sessions with 125 milligrams of MDMA, plus 62.5 after two and half hours, and the placebo subjects can enroll in open label. All but one of the placebo subjects has done so.

We found that when they do this after an extended period of time, the temporary gains they made from the nondrug psychotherapy go away. In most cases, they've gone back to baseline, so that there is a placebo effect, but it doesn't seem to last very long, and by the time they go into the second phase, the average scores of the placebo subjects were almost identical to the average scores of all the subjects when they enrolled in the study.

We have now had four amendments to our study protocol. Our current protocol outlines enrollment of a total of twenty-four veterans, firefighters, or police officers with chronic, treatment-resistant, service-related PTSD. Twelve subjects receive 125 mg [full dose], six subjects receive 75 mg [medium dose], and six receive 30 mg [active placebo], with supplemental doses equivalent to half of the first dose available 1.5 to 2.5 hours after the first dose. After unblinding, full-dose subjects will complete the third open-label experimental session in stage 1. Medium-dose and active-placebo subjects will have the opportunity to continue to open-label stage 2, following procedures similar to the full-dose group in stage 1, but with participants receiving open-label 125 mg, possibly followed by 62.5 mg, in three MDMA psychotherapy sessions.

What were some of the factors that were measured in the study?

RICK: Michael Mithoefer's studies use the CAPS scale to measure PTSD—which is the gold standard in terms of measuring PTSD—and there are three basic clusters within it: hyperarousal, emotional numbing, and avoidance. So hyperarousal means they startle really quickly. They have nightmares. They can't sleep.

There's all these things that remind them of the past trauma. They're constantly on edge, with many violent outbursts of anger and intrusive thoughts. There's a whole subset of symptoms associated with hyperarousal. Then there's emotional numbing, close to not caring or not feeling, shutting down.

We have a blinded independent rater, who rates everybody before they go into the MDMA session, to see a baseline. The subject has to have 50 or above on the CAPS score—which means moderate to severe PTSD symptoms—in order to qualify for the study. Then the subjects get rated at various times throughout the therapy. It's a symptom-based evaluation system, with some scores also for subjective measures of their emotional landscape. The CAPS scoring system is translated into multiple languages, so we have the CAPS in German for the Swiss study, and in Hebrew for the Israeli study.

Michael's study is our cornerstone, and Michael is going to be the trainer for future therapist teams as we expand into the phase 3 studies. We need probably twenty different locations and twenty different therapist teams, so the issue will become, How do we train them? And how well do they follow the method? And what is our method?

So we have a whole cluster of things going on. We have a team of people working on the treatment manual, and here we fall between the FDA and National Institute of Mental Health. When the NIMH focuses on evaluating psychotherapies for depression, or anything like that, they have a treatment manual. You have to have standardized therapies, and you have to have ways to look at videotapes of people doing the therapy and score them on how well they are doing it. That's how they do the cognitive-behavioral therapy, or any kind of method. They need to make sure the therapists are adhering to the method.

But when you come to the FDA, their whole focus is just, What drug are you giving? And how are you standardizing the drug? They haven't really approved drugs in conjunction with therapy, so they don't tend to pay attention to that. We hope to get an NIMH grant, but we also want to be able to make sure that we have a consistent therapy that maximizes the potential of MDMA that's practiced by all of these different therapeutic teams.

So we have a treatment-manual team. We have other teams looking at transcripts and categorizing defense mechanisms that are used. So we're looking at process variables to try to explain to skeptical people why this might work. All twenty-one subjects with treatment-resistant PTSD, as a result of sexual abuse, crime, or war, have completed the experimental treatment. The study was completed in September 2008 with remarkably promising results. We now have three phase 2 pilot studies, and with each of these we're tinkering with different things, so that we try to get the best idea on how to go forward into these large-scale phase 3 studies. That's where the millions of dollars are going to come in.

In Michael's study, because it was the first, we had to say that our male-female cotherapist team was at every meeting—all of the nondrug meetings and all of the basic sessions. In the Swiss study we said that one or the other of the therapist team had to be part of the nondrug sessions, but the patient met up with both male and female cotherapists before the first MDMA session, and we were able to get out from under some of the health and safety requirements.

We didn't need an ER doctor or nurse in the next room in Switzerland, according to the Swiss authorities, where it's very near a hospital, even though it's still also in a clinic center. The Swiss study included twelve subjects. It concluded in 2010. We found that while we had a small sample size, the study had a large effect size.

I should go back and say that in 2001, or around the time, Michael approached me about what to do. We had a study on MDMA for PTSD, the first one ever approved in Spain, and that was going to be a dose-response study, actually testing doses up to 150 mg. In that study about five patients were treated, and there were no problems whatsoever, but then the study was covered in the Spanish media. As a result, the Spanish antidrug authority got motivated to shut it down, and they succeeded in doing so.

So that study has been squashed for political reasons. We hope to start the Spain study up again, but we had to focus on the Swiss study. Then there was the Israeli study. It was limited only to people with war and terrorism PTSD, and was going to be twelve subjects. We had a male-female cotherapist team all picked out, and they came to see Michael in the U.S. They observed him running a session, but then there was a problem. We had our meeting in October. The study-initiation meeting was fully approved, the MDMA was there, and then we found out that the male therapist didn't feel capable of doing the therapy. He'd never done MDMA and he didn't really want to do so. We've learned from this and started a training protocol for researchers study, also in Charleston, so that researchers can experience, first hand, the MDMA therapy. This has been a great success so far and is helping us develop new studies in the U.S. and internationally.

We're in progress with an MDMA-assisted psychotherapy for PTSD study in Boulder, Colorado, we have a research team preparing in Canada, and study design happening in Australia. We are currently designing an MDMA for end-of-life anxiety study in the San Francisco

Bay Area, and have started an MDMA for social anxiety in autistic adults at UCLA. As of March 2014 we received NIDA approval to study marijuana for PTSD. We're heading toward phase 3 for MDMA-assisted psychotherapy for PTSD and a therapist training program. Our research has expanded incredibly!

Why do you think that psychedelic drugs have therapeutic potential, and what do you think that psychedelic agents have in common that gives them potential as therapeutic agents?

RICK: For me, Stan Grof explained it the best: that there's this barrier between the conscious and unconscious mind, and this barrier becomes more permeable under the influence of different psychedelic drugs.

But that's what they have in common. They are called *psychedelic* because they are mind manifesting. They make this transfer of information and emotion through the unconscious to conscious mind, more likely—similar to dreams, that you can have all different kinds of dreams. But everybody is comfortable, or everybody is aware that there is this doorway between the conscious and unconscious, that we all have access to in our dreams.

Most people don't remember their dreams, and their dream life is hardly at all part of their real life. But when you go to therapy, working on dreams and things like that, it is the royal road to the unconscious. Psychedelics have the common thread of opening the door to the unconscious, and they each have their selective ways of doing it. So it's like a rainbow of colors, of themes, of tones, opening up the unconscious.

But in that way, psychedelics are distinct from other psychotropic medicines that mean to move the mind. There's a lot of ways you move the mind. With stimulants you speed up the mind or you give it energy, and with depressants you tranquilize it. But those aren't drugs that really enhance this flow of the unconscious to the conscious, and that's where psychedelics are unique.

In addition to the studies that are to be done with MDMA and PTSD, what are some of the most important potential therapeutic applications that you see for psychedelic agents? And which psychedelic agents do you think hold the greatest potential for therapeutic application?

RICK: I think the other main aspect that we're trying to implement is psychedelics to help people deal with the anxiety around end-of-life issues. There's something about both bringing the fears up, so that they can be looked at, as in PTSD, and also this sense of connection. And here we get back to the reason why for thousands of years people have used psychedelics for religious experiences.

When you open up the unconscious, in a certain way, there can be this beyond-ego sense of connection with the whole sweep of life, a sense of unity, and a certain kind of time and space transcendence that can help people see life-and-death cycles with a little more equanimity, so that they are not as scared of dying.

For political reasons, I think that helping a scared population deal with dying will overwhelm their fears of drugs. If we can show that we can be helpful to people who are facing anxiety because of end-of-life issues, that will go a long way, more than anything else, more even than the PTSD, toward helping to integrate these drugs into our culture.

Now, another aspect of this, which I think is, again, in a sense, related to spiritual experience, is the treatment of addiction. We have the early work using LSD with heroin addicts and alcoholics. When you look at the research, you see that it did work out, but the benefits of the LSD tended to fade after around six months. So the control group and the experimental groups were divergent in their sobriety from the time of treatment to around six months.

But what was being tested was, again, this flaw from the 1960s, that there is a single-dose miracle cure. Now we understand more, that if we were to supplement the initial psychedelic experience with one or two more, then I think that the results would be better, long-lasting, and still cost-effective.

After he was sober, Bill W., who started Alcoholics Anonymous (AA), tried LSD in the 1950s, and he felt that it was very helpful to him, and he thought that LSD could play a role in AA. That was too controversial an idea for AA at the time, and it never got implemented, but it's like Carl Jung's advice to Bill W. that religious mania is the cure for dipsomania; you can help people have a sense of connection—that's often what they're seeking in the alcohol or other drugs. I think treatment of addiction is really important.

Can you tell me a little about the study that's going on in British Columbia using ibogaine to treat opiate addiction?

Rick: Yes, the ibogaine project is a really good example of how psychedelics can be used to treat addiction. But let me just back up first and say one thing about the work with the terminally ill, and then we'll get to this. We've got studies on psilocybin, LSD, MDMA, and what we're eventually moving toward is not isolated psychedelics in therapy, one versus another, but the practice of psychedelic medicine. This is because each of these drugs have different "flavors" or a different focus. MDMA is more supportive and positive, and LSD is more neutral, as Stan Grof called it, a nonspecific amplifier of the unconscious.

We'd really like to be able to practice psychedelic psychotherapy, and at different stages in a person's psychological process you might use one drug or the other. So, hopefully, if we can prove that each one of them are sufficiently safe and effective used by themselves, then we can go to the FDA and say, "Now we want to give therapist-clinical judgment about which one to use and which time in the process."

So we were talking about LSD being used as a treatment for alcoholism and heroin addicts. Now, ibogaine has unique properties. It reduces the craving for opiate addicts. In particular, it helps people go through opiate withdrawals and it promotes this insight, this emergence into the consciousness of repressed material.

Drug addiction and denial go hand in hand, and if you can get people with addictions to face what they've been doing to themselves and others, that can be very helpful. Ibogaine seems to be uniquely helpful for opiate addictions, and for whatever reasons, it's not scheduled internationally. This is in part because it's not a recreational drug; it's a really hard experience. It's hard to find, but it's legal in Canada, Mexico, England, and much of Europe, and there are ibogaine clinics that have been set up in these places.

We're doing an outcome study with various uses of ibogaine. With all of the uses of ibogaine, and with all of the talk about ibogaine over the last twenty years, there hasn't been one single prospective study on the efficacy of ibogaine. There are clinics that keep some track on their clients somewhat, but they've never published anything, so we really have no idea how effective it is and what percentage of the population can be helped by it. We know that AA works for some people, and other people go to AA and are turned off by a higher power, God, and it doesn't work for them. It's a question of matching people to the right therapy.

We're trying to do the first study with ibogaine, to see how that works with the treatment of heroin or opiate addiction. Now, there are other areas. If we look at MDMA, a key aspect is self-acceptance. MDMA really helps people settle into themselves and accept themselves.

So women with anorexia or bulimia, I think, can make use of MDMA. For people with eating disorders, this is a natural, ready to be explored, and I think that there would be great potential there. Another potential application is depression and anxiety. Many people are saying that there's a biological basis, organic problems that cause depression and anxiety. We're not ever really proposing any of these psychedelics for daily administration. For anxiety and depression, the model that we're talking about is really different, in that it's not daily administration. It's maybe three or four therapy sessions to get at the core personality factors that lead to this anxiety and depression.

I think we have a materialistic sense that everything is biological.

The extreme of this theory is that addiction is a brain disease, and that there's no sense of personal responsibility. And that's what some of the debate is: the government wants to move into this idea that addiction is a brain disease, and to destigmatize addicts so that there will be more compassionate treatment toward them.

That's because we're engaged in this whole prohibitionist mind-set, where the drug users are the enemy, and we're really mad at all these people that have caused themselves harm. So this idea of addiction as a brain disease is an attempt in some ways to provide people with another rationale for being compassionate helping treat addicts, but I think it also becomes distanced from personal responsibility.

This issue of personal responsibility and personal choice is made harder by brain changes, but still people have this choice. So what I'm saying is, in terms of anxiety and depression, that even if there is a biological basis to it, sometimes psychotherapy—particularly MDMA-enhanced or LSD-enhanced psychotherapy—might be able to help people with anxiety and depression to the point where they wouldn't need a daily medication, because they would have addressed the symptoms.

Now, these are more difficult issues to prove. There are a fair number of currently accepted medications for it, so I think that these will be issues that will be looked at later in the process of research, as we try to focus drug development. The greatest benefit from MDMA comes in situations where patients are not adequately treated by currently accepted treatments. That's where PTSD is so good and anxiety associated with end-of-life issues is so good. Eating disorders are also not so easily treated. So I think that's a fair, brief range of the potential uses right now.

One more thing: now in medicine there's this whole thing about personal-growth training, of therapist spiritual experiences. Roland Griffiths did that with his psilocybin studies. So I've just been really focusing on the drug-development, FDA route, but there are a lot of other creative uses that I think our society will benefit greatly from, once we get over our fears about this work and start opening the door to further psychedelic research.

Why do you think that the U.S. government has been so opposed to psychedelic drug research and has created so many obstacles? Do you see that changing now?

RICK: Yes, I see it as definitely changing. I think the reason is that LSD became part of a symbol of the social rebellion of the sixties; there's no doubt about that. Nixon talked about Timothy Leary as the "most dangerous man in America." You had the "We are coming for your children, and will leave you behind to start our society" kind of mind-set. So part of it was the counterculture withdrawing from the mainstream culture, for our own private utopia. So I think that was another one of the fundamental mistakes of the 1960s—this idea that you could ever have a private utopia.

Aldous Huxley wrote about this in his novel *Island,* where he attacked that very idea that you cannot create this private utopia, separate from the world, without the world eventually coming down to crush you. So you have to work within it. Herman Hesse talked about it in *The Glass Bead Game,* which was written in the middle of World War II. This whole effort that had created a channel for the aggressive energies into an intellectual game, how that became the substitute for war, and how even that became isolated and too esoteric, and didn't serve a purpose.

So, really, the change has to come from the center of the culture, and becoming part of it, rather than trying to remove from it. I feel that LSD and other things became symbolic to policy-makers, politicians, and parents, as a symbol of something that is both destroying society, by taking people and focusing them on their private utopias, and also destroying individuals through making them crazy at the same time.

There was a link between the civil rights movement, the antiwar movement, the Beatles, LSD, the environmental movement, the opposition to ballistic missiles, and Earth Day. A lot of these things were affiliated with psychedelics. When you have this sense of connection, this universal sense of connection, that does indeed have political implications.

So I think that the early thesis that I had was limited. The thing that I had been hearing in the 1960s was that psychedelics can change the world, that psychedelics can change individuals in their consciousness in a deep way and make them more open—and that idea really fueled a lot of the progressive, but also divisive, movements of the sixties.

To the people holding on to the status quo in America, you're not supposed to throw people in jail for their ideas, but if you can throw people in jail for their drugs, then that's okay, and that's the whole history of the drug war. The early laws were targeted against the Chinese laborers. They came to build the railroads, and when the railroads were done and they were competing with other Americans for low-wage jobs—and they smoked opium—the authorities said, "So let's go after opium."

Supposedly it was Mexicans who were the pot smokers in the 1930s, so let's go after them! Then with blacks and the drug war, it is just as racist. Population control is a common theme of the drug war. However, what shifted during the 1960s was that it wasn't just these racial minorities—now it was the white middle class going after their own kids! And that's what made it such a total hot-button issue. As the leader of the drug war spirit from the late 1960s, early 1970s, the U.S. then pressured people in every nation, through the international drug-control treaties, to block psychedelic research all over the world—and it was completely successful.

The research went from thousands of studies in the 1950s and 1960s to nothing, starting around 1972. Now, that began to change in the U.S. around 1989, 1990, with a different group of people at the FDA. This shows what people lower down in the hierarchy were thinking. You don't need the words to come down on high for bureaucracies to open the door to some previously suppressed thing.

They have to have sufficient support, and that's what my dissertation is about, why this group of people at the FDA opened the door to psychedelics and how durable that is. But the conclusion that I drew was that they had done their work in a careful, methodical way.

They created a series of rulings from advisory committees and NIDA, to set various precedents to underscore their opening the door to this field. So at the FDA we have had science over politics since 1989 to '90, as it relates to both medical marijuana and psychedelic drug research, and that has had an impact all over the world. People are looking at us now. They're looking at the National Institute on Drug Abuse, NIDA, the office of National Drug Control Policy, and the Drug Enforcement Agency, DEA.

When it comes to illegal drugs, the DEA is putting politics over science. They block research, saying, "We don't need it, we won't fund it, and we're going to make it hard for you to conduct it." That's still the case, but with the FDA opening the door to science and permitting the protocols to go forward, we've had a flourishing of psychedelic research. But that's because we have our own independent sources of supply. However, with marijuana, the FDA has approved several studies, and NIDA held the monopoly on the supply of marijuana, refusing to give it to researchers. That changed in March 2014, when NIDA finally approved of our marijuana for PTSD study. There is still a question of quality of NIDA marijuana, but we've made a breakthrough, at least in their approval.

So what we see in our society, as far as medical marijuana goes these days, is twelve states have approved medical marijuana laws and there are all these initiatives. There's been fifteen million dollars spent on these state medical marijuana struggles so far, but that's because the FDA route is blocked by NIDA, who holds a monopoly on the marijuana that can be used in FDA-approved research. But because there are private suppliers of psilocybin, LSD, MDMA, ibogaine, and all these other drugs, psychedelic research goes forward without having to be ruled on in a major way by the parts of our government that are still putting politics over science.

We still need DEA approval for the researchers to handle the controlled substances. The DEA can be very slow in giving those licenses, but once the FDA has said yes, the DEA is really limited to divergent control issues.

So we now have the situation where research has flourished in the U.S., in multiple, different ways, in both looking at spiritual experiences and at therapeutic outcomes with a variety of psychedelics, and that has impacted researchers in Switzerland, Germany, Israel, Spain, and elsewhere, to get involved. The trend now is very hopeful toward the expansion of psychedelic research even further, but the big issue is that in order for us to really expand it, we have to focus on drug development as the FDA wants it to be practiced.

We have to speak the language of the FDA, and we have to raise large sums of money. At this point we're not able to raise it from the pharmaceutical industry, because these drugs are off patent, not patentable, and they compete against pharmaceutical industry drugs for a variety of things. We're also not able to get money from the government, because it goes against government propaganda at this point. However, the work with ketamine is exciting, and it just shows that there may be an awareness that we can learn from psychedelics. But we're still not at the point yet where we can get government grants for the research, or from the major foundations, like the Ford Foundation, the McCarthy Foundation, or the Howard Hughes Foundation, that support medical research.

We've not been able to break into those foundations to get any money, at least not yet, and so the only thing that's left is the nonprofit drug development through private individual donations and family foundations. That's what's taken us so far.

We're hoping that, as our pilot studies generate more and more favorable data, as we get more attention for this field from the research, then the baby boomers will start saying, "Hey, I'm about to die. I'm really scared, and LSD will help me. I did it when I was younger and I know it."

I think there's going to be a major demand on the part of boomers for more enlightened death and psychedelic retirements. My wife and

I joke about how we're going to have a psychedelic retirement. I think that there are millions of people who are more open to this life-death transition mediated with psychedelics, both for the mystical experience and for the whole emotional aspects of it.

How do you envision the future application of psychedelics for therapeutic use?

RICK: There are several things to say here about the way I envision it. The first is that we're talking about something that is highly stigmatized, that I believe should be introduced in a gradual, step-by-step basis. We want to avoid the backlash we saw. By the end of the 1970s, there was growing support all over the country for the legalization of marijuana, but there was also the rise of the parent groups. There was backlash. Now we're twenty-five, twenty-seven, twenty-eight years past the backlash, but we've not yet even recovered that much, to the point where we were then. But we're close. Actually, the percentage of people who are in favor of marijuana legalization is growing by around 1 percent every year. There is general support for change in drug policy. But my point here is slow, gradual change.

So the way that I envision psychedelics as medicine—and this is elaborated on in the last chapter of my dissertation—is limited to people who have received special training. *People* meaning "doctors and psychologists who have received training with how to work with psychedelics." We would be administering these drugs in special treatment facilities: psychedelic clinics—like methadone clinics. That's the model now. I don't think that it will stay that way. I think that we will eventually have doctors that would be able to prescribe psychedelics, perhaps out of their own offices, but it would all depend on the risks of the different drugs.

There will be requirements. If you look at the requirements to run a nursery school or a day-care center, there are loads of them. I think a psychedelic clinic would have lots of requirements. One of the sad things is what we saw in the early 1980s, when some of the people who were the prime advocates of MDMA were accused of sexual abuse on their patients. So one of the things is a male-female cotherapist team, two therapists, so the patient is never left alone with a therapist. There are two people there to, in a way, protect the patient from being exploited.

I think that the FDA is more and more interested in what they call a risk-management plan. It used to be that they would approve drugs, and then any doctor could prescribe it for any purpose. But more and more this is changing, as with the return of thalidomide as a prescription medicine. Thalidomide being the main demonized drug of the 1960s that caused birth defects and was prevented from being marketed in the U.S. by the FDA, but now it has a role in the treatment of cancer and leprosy.

So thalidomide has returned as a prescription medicine, but under a whole series of educational requirements—of the pharmacist's education and of the doctor's education. This includes monitoring the patients' single pharmacy, tracking everybody who's ever taken thalidomide and looking for evidence of birth defects. These risk-management plans are the way the FDA has moved to approve riskier drugs, by trying to mitigate those risks. So how psychedelics will be prescribed is going to primarily be the result of these debates and discussions with the FDA. The DEA has a role, but only as a diversion. The FDA role is about how to develop these risk-management plans.

Now, if we develop MDMA, we'll have our treatment manual and a standardized treatment for everybody who does the clinical trials in our different phase 3 studies, the multisite studies. We're going to say, "Hey, it's not just that you give MDMA to patients and it enhances cognitive-behavioral therapy, or you give MDMA to them and it enhances this kind of approach." We're going to have one approach, and we're going to have a standardized treatment manual.

In evaluating people, the question is, Will the FDA say that only people who practice that method can practice MDMA therapy? And our view is going to be, "No, what we want is people to have been trained and licensed in our method, so they know the basics, but then they can go off and do whatever method they want." Maybe they can figure out a better way to do it. But, initially, for the first couple years, there will be a single pharmacy; all of the off-label uses of MDMA will be tracked. If we get it approved for PTSD and somebody uses it for eating disorders, that's okay. We don't want to stop that, but we want to gather information about that.

So here's the model that I imagine. In 1974 there was one hospice center; by 2004 there were about 3,500 of them. The movement to incorporate death continues, bringing it out of the shadows. This took place over a thirty-year period, to where there's hospice centers in most every community of a certain size in America. I think that's what we're going to do with psychedelic clinics, and it may take another thirty years to do that.

But I think that goes back to the original vision, which is that if we can use it for therapy and if enough individuals become more comfortable with this conscious-unconscious flow, then it will grow into other areas. We have a clinic model that can expand, initially to people with the designated disease, then family members—a lot of family members. In fact, a psilocybin study that we're going to try to get approval for with cancer patients is where we're also going to be testing the primary caregiver on their levels of anxiety, to see how they change as we do work with the patient.

So with these psychedelic clinics, first off they'll be the site of the treatments for the patients. Then we'll start bringing in family members. Then people will start coming for personal-growth issues, and then I think it's the doorway to broader legalization. I guess this is controversial, but I think it's really a fundamental human right for people to be able to change their consciousness in ways that they see valuable to themselves. People should have the right to practice their own religion. They should have that right.

I think that this is different, and beyond medical, but that these psychedelic clinics will become like the driver-license exam. You want to ride on the road? You got to show proof that you can drive, and somebody actually sits in the car with you. Then you go and drive and prove to them that you can drive. Then you take this little test, and it's not that hard to get the license.

But there are all these people out there, patrolling police cars and everything, so if you screw up on the road, you get points and you can lose your license. I think similarly with drugs; we'll have these centers initially, where people go and they say, "I want to try LSD." So you get LSD, under supervision, with people who know how to use it safely so you don't flip out. You get a general sense of it, and then you get a license to use it on your own. If you misbehave, then the license is taken away.

The integration of psychedelics into medicine is what I would say that most of the MAPS members—of which there's only about 1,500— are sympathetic to. This is with both medicine and the human rights of people to alter their consciousness, but not all of them want to see it go beyond that. There are some that are only willing to go so far as making these drugs available to medicine.

But what I had been saying about social change being instrumental and step-by-step, we have to be very careful to avoid a backlash. As we have seen, these backlashes have enduring power, and to get out of them is just horrendous—really slow and expensive. So we are getting out of a backlash, and there is more and more appreciation and support for this research. But we have to be very careful. So that's why I think we should be researching medicine initially through these clinics that control who uses psychedelics, who can prescribe them, who can do the therapy, and where. So that's the big-picture vision.

What do you think happens to consciousness after the death of the body?

RICK: I think it's gone. I don't personally believe in the survival of the individual entity. But what I also believe is this. This is a crude analogy: I've heard that if you're out in space somewhere you can pick up television channels from the Earth, and that everything that has ever happened has waves that radiate. We're talking about picking up leftover radiation from the big bang, so I think that every life is, in a sense, eternal. You have your brief period here on Earth, in this particular body package, and then whatever you do in some ways lasts forever.

It's a little bit also like the holograms where there's distributed memory, where you can see the whole picture, but then you can take a little bit of it and then you could generate the picture from it, but with slightly less detail. This is somewhat similar to DNA analogy, where every cell has the ability to re-create the whole body, or at least the information for that. So I think that consciousness, I think that once our bodies are gone, I don't think that there's an independent entity that's my ego that survives, but I think that the things that I have done while I was alive still radiate. And I think that now if I were to take LSD, I could tune in on this emotional-resonance level between emotional issues that I'm working on, and I could have a past-life experience that could be real.

I think that there's a way to tap in to that information, and it's not always perfect, and it's not always at the same level of detail, but that you can actually tap in to somebody else's life and reexperience it. It's the emotional resonance between that life and our life that's really the key, and I don't think that that person that lived back then is still alive now, off in Heaven, waiting to welcome their relatives. For me the issue is not something that I wrestle with because these moments, this world, is a reward enough. Life is intrinsically worthy, because of love, because of caring, because of this social milieu that we're in, and because of the mission to try to make it better. That's how, for me at least, I approach it.

What is your perspective on the concept of God?

RICK: Again, I think that there's this unity that exists, that weaves us all together, and that's what I would call God. I don't personify it. I think that there are all these levels and hierarchies, just like the way that there's constellations and galaxies in the sky. I think that much of what people say is God is merely an internal projection outward—particularly when we talk about psychedelics.

All these alien spirits that people see under the influence of DMT often cause them to wonder if they somehow have an independent existence or not, or are they part of our consciousness? For me it's just the unity. Another way to explain, I guess, is I took MDMA one night, all night, and tried to imagine what it would be like to be Brother David Steindl-Rast, what it is like to be a monk. How could I live without women? How could I live without that emotional contact with another human being? I did this on the edge of a cliff at Big Sur at Esalen. I did it in the middle of the night, and at one moment I felt like I was going to lose myself. I felt like I was just going to float away, fly apart, into the vast cosmos, into the sky, into the ocean.

I felt like I was just being swept away into the magnitude, but then I realized I wasn't. There was a part of me that was still right there, that was anchored there, and that I could appreciate the greater world, but that I was still me individually. And I felt that there was a force of gravity that was holding me there, and without that, without gravity, I'd be gone. There would be no humans, no condensed matter and stuff like that. I'd just be scattered, and this force of gravity was a loving force that made my life possible. I felt it as if the image was cradled in the arms of gravity, that the loving structure woven into the universe was nurturing, and that there was this love aspect to the universe. So, in a way, that's what I called God. It's like this generic unity built into things, but I don't particularly think that this is the God who wrote the Bible, for example.

What are you currently working on?

RICK: It's the most mundane of things. I'd say the top priority for me is management, learning about running an organization, directing the work, giving feedback, and trying to figure out the priorities. So it's really business. I'm building a nonprofit pharmaceutical business, and it's very mundane and far away from the mystical things—but it's inspired by that and infused with that.

So that's the main thing. Plus the other big thing that's been occupying my mind a lot is my son's bar mitzvah. He's twelve and a half, and it's going to be in December. As I started saying earlier, the bar mitzvah I had did not turn me into a man, and I don't think his will either. So his mother and I and some of the other moms and dads, we're going to have an all-night ceremony for them. Because the boys, when they go do their sleepovers with their friends, it's always a big contest—who can stay up all night, and can they see the sun rise.

So then his bar mitzvah is during Hanukkah, during December, the Festival of Lights. We're going to combine not sleeping all night with fire as the two main tools. No drugs at all. The parents would flip out, of course, but trying to design a ritual where there is this kind of rite of passage. Something is going on with these kids' lives as they turn thirteen. So trying to bring the psychedelic consciousness into suburban PTA life, in a way where I don't flip out the moms and I also don't flip out the boys, and where it becomes something organic and helpful, is what I'm working on a lot.

14
Psilocybin Studies and the Religious Experience

*An Interview with **Roland Griffiths***

Roland Griffiths, Ph.D., is a psychopharmacologist and professor of behavioral biology at Johns Hopkins University in the departments of Psychiatry and Neuroscience. Although Dr. Griffiths' psychopharmacology research has been at the cutting edge of neuroscience for more than thirty-five years, he is probably best known for having led the landmark study with psilocybin, published in the August 2006 issue of *Psychopharmacology* under the title "Psilocybin can occasion mystical-type experiences having substantial and sustained personal meaning and spiritual significance."

This study confirmed what many people had long suspected, and it also helped to join Dr. Griffiths' two most passionate personal interests: neuroscience and meditation.

---- © ----

I interviewed Roland on December 18, 2009. He was very gracious and reflective and appeared to choose his words carefully. We spoke about his research with psilocybin, his interest in spiritual experiences, and how psychedelics may provide help for people who are dying.

How did you become interested in doing psilocybin research?

ROLAND: I'm trained as a psychopharmacologist. I was trained in both experimental psychology and pharmacology. For the past thirty-five years I've been doing work in both the animal lab and the human lab, characterizing the effects of mood-altering drugs, mostly drugs of abuse.

About fifteen years ago I took up a meditation practice that opened up a spiritual window for me and made me very curious about the nature of mystical experience and spiritual transformation. It also prompted an existential question for me about the meaningfulness of my own research program in drug abuse pharmacology.

On reflecting about the history of psychopharmacology and the claims that had been made about the classical hallucinogens occasioning mystical and spiritual experience, I became intrigued about whether I could turn the direction of some of my research program toward addressing those kinds of questions. Through a confluence of interactions and introductions, I first met Robert Jesse of the Council on Spiritual Practices, and he introduced me to Bill Richards, who had a long history of working with these compounds from the 1960s and '70s. We decided that we would undertake a research project characterizing the effects of psilocybin.

The initial study that we undertook was really a comparative pharmacology study aimed at rigorously characterizing the effects of psilocybin using the kinds of measures that have been developed in clinical pharmacology over the last fifty years—measures that we had used extensively in our past research. However, we added another piece to that study, which came from my interest in spirituality. It really provided an opportunity for me to start reading about the psychology of religion, and looking closely into kinds of measures that might tap those type of experiences.

So the final publication of that first study, which came out in

2006, really reads as though it were intended to focus exclusively on mystical experience. The title of that paper, "Psilocybin can occasion mystical-type experiences having substantial and sustained personal meaning and spiritual significance," underscores the most interesting finding from the study. But, in fact, I went into that study, although very curious about spirituality, completely agnostic about the outcome of the study. I didn't believe, necessarily, that psilocybin would occasion compelling mystical experiences of the type that I had become so interested in through meditation.

How did the findings from the first study motivate you to do additional research, and can you talk a little about the more recent psilocybin studies that you're involved in?

ROLAND: After completing our first study and then publishing a fourteen-month follow-up report, we conducted a psilocybin dose-effect study in healthy volunteers that we have yet to publish. Currently, we have a study in anxious cancer patients that's ongoing, and with Matt Johnson we are also conducting a small pilot study examining psilocybin-facilitated cigarette smoking treatment. We also just initiated a study that will focus on psilocybin and spiritual practices. We will be giving psilocybin to people who are interested in undertaking meditation and spiritual-awareness practices to determine how a psilocybin experience impacts their engagement with those practices.

Let me back up just a little bit. The first study showed that psilocybin can, with high probability, occasion mystical-type experiences that appear virtually identical to naturally occurring mystical experiences that had been described by mystics and other religious figures throughout the ages. We knew that these mystical-type experiences spontaneously occurred occasionally, although unpredictably. It seems that the frequency of such experiences increases under conditions when people fast, meditate, or engage in intense prayer or other kinds of ritual or spiritual practice. However, these experiences still occur at a relatively low rate.

Roland Griffiths

What our studies are showing is that such experiences can be occasioned at relatively high probability. In the most recent study that we conducted, more than 70 percent of our volunteers had complete mystical experiences as measured by psychometric scales. An important implication of demonstrating that we can occasion these experiences with high probability is that it suggests that such experiences are biologically normal. Another important implication is that it now becomes possible, for the first time, to conduct rigorous prospective research, investigating both the antecedent causes as well as the consequences of these kinds of experiences. With regard to antecedent causes, it becomes possible to ask what kind of personality, genetic, or disposition characteristics increase the probability of these experiences. We described some of the consequences of the mystical experience in our first study, and certainly they've been well described in the broader literature on religion, mysticism, and entheogens. These involve shifts in attitudes and behavior, and some cognitive functions that appear quite positive.

Our interest in examining the effects of psilocybin-occasioned mystical experience in anxious cancer patients was that it appeared to be an immediately relevant therapeutic target. It's very common for patients with cancer to develop chronically and clinically significant symptoms of anxiety and depression that have a significant negative impact on quality of life.

The existing pharmacological and psychological treatments for depression and anxiety in patients with cancer and other terminal illnesses are currently very limited. Epidemiological data show that spirituality has a protective effect on psychological response to serious illness. We also know that spiritual well-being is negatively correlated with hopelessness in cancer patients, and that cancer patients are interested in addressing issues of spirituality.

Importantly, there had been substantial previous work in cancer patients in the 1960s and early 1970s with LSD and other classical hallucinogens. Research had been done by Bill Richards, Stan Grof, and others at the Maryland Psychiatric Research Center. In fact, Bill's Ph.D. thesis research focused on this topic. So there was a very good clinical sense that cancer patients would be an interesting target group.

Also, having personally looked closely at the spiritual experiences that people in our first studies had reported, it seemed obvious to me that psychologically distressed cancer patients were a very appropriate group to study.

Have you seen anything in your sessions that influenced your understanding of or perspective on death?

ROLAND: The hallmark feature of the mystical experience, that we can now occasion with high probability, is this sense of the interconnectedness of all things—a sense of unity. That sense of unity is often accompanied by a sense of sacredness, a sense of openheartedness or love, and a noetic quality suggesting that this experience is more real than everyday waking consciousness. I believe that the experience of unity is of key importance to understanding the potential existential shifts that people can undergo after having these kinds of experiences.

Within the domain of the psychology of religion, scholars have described two variations of this experience of unity: something called introverted mystical experience and another called extroverted mystical experience. The extroverted version of this sense of unity was assessed by items in one of the spiritual questionnaires that we used, the Hood Mysticism Scale.

I'll read you a couple of items. One is, "An experience in which I felt that all things were alive." Some of the others are: "An experience in which all things seem to be aware." "Realized the oneness of myself with all things." "An experience where all things seemed to be conscious." "An experience where all things seemed to be unified into a single whole." "An experience in which I felt nothing was really dead."

So this feature of mystical experiences point toward the nature of consciousness, and an intuition that consciousness is alive and pervades everything. From there, it is not a great stretch to contemplate the possibility of the continuity of consciousness—or, more traditionally, immortal soul. Such an experience can break down a restrictive sense of being defined by your body, in a total materialistic framework. So I think that it's these subtle and not-so-subtle perceptual shifts that could be at the core to rearranging someone's attitude about death.

Is this why you think that psychedelics can be helpful in assisting people with the dying process?

ROLAND: It's very common for people who have profound mystical-type experiences to report very positive changes in attitudes about themselves, their lives, and their relationships with others. People often report shifts in a core sense of self. Positive changes in mood are common, along with shifts toward altruism—like being more sensitive to the needs of others, and feeling a greater need to be of service to others.

It is not difficult to imagine that such attitudinal shifts flow directly from the sense of unity and other features of the mystical experience—a profound sense of the interconnectedness of all things packaged in a benevolent framework of a sense of sacredness, deep reverence, open-hearted love, and a noetic quality of truth. So it's quite plausible that the primary mystical experience not only underlies changes in attitude toward death specifically, but also changes attitudes about self, life, and other people in a way that's dramatically uplifting.

What sort of promise do you see for the future of psilocybin research?

ROLAND: I'm trained as a scientist, so I'm very interested in all of the scientific questions that can be asked of this experience. I'm interested in the neuropharmacology of the experience. I'm interested in the psychological and physiological determinants of this kind of experience. And then I'm interested in the consequence of this kind of experience, not only for healthy volunteers, but also for distressed individuals who might have a therapeutic or clinical benefit. Now, whether or not unpacking those scientific questions will lead to approval of psilocybin as a therapeutic drug, I don't know—and, in some ways, it's not important one way or another.

For me, what's most important is understanding the mechanisms that occasion these kinds of experiences. So I will not argue the future is with psilocybin per se. But it does appear to be an amazingly interesting tool for unlocking these mysteries of human consciousness. As we get a better understanding of the underlying neuropharmacology and neurophysiology, it may be that better compounds or nonpharmacological techniques can be developed that occasion these experiences with even higher probability than we can right now with psilocybin.

Frankly, I can't think of anything more important to be studying. As I've said, the core feature of the mystical experience is this strong sense of the interconnectedness of all things, where there's a rising sense of not only self-confidence and clarity, but of communal responsibility—of altruism and social justice, a felt sense of the Golden Rule: to do unto others as you would have them do unto you. And those kinds of sensibilities are at the core of all of the world's religious, ethical, and spiritual traditions. Understanding the nature of these effects and their consequences may be key to the survival of our species.

That was precisely the point that I was trying to make when I edited the MAPS Bulletin about ecology and psychedelics. Psychedelics have played such an important role in inspiring people to become more ecologically aware.

ROLAND: Yes, that follows from the altruistic sensibility that may flow from these types of experiences. Ecology can become a big deal with these experiences. If you really experience the interconnectedness of all things and the consciousness pervades all things, then you have to take care of other people and the planet, right? And to bring this back around to death and dying, if everything is conscious, then death and dying may not be so frightening. There is a big and mysterious story here.

15
Music, Creativity, Shpongle, and Psychedelics

An Interview with **Simon Posford**

Simon Posford (a.k.a. Hallucinogen) is a British musician and producer specializing in psychedelic electronic music spanning many genres, from psychedelic trance (psytrance), to rock and electronica.

Posford's first studio album, *Twisted,* was released in 1995 under the artist name "Hallucinogen." *Twisted* is considered one of the most influential albums in the genre of psytrance, and Posford's connection with psychedelics was evident from the title of the very first track, "LSD," which, to this day, remains the defining sound of a form of electronic music that originated during the late 1980s in Goa, India, called Goa trance.

In 1996, Posford and Australian musician Raja Ram created one of the most popular electronica music projects of all time: Shpongle. Arguably not since the Grateful Dead has a brand of popular music been so lovingly associated with psychedelics as Shpongle has. Psychedelics have played a huge role in the creation, performance, and experience of Shpongle's music, which is extremely popular among members of the psychedelic community.

Posford is generally responsible for coordinating the synthesizers, studio work, and live instrumentation, while Ram contributes broad musical concepts and flute arrangements. Shpongle's unique style combines Eastern ethnic instruments, flute riffs, and vocals with contemporary Western synthesizer-based electronic music, hyperdimensional alien-space acoustics, sound clips from television shows, and spoken words. Truly genre-defying, Shpongle contains elements of jazz, classical, dub and glitch, among other musical forms.

Shpongle performs live with different musicians, dancers, and other performers, while Posford masterfully controls an electronic sound board, alchemically mixing and remixing the music, engineering, tweaking, and orchestrating the highly textured, multilayered music that emerges. Shpongle's studio albums include: *Are You Shpongled?* (1998), *Tales of the Inexpressible* (2001), *Nothing Lasts . . . But Nothing Is Lost* (2005), and *Ineffable Mysteries from Shpongleland* (2009). Posford also frequently tours as Hallucinogen. To find out more about Shpongle see www.twistedmusic.com and www.facebook.com/shpongle.

I interviewed Simon on July 26, 2011. Since Simon's music has served as the soundtrack for numerous personal psychedelic experiences, this was a special interview for me. It was great fun to, as Simon put it, "intellectualize the abstract" and "muse over the ineffable" together. There's a delightful eloquence to the way that Simon expresses himself, and a vibrant sense of creativity continually comes through his words. We spoke about how his psychedelic journeys have affected his creativity and his experience with music.

What inspired your interest in music?

SIMON: When I was just growing up there was always music around my house. My parents were very young. My mom was nineteen and my dad was twenty-one when they had me, so there was always music on the stereo, and it obviously caught my ear. I have fond memories of the speakers booming late into the night, in spite of the fact they were playing the likes of Donna Summer, Queen, Elton John, and ELO. My grandfather was a composer in the forties. He wrote for musicals featuring stars of that era, such as Bing Crosby and Vera Lynn, but I never knew him, so I don't know if there's any genetic link or even if there's any validity to that idea. I would say that my interest was probably more just the result of being constantly surrounded by music as I was growing up.

How did you become involved with creating Shpongle?

SIMON: That was when I got together with Raja Ram in 1996. We went to the Glastonbury Festival, which is a huge festival in the U.K. In those days, they got up to around three hundred thousand people going, because they had a hard time keeping people outside the gates from sneaking in for free. Now it's more regimented. They've got two double fences and it's really hard to get in without a ticket, so there's only around 170,000 people going now. The festival takes place on a huge farm in the rolling hills of Avalon, and right at the top of site they have built a large stone circle, which normally hosts a variety of drummers, druids, and lost souls trying to escape the general mayhem and seek some sort of refuge.

I remember clearly, Raj and I were sitting there, watching this Celtic harp player, and I think that we'd both taken some psychedelic substance. I'm not sure what it was; probably acid. We were listening to this beautiful music emanating from this fairy goddess and her wooden harp—we were just fascinated by her. We became obsessed with her pulchritude and grace, falling in love with her, lured like Odysseus to the Sirens' song. She was so exquisitely beautiful—we never even saw her face; we were sat behind her—but she sat so upright, and this music was divine.

Raja and I had made only trance music together up to this point, but during that performance we thought it would be really nice to try to capture that particular moment. It wouldn't have to be dance-y, but

Simon Posford

just something that reproduced the energy of the stone circle and tribal beauty of the bonfires, the smoke mingling with the mist rolling in through the valley, and the honeyed tones of our Celtic muse.

What do you think makes Shpongle's music unique?

SIMON: That's a tricky one for me to answer, because I'm obviously so involved in it. But I would say that what makes anyone's music unique is that it comes from deep within the soul of the writers. The KLF wrote in their inspirational book, *The Manual,* that two artists could each make a track using only a single kick drum, the same sound, at the same tempo, yet undoubtedly one would *still* be better than the other. You could listen to both tracks and you would surely prefer one over the other. Maybe because no matter what you do or whatever you write, the musician's character and soul shines through, and some people you resonate with and some people you don't.

What inspired the name Shpongle?

SIMON: The name Shpongle came from my partner Raj. One day he had taken some acid, and . . . [*Laughter heard in the background.*] My girlfriend is just laughing. [*Explaining to girlfriend.*] This is for a psychedelic site; it's for MAPS. I guess all of these drug references are okay? My girlfriend is just laughing at me. [*Pauses, as laughter sounds in the background.*]

GIRLFRIEND: 'Cause I'm on acid now!

SIMON: She's on acid now, driving the car [*laughter*]—not really, don't worry. Anyway, Raj was tripping one day, and he said, "Oh, Si, I'm feeling really shpongled." This word was a mixture of a lot of other words that we were using at the time—like *spangled, stoned, monged,* and *mashed*—and all of these came out as one word: *shpongled.* So I said, "That's a great word. Maybe we should use that as a band name or track name," as it captured the essence of the message we were trying to get across, without a tired history of associations and expectations that existing words are weighed down by.

That's so appropriate too, since your music blends so many different styles together. In general with Shpongle, how would you describe your creative process?

SIMON: Raj will turn up, sometimes with a load of samples or recordings. One time he went to Brazil and recorded some stuff there.

Otherwise he'll record stuff off TV shows, some spoken words, or bamboo forests creaking in the wind—something like that. So that might spawn an idea for a track.

Raj is a very visual person and he's a fabulous painter, so he might come up with a visual image that, in time, I'll translate into music. Over the years he's come up with some inspiring imagery, such as a lake shimmering in the sky. Our most recent one was about CERN, [home of] the Large Hadron Collider in Switzerland, and about the idea of particles colliding at high velocities, neutrinos, protons, and neutrons smashing into each other, creating black holes, explosions, and new universes. Stuff like that.

So we'll have a visual image. Then, when I can finally get him to shut up, Raj will sit on the sofa and do a thousand drawings into his notebook, while I'll sit at the computer and get about translating our images into sound. I generally do the programming, playing, and production, because Raj can't work the computer or any of the equipment, but he's the inspiration and the muse, and will play flute or jabber strange vocals into the mic, being the cunning linguist he is.

We start with just a blank canvas, an empty computer screen, and just add more and more sounds until it's time to go home, I'm either sick of having him in my house, or he's sick of sitting on my sofa, listening to me torture him with various obnoxious instruments. Then we stop, and later we mix it. Then we give it the acid test. He'll take some LSD and put the headphones on when I'm ready to mix. Then I'll play it to him at high volume, and, judging by the state of his eyeballs and his face afterward, I'll know whether we've got a good one or not. [*Laughs.*]

I love it! This leads right into my next question, which is, How have psychedelics influenced your experience with music, and how has it affected your creativity and your performance?

Simon: I would say massively, and on a profound level. In fact, so fundamentally that I didn't even really like the type of music that I now create before I took psychedelics. I liked bands and music with singers and stuff. I never got into Kraftwerk or Depeche Mode or any of the well-known electronic bands that my friends would listen to. Then, once I took psychedelics, I really went off that for a while and only wanted to hear the alien, otherworldly, futuristic sounds of electronic music, and it's what inspired me to start making the music that I'm doing now. In a way, it's foundational to what I'm doing, because it pushed me down this path.

Also it changed my appreciation of music in general. I think that listening to music in an altered state of consciousness can either magnify the music or it can really leave you cold. Hopefully it will enrich the experience, and, hence we have what we call psychedelic music, which is designed to do so. I think that electronic music can certainly enhance a psychedelic experience.

I probably shouldn't mention the artist, but there's a particularly commercial band who sold a lot of records in the eighties and early nineties, and I made the terrible mistake of listening to their music while trying to have a psychedelic experience in my parents' house when I was a teenager. I put on this CD while I was tripping, and truly heard it for the bland, potbellied, corporate, insipid, vapid nastiness that it was. So our only concerns now are, What do we need to do to make this sort of kaleidoscopic music that really expands the brain, in the same way that, I think, psychedelics do?

I think that's really important. One of the reasons that I love your music so much is because I feel really vulnerable when I'm tripping, and it seems just so vital to have the properly supportive music. I was listening to some of your music recently and was thinking that some of it reminded me a bit of Pink Floyd, one of my favorite bands in high school. They developed sophisticated acoustic techniques for beautifully heightening consciousness with their music, but much of it feels so sad to me, like I'm floating all alone in outer space, haunted by loss of cosmic proportions. You seem to have developed similarly layered acoustic techniques for heightening consciousness with your music, but much of it has an upbeat, joyful exuberance, which I totally love and appreciate immensely.

Simon: What's amazing about Pink Floyd is that they managed to capture it with lyrics as well, which I find quite hard to do—because lyrics often distract me from the exact feeling that you were describing. This is why I never got, for example, the Grateful Dead, or some of the jam bands over here that were touted as so psychedelic. The Grateful Dead weren't as big here in England, but they certainly weren't around me and my friends when I was growing up. So when I finally did have an experience with them and then someone told me, "Oh, that's the Grateful Dead," man, I was disappointed. To me it was just blues-folk music. I just didn't get it. . . . Apparently it sounded best from the car park, which I could understand!

Trippy, blues-folk music, but, yeah, it's pretty old fashioned compared to electronic music. There's such a rich tapestry of acoustic variation and so many dimensions to your music that it really comes close to capturing the multidimensional state of consciousness that one is in during a psychedelic experience. I'm sure that's why so many people love it.

Simon: You know the old cliché about gazing at your shoelace for ten hours when you take psychedelics? I always like to have a similar experience with music while I'm tripping, where I really get into each and every guitar note. Each note will be analyzed, affected, and tweaked out, with layer upon layer of instrumentation—tambourines turned into liquid drops of nectar, vocals converted to voices of the cosmos.

Right, and there's such an incredible sense of time dilation. Everything seems to slow down, and there's a lot more going on in each moment, so you can analyze every detail more easily. Normally, it all just flies by so much more quickly.

SIMON: Yeah, I guess that's why it takes me so long to make an album. I like to spend a lot of time on each track. I think that you should be able to listen to a good track many times and hear something new in it each time. It should be composed so that you hear something new in it if you listen to it on headphones, or on a good sound system or in the car, alone, or with friends. It's got to keep you interested and tickle the brain cells as long as possible.

How have psychedelics affected your audience and your interaction with your audience?

SIMON: I don't know if I can really speak for my audience, because the psychedelic experience is a very personal journey. But I would say that quite a large percentage of our audience appears to have certainly had that experience, and I think that it provides a way to relate. Our music creates a common thread and instant bond of alliance to other people who have had a psychedelic experience, in the same way that, say, traveling might.

I think that I get on better with people if they've done psychedelics and traveled, because it opens your mind up in a way that is unequivocal. It makes one adept at relating and interacting in a playful, intangible, broad-minded way that perhaps you don't have with people that maybe haven't had those experiences.

I think that there's something very similar about traveling and tripping, because they both help you to become more culturally transcendent. They allow one to dissolve and transcend the boundaries of culture, and most people don't even know that culture creates limitations until they are free of them.

SIMON: Yeah, so it does mean that then there is a bond with the crowd, and my interaction with them. I only really make music that I want to hear myself. Because I want to hear that tricked-out, tweaked-out, psychedelic, trippy sound, I hope that many other people will want to hear that as well, and that my personal taste isn't so weird that no one else will like it.

You're definitely tapping in to something that's really hitting a chord with a lot of people.

SIMON: A lot more people might have done psychedelics than, perhaps, we might imagine. It's also a lot less taboo just to talk about it now than it used to be.

Could you talk a little about some of your most significant personal experiences with psychedelics, what you learned from them, and how they affected you?

SIMON: You mean like tripping tales—that kind of thing?

The experiences that have influenced you the most.

SIMON: I guess sometimes the greatest influence has not always come from the best trips. My friend says that there is no such thing as a bad trip. When you're absolutely terrified, in a complete state of jelly, then it may be hard to agree with that. But I think that when I view my experiences with a regard for what I've brought back from them, I see that sometimes the bad trips have been the most productive, and the most mind-expanding in a way, because they taught me the most about myself.

Like that trip at my parents' house, which I just mentioned, listening to the bad eighties music. It was superweird, and, at some point, I realized how someone could even prefer death to this, but I just chose not to go that route. Then, after I came down, it really gave me a new joy for life, and a fresh perspective on everything. I was able to think, "I'm so glad to be alive and *not* on acid!" for the next six months. I had heard music that sounded terrible and curdled my blood, and I had imagined music that would elevate me to the stars and stir dormant neurons into life.

But then there's also peak experiences on psychedelics, like with DMT, which for me, I think, is by far the most profound of all the psychedelics I've tried. With DMT it was just revelation after revelation, both personal and universal stuff. I had time explained to me.

Did you do it with harmaline, as ayahuasca, or on its own?

SIMON: No, I vaporized it in a pipe. Raj was with me, and a lot of my friends had done it. I was scared to do it. It had been around for a long time, and I knew that it was going to be a big experience. Having done other psychedelics, I was nervous to do it, so I waited awhile. Then, suddenly, I thought, *You know what? The time is right now!* I was in my house with my dear friend. All was quiet. It was just before dawn, and—because it was summer—the birds would come out and start singing as I returned to reality.

So I did it. We did a little meditation first and approached the experience very much as a vision quest. I was a little scared going in to the experience. As Terence McKenna said, "If you take a psychedelic and you're not afraid you did too much, you didn't do enough." Supposedly, the DMT that I did that day was from Terence McKenna's personal stash. Although I'm sure that there's a lot of DMT from Terence McKenna's stash, the experience that I had with this particular material was certainly the strongest that I've had out of all my DMT experiences.

With one toke I was already possibly higher than I'd ever been before, and was hurtling through the universe hanging on by a mere thread. Then I took another toke, even though I'm already feeling like I can't take any more—I mean, I couldn't even see properly by this point! I held it in for a really long time, and when I exhaled, I hear this voice echoing through the ether, saying, "Have another one, Simon." So as I feel the pipe hit my lips, I inhaled really deeply on it again.

By this point, I'm beyond my body, so it's really easy to take in that mothball-y, acrid, chemical taste. I could just suck it to the depths of my lungs and my soul, and really hold it for a long time. Then I got to the third toke that McKenna talks about and just laid back on the sofa in silent darkness.

First of all, I had that initial rush, which is fiercely intense. Then I sort of plunged into this portal, about where my third eye was and yet out in deep space, where I was met by these entities. I can only describe these beings as entities; they were without bodies or physical features, more like a collection of intelligent energy continually shape-shifting, that communicated with me through a variety of mediums, not all of them language, sometimes color, sound, or a form of telepathy that I cannot describe with mere words. One of the things they said to me was, "Oh, we're so glad to see you! You made it! You're here."

Then they started examining me in a very frivolous, excited, joyful, and playful kind of way. When I say *examining me* I don't mean physically or medically, which would be horrible. Rather, it was like all of the information in my brain was accessible to them. The hard drive was open, so to speak, and they were rebooting me. They were feeding me information, nourishing me, and then they asked, "What do you want to see?" For some reason, I thought, *Time.* I don't know why I thought *Time,* but they replied in a slightly ominous way: "Okay, we're going to *show* you time!" Although I can't conceive of it in my head now, or transcribe it with such a limited form of language—maybe that's what music is for?—but in that moment, I *totally* understood time.

They showed me the universe without time, which was the clincher that made me think, *Okay, I get it. If I'm able to step outside the universe, I see the cogwheel of time and how it fits into the larger cosmic machinery.* My memory of it is that it's a method or a required construct to keep us in this dimension—while we are here with our bodies on planet Earth—in order to witness the universe that we see every day. Or possibly nature's way of preventing everything from happening at once. Ha-ha!

With that, they also reminded me that I'm really so lucky to have a body for this transitory period of—what?—eighty years, if you're lucky, and really, you should be making the most of it. You should just be experiencing everything in life, all of it: love, joy, pain, anger, sorrow, bliss, enlightenment. Everything that you experience—that's really why we're here, because at some point you'll return to the source, and we won't have these bodies to be able to savor these experiences from the Garden of Earthly Delights. It was just revelation after revelation. It was very much like a near-death experience or an out-of-body experience.

People speculate that a chemical very similar to DMT is released in the brain when we die, and it felt a bit like that. In a way it felt like I was dying. I was communicating with what might be souls or something—I don't know. There are definitely energies out there that communicate and see stuff that I have achieved in my life, and will, perhaps, reprimand me for the bad things that I've done. It tied in with the Christian idea of Heaven and Hell, where you're there for eternity. When you die your heartbeat stops, your body is still, and you have no reference to any time whatsoever, and yet this chemical might be coursing around your dying brain. At least during my DMT journey I had my breath and my heart was beating, although I wasn't really aware of how long I was out there.

If your brain is active after you die, for between five and fifteen minutes, as some medical professionals suggest, then you're effectively there for eternity, experiencing what could very easily be your own personal private Heaven or Hell in this psychedelic state. So it raised the question to me, Is consciousness chemical in nature? Really, the whole experience raised far more questions than it answered—although it provided me with a lot of personal revelations about my life, including behaviors I could perhaps improve, even down to the song that I was working on.

I could see the music we had been working on leaving my head as a flowing liquid mercurial stream of holographic, colored symbols, and these machine elves, as Terence McKenna calls them, appeared to be getting off on it. They were dancing, laughing, and enjoying it. There was a little flute riff in there that we could all see; it was red and blue and melting like one of Dali's clocks. These creatures suddenly turned serious and told me, "You have to go back and find this particular flute riff. It is the divine riff, and this is the one that you have to use."

So when I came down, I went through one of Raj's takes to find it.

When we make music, Raj will just play and I'll record him for around twenty minutes. Then I'll edit it and find the juiciest chunks to put into the track. So I was searching very specifically for this particular bit that the entity explained to me on DMT that I should use, and, sure enough, there it was. But he fluffed it a little bit in the playing, so I tried to get him to replay the melody. Raj is a very improvisational player. He can never play the same thing twice, so to get him to be specific and really try and play this riff was very hard. But he got pretty close—as close as we could get. The tune was "Behind Closed Eyelids," and the flute riff that appears in that track was an imitation of the riff we had been instructed to use by the alien creatures we encountered on DMT.

It affected me so deeply, on so many levels—from what I was working on right then down to my core beliefs and all of the paradigms of the universe that I've encountered, from Buddhism, Christianity, religion, science, and the various different interpretations that people make in trying to explain the world. It provided a model of the universe that could fit comfortably—or relatively comfortably—in my small human brain.

That's extraordinary that you were able to bring so much back from such a powerful experience.

Simon: It has taken a long time to assimilate it. I still think about it every day. Initially when I came down I thought I would never speak again. What's the point? Words . . . they are so inadequate, lifeless, and stultifying. I spent a day in silence before admitting that I have to try to express myself, and share these experiences.

Even this single moment made the whole experience worthwhile: I received the message to "just be." Amongst all these crazy, hyperdimensional visuals, universes being created and exploding around me, suddenly a phrase I'd maybe picked up somewhere about an aspect of enlightenment is to "just be." And suddenly I just was! I literally had no thoughts. There was no me. There was obviously no ego remaining, but really there was no thought, no body, no universe . . . no thing. It was like thirty years of yoga and meditation practiced every day to try to get to that point, and suddenly there I was.

All of the visuals up to that point had been very intense, and this was just white light. It was just *Just be,* and all it was was white light, with no me—nothing. I realize I'm gabbling now, but I can't even really put it into words. I would imagine that that's the closest that I've ever come to some kind of enlightened bliss state which people have described. Then, suddenly, I had the thought, *Oh, this is it! I'm just being!* But by then, of course, you've lost it—because you've got a thought and you're already analyzing your own experience.

Did this experience influence your thoughts about what happens to consciousness after death and your perspective on the concept of God?

SIMON: As I say, it raised more questions than it answered. I mean, I'm still thinking about what happened during that experience now. I'm still wondering, as I said, *Is consciousness chemical in nature? Is God chemical in essence?* Here I am, a load of chemicals, and I believe in science. I take another chemical, and then suddenly I'm in this other universe—which is *so* real, so convincing, so familiar in a way, and yet also so alien. But certainly as authentic as the universe I witness every day, without chemical assistance. That experience still confuses me in that I'm not sure if I particularly believe in God. But it's hard to say that when you've met some kind of, what appeared to be, God. Or maybe more like a goddess, as it was a more feminine energy.

What type of relationship do you see between psychedelics, music, and shamanism?

SIMON: If you had a Venn diagram of the three, there'd be this huge overlap, because shamanism obviously uses music and psychedelics. It's heavily based in ritual, and music and psychedelic plants are often a part of that ritual. There's obviously music without shamanism and psychedelics, but I would say maybe avoid some of that music. [*Laughs.*] Psychedelics make music sound great, and they work really well with music. But then there is a whole spiritual side to shamanism. I think that psychedelics probably help you to connect in some way to the shamanistic spiritual side of the sound and music. To articulate how they all interact is probably a little bit difficult; that's probably more up your alley than mine. I'd have to think about that a little bit more. There's clearly an overlap between all of them.

In pictures of shamans around the world—from Siberian, Native American, Russian, to South American—they are usually depicted holding a drum, so there appears to be some kind of connection of a beat to the spirit world. When a shaman wants to communicate in the voice of the spirit world, he/she will often use music or glossolalia—speaking in tongues; wow, I've always wanted to get that word into a sentence!—instead of language. Taking psychedelics clearly is a gateway to the spirit world, but to weave all these elements into a cohesive unified theory should probably be the subject of a book. . . . I'm not qualified or knowledgeable enough; I'm just excited to be able to use the word *glossolalia,* a word I learned from the English TV show *QI*! I guess TV isn't all bad, despite how it seems whenever I switch it on in the USA . . .

How do you envision the future of your music evolving?

SIMON: I don't know. I guess my taste changes throughout the years, with the influences that I have, so it's hard to say. All I can say about my music is that I will only ever do something that I want to hear at that time—and that's all I really think an artist can do. If you're trying to do something to please other people, or to appease the myriad cast of characters that one inevitably has sitting on one's shoulder while you're making a tune, judging you, as I'm sure any artist has, then I think that you'll run into problems.

When you're doing it, you have to ignore them, and basically just do what you like and what you want to hear, and hope there's a resonance with your audience. As I mentioned before, I just have to hope that my taste isn't so obscure and off-the-wall that no one else will like it, and that there will be a few hundred souls that will relate to it and enjoy it.

And isn't that just so beautiful when that happens?

Simon: Yup.

Is there anything that we haven't spoken about that you would like to add?

Simon: Yes, I'd like to think a little bit more about psychedelics and art, generally. What might be interesting to examine, which we haven't really discussed, is how the psychedelic arts also seem slightly bound to the culture from which they originate as well—even though there is a common theme.

If you look at aboriginal art and that Mexican Indian art that they do with the beads, you'll see what I mean. They make those masks with the beads. I forget the tribe—do you know who I mean?

Do you mean the Huichol Indians of central Mexico? They do those brightly colored yarn paintings of their peyote visions.

Simon: Yes, exactly. They also make these very colorful masks with tiny beads and sculptures. But there's an overlap. Both share themes common to psychedelic artwork, such as fractal-style patterns and spirals or concentric circles. I'm pretty sure the Mexicans took peyote, but I don't know about the aborigines. Did they take psychedelics? Certainly it seems like the ancient Egyptians did, or the mushroom drawings in the Tassilic caves. Also it would be interesting to look into the hallucinogenic effects that laudanum and absinthe had on those poets we so revere today. In fact, the more I think about it, the more I realize psychedelics have probably had a huge impact on art and artists. When will it start to affect our governments and politicians? That's what I'd like to know!

Me too! There's definitely something universal and archetypal about many of the recurring psychedelic motifs in art and music around the world. Not long after I had my first psychedelic experience as a teenager, I realized that when looking at a piece of artwork or hearing a piece of music I could tell, with a high degree of accuracy, whether or not that artist had ever had a psychedelic experience. People who have experienced psychedelics seem to pick up on signals that may be completely invisible to others.

SIMON: Yeah, it really is like lifting a veil to another world. I think that once that veil has been lifted you can never really put it back. Maybe that's what scares people who haven't tried psychedelics: What if it changes me?

And it will! [Laughs.]

SIMON: But, I think, generally for the better.

I do too. Is there anything else that you wanted to say about psychedelics and art in general?

SIMON: On a slightly sad footnote, it's such a shame that Bill Hicks isn't alive. To be able to speak to him about it would be amazing. You're familiar with Bill Hicks, right?

Bill Hicks is my very favorite comedian of all time. Absolutely brilliant and totally hilarious.

SIMON: He popped into my head when I was saying that I think perhaps more people have taken psychedelics than you realize. That famous last film show that he did at the Dominion Theatre in London was the big venue, and he's up there as a stand-up comic, talking about psychedelics and the experiences of taking acid. As a comic you're going to want to be able to relate to your audience, and I think his confidence in doing that just shows that there are plenty of people out there who have had the experience that unites us.

I'm glad that MAPS, among others, are reminding us it's okay to experiment with our minds—in fact, for the spiritual evolution of mankind and art it might even be a requirement. So to finish up I would just like to [paraphrase] Bill: it's just a ride. We can change that ride anytime we choose. [It's a] simple choice between fear and love.

About the Author

Photo by Danielle DeBruno

David Jay Brown is the author of *The New Science of Psychedelics: At the Nexus of Culture, Consciousness, and Spirituality* and *Psychedelic Drug Research: A Comprehensive Review*. He is also the coauthor of four bestselling volumes of interviews with leading-edge thinkers: *Mavericks of the Mind, Voices from the Edge, Conversations on the Edge of the Apocalypse,* and *Mavericks of Medicine.* Brown is also the author of two science-fiction novels, *Brainchild* and *Virus,* and is the coauthor of the health science book *Detox with Oral Chelation.* Brown holds a master's degree in psychobiology from New York University and was responsible for the California-based research in two of British biologist Rupert Sheldrake's books on unexplained phenomena in science, *Dogs That Know When Their Owners Are Coming Home* and *The Sense of Being Stared At.* His work has appeared in numerous magazines, including *Wired, Discover,* and *Scientific American,* and he is periodically the guest editor of the *MAPS Bulletin.* Brown writes a popular weekly column for Santa Cruz Patch called "Catch the Buzz," about cannabis and psychedelic culture, and in 2011, 2012, and 2013 he was voted Best Writer in the annual *Good Times* and *Santa Cruz Weekly*'s Best of Santa Cruz polls. His news stories have been picked up by *The Huffington Post* and *CBS News.* Brown is currently coleading workshops about navigating altered states of consciousness with psychotherapist Meriana Dinkova. To find out more about his work see www.mavericksofthemind.com.

BOOKS OF RELATED INTEREST

The New Science of Psychedelics
At the Nexus of Culture, Consciousness, and Spirituality
by David Jay Brown

DMT: The Spirit Molecule
A Doctor's Revolutionary Research into the Biology of
Near-Death and Mystical Experiences
by Rick Strassman, M.D.

DMT and the Soul of Prophecy
A New Science of Spiritual Revelation in the Hebrew Bible
by Rick Strassman, M.D.

LSD: Doorway to the Numinous
The Groundbreaking Psychedelic Research into
Realms of the Human Unconscious
by Stanislav Grof, M.D.

LSD and the Divine Scientist
The Final Thoughts and Reflections of Albert Hofmann
by Albert Hofmann

Plants of the Gods
Their Sacred, Healing, and Hallucinogenic Powers
by Richard Evans Schultes, Albert Hofmann and Christian Rätsch

The Psychedelic Explorer's Guide
Safe, Therapeutic, and Sacred Journeys
by James Fadiman, Ph.D.

The Pot Book
A Complete Guide to Cannabis
by Julie Holland, M.D.

INNER TRADITIONS • BEAR & COMPANY
P.O. Box 388 • Rochester, VT 05767
1-800-246-8648
www.InnerTraditions.com

Or contact your local bookseller